Conflict Management Skills for Law Enforcement

Professor Terri M. Geerinck

Sir Sandford Fleming College

Constable Geoff J. Stark

Peterborough Lakefield
Community Police Service

Prentice
Hall

Toronto

To my family, as always. —T.G.

To Susan, Nicholas, and Madeleine.
For the gift of time. —G.S.

National Library of Canada Cataloguing in Publication Data
Geerinck, Terri, 1958–
    Conflict management skills for law enforcement

Includes index.
ISBN 0-13-093074-1

    1. Conflict management. 2. Police. I. Stark, Geoff. II. Title

HV7936.P75G42 2003   363.2'3   C2001-903773-2

ISBN 0-13-093074-1

Vice President, Editorial Director: Michael J. Young
Acquisitions Editor: Sophia Fortier
Marketing Manager: Sharon Loeb
Associate Editor: Meaghan Eley/Craig Pyette
Production Editor: Cheryl Jackson
Copy Editor: Ian MacKenzie
Production Manager: Wendy Moran
Page Layout: Heidi Palfrey
Art Director: Mary Opper
Cover Design: Amy Harnden
Cover Image: PhotoDisc

4 5 6 DPC 10 09 08

Printed and bound in Canada.

Contents

Chapter 8: Negotiations and Mediation   144

Chapter 9: Dealing with Domestic Abuse and Family Abuse   168

Chapter 10: Managing Stress   187

Preface

Welcome to *Conflict Management Skills for Law Enforcement*. We are pleased that you have included our text in your studies toward a career in law enforcement. This was truly a team effort between an experienced police officer and a professor and writer who teaches psychology and interpersonal dynamics. We both learned a great deal about each other's professions, which enhanced this effort. Thus this text balances teaching with the realities of being a police officer in Canada today.

This was not an easy text to write as we struggled with what to include in a book on conflict management skills when many situations in policing can be classified as conflict-prone and/or confrontational. As police officers, you must be ready for a conflict at all times; even routine calls can escalate quickly into tense situations. While there are special teams that manage incidents such as hostage-taking, potential suicides, and barricaded suspects, you may be the first officer on the scene. You will need to have some basic conflict management skills to ensure your safety and the safety of others. While not everything will go as outlined in this book, our primary goal was to give you some strategies and skills that will help you handle conflicts. Our secondary goal was to assist you with self-awareness: If you are aware of how you react conflict, stress, or aggression, you will be in a better position to cope with these types of incidents. So with these goals in mind, we began to write.

Chapter One introduces you to conflict focusing on conflict escalation and the management skills and techniques that will be discussed in the next nine chapters. In Chapter Two, conflict is more carefully examined as a dynamic process between people within a context and culture. Chapters Three and Four incorporate a variety of techniques that you can use to manage conflict in a variety of situations. The focus is on conflicts that have not become violent and the techniques include both verbal and nonverbal interventions. Due to the high amount of aggression police officers must manage, Chapter Five explores aggression in some detail. An understanding of aggression will assist you in managing conflicts that increase in hostility and violence while it answers some questions about why people are aggressive. Chapter Six introduces alcohol abuse and techniques for dealing with the abusers, who make up a large percentage of a patrol officer's "clientele." Chapter Seven provides information on people with mental health disorders. With ever decreasing health care resources, police officers come into contact with more and more such cases on a regular basis. Negotiation and mediation skills must be used daily by the officer on the street. Chapter Eight addresses everyday negotiation issues as well as some of the characteristics of crisis negotiations. Domestic disputes and domestic and family abuse are introduced in Chapter Nine. These scenarios are among the most challenging for officers to deal with. The final chapter is a chapter to help you manage the stress of policing. Policing is a stressful profession and an understanding of stress and techniques to reduce stress will be beneficial for you to learn *before* your stress levels escalate during the job.

This text is "hands on" and incorporates experiences of real officers and real situations in a feature called "Consider This …". The "Points for Pondering" feature highlights recent research, issues, or techniques related to conflict management. We have avoided long and wordy theories while still providing the information necessary to enhance your understanding of many techniques, all of which are currently used by police services across North America. Many chapters also include opportunities for practicing some skills you may not have previously used.

We wish you success and hope that this book will assist you in the development of a career in law enforcement!

Terri Geerinck, Professor
Sir Sandford Fleming College
Peterborough, ON

Geoff Stark, Constable
Peterborough Lakefield Community Police Service

Acknowledgments

This book could not have been completed without the assistance of a large team of people from Pearson Education. This includes David Stover, Sophia Fortier, Meaghan Eley, and all the others behind the publishing scene. Thanks also to copy editor Ian MacKenzie. We would also like to give our thanks to Roland Ouellette and Ed Nowicki. A very special thanks goes to all of the officers who shared their experiences and their knowledge, especially Gene and Ken Rogers who shared their experiences of Posttraumatic Stress Disorder. Thanks also to the Peterborough Lakefield Community Police Service for the pictures that we used in this book.

Thanks also to our families, friends and colleagues who supported us in this endeavour.

chapter one

An Introduction to
Conflict Management

Courtesy Peterborough Lakefield Community Police Service

LEARNING OUTCOMES

After studying this chapter, you should be able to

• Describe the various types of conflict in policing and how they differ from other types of conflict.

• Define conflict.

• Outline the continuum of conflict.

• List the basic causes of conflict.

• Differentiate between productive and destructive conflict.

• Understand how this text will assist in developing conflict management skills.

On-the-Job Scenario

WOMAN: I don't know why you pulled me over! I was hardly speeding. Lots of people passed me! What is it? You don't like women drivers?

OFFICER: I'm sure there were others speeding as well, but you were the one I caught this time.

WOMAN: Hurry up! Just write the !!@$@$!! ticket and let me get to work. I don't have all day. I have a real job to go to. I don't get to sit around all day and eat doughnuts!

Conflict and managing conflict is an everyday part of policing. Some conflicts may be quite minor like this one and can be easily shrugged off by maintaining a polite and impartial demeanour, not taking the bait, or avoiding arguments. However, some conflicts may not be so easily dealt with and take skilful management to keep you and the other parties safe. Calls that involve weapons or hostages or other unknowns (Are there weapons? How many subjects, parties, or suspects? Are people under the influence of drugs or alcohol, or are they anti-police?) are just a few.

This text focuses on conflict, although the authors do realize that not all policing involves conflict or the potential for conflict. However, the very nature of policing, including the perception of the power that police officers hold, brings officers into more conflicts than are encountered in many other fields of work. Research also indicates that many police injuries occur when officers intervene in conflicts between individuals who know one another. As well, with mental institutions and other agencies discharging patients and clients, police are called upon to deal with increasingly complex problems (Consortium, 2000).

Police conflicts are different from other conflicts in many respects. First, officers are often requested to get involved in ongoing battles such as domestic disputes or other confrontations or disturbances. Second, the conflict is rarely started by the police officer, and the officer must often get involved in a conflict that he or she knows very little about. Thrown into the middle of a battle, the officer has little or no knowledge of its cause, what it is about, or how long it has been going on, and knows virtually nothing about the disputants. Third, the officer may be unwelcome if the call came from a witness or other third party to the dispute, and the conflict may turn onto him or her, making the officer the unintended focus of both persons' anger. Fourth, an officer cannot always predict when a confrontation may turn violent and require an escalation to use of force. Thus, conflicts can pose a serious threat to police officer safety. As well, officers first to arrive at a scene may have to deal with potential suicides, hostage takers, people completely out of control, and other crises that are truly challenging to manage without harm to any of the involved parties. To minimize the threat and potential for injury, conflict management skills are essential. When an officer is armed with these skills, the potential of increased violence is reduced, and the chances of a successful outcome are enhanced in such conflicts.

On the other hand, community policing has increasingly involved police personnel in functions beyond those described above. Programs in schools, agencies, and other community initiatives require that officers have excellent communication skills, which are essential for resolving conflicts in the community. Thus this book, although focused primarily on conflict, also includes a wide variety of communication skills to enhance your work with the public.

This first chapter introduces the area of conflict and conflict resolution. We begin by defining conflict, defining the continuum of conflict, and outlining the causes of conflict. Next, we examine productive conflict and compare it to destructive conflict—the type of conflict most often handled on police patrol—and both its positive and negative aspects. Then we look at the changing role of the police officer and how this affects conflict management. Last, we describe the content of this text and how it will assist you in becoming more skilled in conflict management.

DEFINING CONFLICT AND THE CONTINUUM OF CONFLICT

In the examples of conflict that we have discussed, there are several clues about its nature. First, conflict is about disagreement, which can range from a mild argument to full-blown violence. Second, conflict involves the perception that one person or group is somehow interfering with the other person or group. In the opening scenario, the female driver perceives that the officer stopped her because of her gender. The officer, however, was simply doing his duty by ticketing a speeding driver and refused to venture further into any argument. Therefore, the officer did not perceive this encounter as a conflict. This leads to a third characteristic of conflict: People engage in conflict when the issue is something they feel strongly about (at least at the time) and feel they need to defend their position about an idea, event, or situation.

Conflict Defined

With these ideas in mind, **conflict** can be defined as a condition where two sets of demands, goals, or motives are incompatible (Dubrin and Geerinck, 2001). Conflict can also be seen as strife, quarrels, and battles. During a conflict, one person or group interferes with, disrupts, or in some way makes the other person or group less effective in a particular area (Dubrin, 2001). Conflict is also characterized by emotions or feelings that range from slight annoyance to uncontrollable violence.

The Continuum of Conflict

There are many ways to look at conflict. In chapter 3 we will look at stages in conflict. Here we will examine the continuum of conflict, which ranges from conflict escalation to de-escalation. However, before examining this continuum, let's explore some of the characteristics or properties of conflict. There are four properties of conflict interaction (Folger, et al., 2001).

1. **Conflict is made up of and sustained by moves and countermoves in interaction.** When describing a past conflict with someone, the conversation usually goes something like, "He said, then I said, then he said, then I stormed out of the room." Sound familiar? How these moves occur depends upon the personalities of the people involved, including such aspects as conflict style, power in the relationship, and the ability of one party or both parties to use persuasion tactics.

2. **Patterns of behaviour in conflicts tend to perpetuate themselves** (Folger, et al., 2001, p. 28). During a conflict, perceptions are heavily involved, whether they are correct or incorrect. These perceptions are affected by assumptions about how messages will be received by the other person. For example, one of our children often starts a request by stating, "I know you probably won't let me, but…" The assumption here is that the answer will most likely be no. It's also a guilt inducer and often quite effective!

   An important note here is that people who are in repeated conflicts tend to repeat the same pattern (often destructive) of interaction. People who have continued interaction with police may adopt the same confrontational style with all officers based on an early negative (or positive) experience.

3. **Conflict interaction is shaped by the climate of the situation.** All situations have a climate inherent to that unique situation. Teachers consciously or unconsciously create climates in classes, and the same teacher can have a negative climate with one group and a positive climate with another. The climate is based on the interaction of all the players, which changes from class to class, meeting to meeting, police encounter to police encounter, and so on. Later, we will examine the importance of a supportive climate for conflict resolution.

Consider This...

When dealing with bar fights, one officer reports, "If you can just get the guys out of the bar or into a quieter area, the fight usually ends right away. They no longer have to be macho in front of their buddies or others. I try to get them away from the bar crowd."

4. **Conflict interactions are influenced by relationships, and relationships influence conflict interactions.** Conflicts are often very tense and emotional, partly because people are trying to get what they want, and partly because conflict has implications for the present and future relationship of those involved. For example, if someone tells you that you cannot be trusted, this has implications for the relationship. You may back down and attempt to persuade the person that you are trustworthy, or you may become angry at such treatment and retaliate. Whichever course you choose, the relationship will be affected. In many conflicts, **face-saving** or trying to protect or repair your image with others can escalate a conflict. When someone accuses us of wrongdoing (whether or not he or she is correct), we may attempt to protect our self-image. This behaviour often leads to a downward spiral in the conflict and continued escalation. For example, an argument about whose turn it is to do the dishes becomes one about not pulling weight in a relationship, then the accusation, "You don't really love me!" Whenever we feel we have to defend our self-esteem, we can become defensive. Such defensiveness does not lead to resolution. It is important, therefore, to be very aware of the escalation of conflict in any relationship—personal or professional.

Conflict escalation and de-escalation, then, are necessary for a more complete understanding of the conflict process. Figure 1.1 is the Continuum of Conflict, which illustrates conflict escalation. It is important that police officers develop a thorough understanding of this continuum in order to use the correct skills to de-escalate a conflict when possible. Let's discuss this continuum in some detail by using an example to enhance understanding. Also, the Points for Pondering box below explores another example of conflict escalation: road rage.

POINTS FOR PONDERING   *Road Rage and Conflict Escalation*

When it comes to conflict escalation, "road rage" is a great example of behaviour out of control. Open up the newspaper or listen to the news and you will discover incidents of stabbings, shootings, fist fights, cars being run off the road, and a host of angry behaviours displayed by disgruntled drivers. Road rage includes aggressive tailgating, honking horns, mouthing and yelling at other drivers, using nonverbal rude gestures, and other behaviours that indicate displeasure with another driver. According to the National Traffic Safety Administration, approximately 66 per cent of traffic fatalities are caused by aggressive driving (State Farm Insurance).

The quick escalation of these incidents is very alarming to police services. A seemingly calm driver can turn into an aggressive driver in seconds at the wheel of a large and fast-moving vehicle. People appear to go from law-abiding drivers to "maniacs" who then engage in all kinds of dangerous driving. At times, one vehicle follows the other vehicle, and the conflict continues as the drivers get out of their cars and continue to fight. Police services all over the country have programs to prevent these aggressive driving incidents, such as "Safe on Seven," a program launched by the Ontario Provincial Police to target aggressive driving on Highway #7 east of Peterborough.

Causes of road rage include misperception of the other driver's motives (for example, one driver was deliberately cut off by another), misdirected bad moods, long and irritating waits (such as traffic jams or long lines at traffic lights), and invasion of personal territory (the immediate space around the vehicle). Whatever the cause, the escalation in these incidents is alarming and illustrates the quick escalation in a conflict.

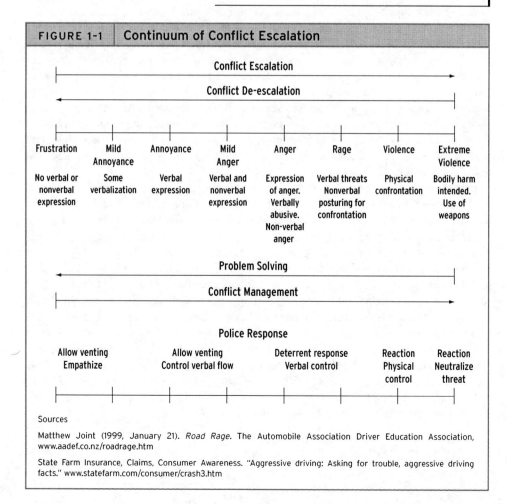

| FIGURE 1-1 | Continuum of Conflict Escalation |

Conflict Escalation →

← Conflict De-escalation

Frustration	Mild Annoyance	Annoyance	Mild Anger	Anger	Rage	Violence	Extreme Violence
No verbal or nonverbal expression	Some verbalization	Verbal expression	Verbal and nonverbal expression	Expression of anger. Verbally abusive. Non-verbal anger	Verbal threats Nonverbal posturing for confrontation	Physical confrontation	Bodily harm intended. Use of weapons

← Problem Solving

Conflict Management →

Police Response

Allow venting Empathize	Allow venting Control verbal flow	Deterrent response Verbal control	Reaction Physical control	Reaction Neutralize threat

Sources

Matthew Joint (1999, January 21). *Road Rage*. The Automobile Association Driver Education Association, www.aadef.co.nz/roadrage.htm

State Farm Insurance, Claims, Consumer Awareness. "Aggressive driving: Asking for trouble, aggressive driving facts." www.statefarm.com/consumer/crash3.htm

At the far left is the mildest form of conflict. Here a person feels mild annoyance or frustration about an event or situation. For example, a person is perturbed by the super-market customer in front of her who has twelve items in his cart in the one-to-eight item express checkout line. At this end of the continuum, we rarely express our feelings and keep them to ourselves. The woman may be thinking that the customer ahead of her is rude or inconsiderate, but she takes no action, and the customer with twelve items will remain blissfully unaware of her feelings.

To move further right along the continuum, mild annoyance increases, and there is some nonverbal expression and perhaps some verbal expression. For example, the woman loudly sighs and rolls her eyes at others who are aware of the situation. The woman may even comment to someone next in line, "Boy, I wish people would stick to the rules about express lanes being eight items or less." At this the point in the continu-um, there has been no direct communication. Perception about the situation is important here. If the woman thinks the customer is deliberately rude, she will need to decide how or when she will engage the other person to point out his wrongdoing. Unfortunately, in many conflicts, people do not think about this and rapidly engage in a conflict that leads to disastrous results.

If the situation is important enough (or we think it is at the time), we move to the next level, verbally expressing our opinions, ideas, and thoughts. How we express them is crit-ical. Say something one way, and the conflict escalates; say it a different way, and the con-flict de-escalates. The woman may say, "Hey, Buddy, can't you read? This is the express lane." If the man ignores her, she may increase her verbal and nonverbal behaviours that indicate annoyance. She may move closer to him, change the tone and pitch of her voice (become louder, talk more deeply, enunciate more slowly and carefully). For example, she may say, "What, are you deaf? I'm talking to you!" If she shouts, she has moved to further escalation. If he now engages, and they both start shouting at each other, others had better move to another line and get out of the way! At this point, many conflicts quickly escalate, and that is one of the reasons why it is so important to get angry people to slow down and calm down, and to get them talking more softly.

At the next stage or level, verbal threats are common, and there may be several non-verbal indicators. Waving a finger at the other person, jabbing the person with a finger, and closing interpersonal distance are indicators that physical violence is likely, and extreme violence such as assault, attempted murder, and murder can occur. While rare in the gro-cery store, there have been outbursts and skirmishes at checkouts.

As police officers and as people, we need conflict management skills to de-escalate conflicts and to be able, in some encounters, to avoid conflict completely. If the woman in our example had decided that the whole situation was not a big deal and waited quietly, the conflict would have been averted. Or she could have verbalized her concern in a less threat-ening manner that would have allowed the man to save face. She could have said, "Excuse me, Sir. You may not be aware of this, but you are standing in the express checkout with more than eight items." The man then could have chosen his response in a better commu-nication climate and may have responded differently. While we are not in control of what others say and do, we are in control of what *we* say and do, and, with good skills, police officers can assist in the de-escalation of many conflicts.

CAUSES OF CONFLICT

While each conflict is often unique to the individuals involved in it, the causes of conflict can be categorized into five sources or potential causes (adapted from Dubrin and Geerinck, 2001).

Competition for Limited Resources

Conflict can occur when people or groups cannot get all of what they want, and the resources have to be shared or divided up. Gangs have "turf wars" when each gang feels it has the right to the same "turf." Divorced or divorcing couples may fight over who gets what from the marriage, children fight over toys, and people who are drunk may fight over who gets the last bottle of beer.

Personality Differences

People are different from each other, and these differences can lead to conflict. Three areas in which people may differ are in their values, beliefs, and attitudes. **Values** are central and enduring goals in life that individuals feel are important and right. For example, most police officers believe in the laws that they enforce, and they value a society with such laws and order. Dealing with others who make breaking laws a way of life creates a potential for conflict.

Beliefs, or the things that you hold as being true or false, right or wrong, can also be a source of conflict with others. Strongly held beliefs have led to many skirmishes between law enforcement personnel and various groups during protests. The more strongly held the belief, the more likely that it will cause significant conflict between people or groups. For example, if you strongly believe that stealing is wrong and you witness a friend stealing a CD from a store, there is more likely to be conflict than if you believe that it is acceptable to "rip off" small things from major department stores.

Differing attitudes can also be a cause of conflicts. **Attitudes** consist of feelings (affective component) and thoughts (cognitive component), and are inferred through a person's actions (behavioural component) (Alcock et al., 1998). Attitudes are pro or con and can vary in strength. Strong attitudes may be particularly important in a conflict, because strong attitudes have a number of characteristics, two of which are relevant to our discussion. Strong attitudes are *durable* in that they tend not to change over time and resist persuasion attempts. Second, strong attitudes are more closely linked to behaviour in that people behave according to their strong attitudes as opposed to weaker attitudes (Alcock et al., 1998). For example, a person whose attitude is very strong against drinking and driving will likely never drive while drinking, is more likely to support groups who advocate this behaviour, and will not allow friends or family to drive while drunk. A person with a weaker attitude may pay lip service to the idea but still drive after having a few drinks. If two people or groups hold strong and different attitudes, and if this difference is stimulated, the potential for conflict is greater than if the different attitudes are weak. We may not even be aware of a difference until it comes up in discussion. This would then be the stimulus that leads to awareness of a difference. For example, a police officer may not be aware of her new partner's prejudice until the partner makes a reference to "welfare scum."

Many conflicts also stem simply from the fact that people do not like each other. A **personality clash** is an antagonistic relationship between two people. This clash can be caused by differing personal attributes, ages, preferences, interests, values, beliefs, attitudes, or even personal appearance.

Cultural Differences

Culture is a learned and shared system of knowledge, behaviour, beliefs, attitudes, values, and **norms.** Norms are unwritten rules or guidelines about what constitutes acceptable or unacceptable behaviour in a group, team, or culture. Canada is a very diverse nation made up of many cultures. These cultures differ in their learned and shared systems and thus behave in different ways and value different things. Such differences can lead to conflicts as many people suffer from **ethnocentrism** or the belief that their way of doing things is better, more moral, or more right than others' way of doing things. For example, a person whose culture values the family more than individual rights may disagree with someone who makes a career choice of which his or her family disapproves. This person would feel strongly that individual career choice must be approved by all family members. While cultural differences do not cause conflicts, such differences increase the potential for conflict between members of different cultures.

Policing Styles

While the majority of conflicts occur between police officers and the public, conflict also occurs between officers who have widely different styles of policing. There is a great deal of literature about styles of policing. One traditional style of classification includes the *crime fighter, social servant, law enforcer,* and *watchman* (Greenberg and Ruback, 1982). The crime fighter's primary focus is capturing offenders, and he or she often has an aggressive nature. Almost the opposite of the crime fighter is the social servant, whose primary focus is to help people, and this officer is friendlier than the crime fighter. The law enforcer is satisfied by enforcing all aspects of the law, which range from municipal bylaws to apprehending offenders. He or she may be semi-aggressive. The last style, watchman, is characterized by an officer who does no more than absolutely required and often conveys an uncaring attitude. The style of a police officer depends upon the officer's personality, attitudes, and ambition. Officers with vastly different styles may create a ground for conflict. For example, the *crime fighter* may be hostile and aggressive with witnesses, offending the *social servant* who believes in individual rights. After such an incident, the two police officers may have a heated debate about the aggressive behaviour.

The Building of Stone Walls

Unlike road rage, with its quick escalation of aggression, this type of conflict grows slowly and has been likened to the building of a stone wall (Mayer, 1990). The beginning of the conflict is a minor incident or *pinch*, which is not dealt with openly. The person who has been *pinched* unconsciously begins to gather data to support his or her own point of view to feel that he or she is right and the other person is wrong. It should be noted that much of the information gathered is distorted by the person's perception of the other person. As a result, a wall is slowly built between the two people that becomes insurmountable. For example, a police officer's partner takes the credit for an arrest that she feels should have been shared by both of them, but she doesn't approach him about it. This *pinch* starts her unconsciously seeking (and finding) information about the selfishness of her partner. After awhile, the resentment begins to show, and she requests a different partner.

PRODUCTIVE AND DESTRUCTIVE CONFLICT

Productive conflict has positive consequences, and destructive conflict has negative consequences. While conflict is usually perceived as negative, when properly managed, many conflicts may have positive outcomes and have productive results. For example, a police officer arrests a youth for a minor crime and subsequently develops a rapport with this young person. Initially the youth is angry with the officer and is rude. However, because the officer speaks calmly to the youth and treats him with dignity, the youth calms down. He tells the officer of his situation at home with an abusive father and alcoholic mother. The officer gives him information for help, which the youth accesses to help him get out of the house. This conflict had a positive ending. If the officer had been aggressive and confrontational, the outcome might have been very different. Here we examine some of the positive and negative consequences of conflict.

Positive Consequences of Conflict

Managed properly, conflict can have positive and productive benefits:

1. **The two sides in a conflict may develop new ideas, change perceptions, solve problems, or make better decisions as a result of conflict.** Many community–police programs are the direct result of initial conflicts between the police and groups in the community.

2. **The two sides may develop new respect for each other and work better together in the future.** For example, historically, many police officers have had conflicts with social workers. However, if a police officer and social worker can have an open discussion about their differences and come to some agreement, the relationship will be better.

3. **A small conflict may bring larger issues out into the open for resolution.** Police partners who argue over small things may be covering over a larger difference. If the larger difference can be brought up with the goal of resolution, the partners will develop more trust in each other.

4. **A conflict may illustrate a need for change in laws, policies, or procedures in a police service or other organization.** As will be seen in a later chapter, changes are required in many services to increase arrests in domestic assaults.

5. **Managing conflicts appropriately may also improve skills and relations in other areas of communication.** With proper training in conflict management skills, law enforcement or other personnel improve their social interaction skills. In New York City, training police officers in mediation skills as well other social interaction skills has promoted more positive and professional interaction with the public (Cooper, 2001). The "Points for Pondering" feature below outlines further interventions to improve skills of police officers in New York City.

POINTS FOR PONDERING   *Should All Police Officers*
                                            Carry "Palm Cards"?

In the wake of the shooting death of an unarmed West African immigrant on February 4, 1999, the New York City Police Department has undertaken several initiatives to prevent a similar occurrence. Amadou Diallo was a 22-year-old West African immigrant who was shot 19 times by four New York police officers who fired a total of 41 shots. He was standing in the doorway of his apartment building near midnight when he was asked to "freeze." Rather than comply, he reached into his pants pocket. The officers thought he was reaching for a gun. Diablo resembled a suspect whom the officers had been tracking. Police later speculated that he had not known what "freeze" meant and that he was actually reaching into his pocket for his wallet to show the officers his identity. Another possibility is that he thought he was being robbed, because the officers were in plain clothes and driving an unmarked patrol car. Regardless of speculation, this incident sparked several protests and underscored a pressing need for changes in how the police treat members of the public, especially those from visible minorities.

Several initiatives have been undertaken to ensure that people of colour are treated more fairly and that cultural differences will not become obstacles to proper treatment by police officers. One especially interesting initiative is the distribution to police officers of "palm cards," which instruct them to behave more politely with all citizens. The palm-sized cardboard cards include such instructions as saying please, thank you, hello, sir, ma'am, and other socially acceptable terms. The cards also provide officers with instructions to respect all individuals and to respect individual differences in culture, customs, and beliefs. These cards can be kept in an officer's pocket or notepad and be used as reference or a continual reminder of how the public should be treated.

Do you think that these "palm cards" will be effective? Do you think all police officers would benefit from carrying these cards in police services across Canada? While we often look at the United States as having more problems with prejudice and discrimination, there is ample evidence of racism and other forms of prejudice in Canada. What other training would assist police officers in developing their skills to interact with a diverse population?

Sources

APB News (1999, March 31). 41 shots heard around the world. www.apbnews.com/newscenter/majorcases/diallo/background.html

Christopher Cooper (2001, January 8). Mediation training to improve police social interaction skills. *Mediation Newsletter*. www.mediate.com/articles/police.htm

Negative Consequences of Conflict

Despite the positive outcomes of conflict, conflict can have many destructive and negative consequences for the individual, the organization or service, and society.

Consider This...

One officer states, "It's the continued daily grind that gets to me. Not the big events, but the hassles with Admin about trying to get my overtime pay, or the smiling at members of the public when you really want to yell at them for their stupidity. These conflicts seem to go on and on and never get resolved."

Many of us can remember conflicts with others that ruined or ended a relationship, had us demoted or fired from a job, or resulted in a reprimand from our superiors. There are several other possible negative consequences of conflict:

1. **Prolonged and unresolved conflict may be detrimental to an individual's emotional and physical well-being** (Dubrin and Geerinck, 2001). Unresolved or continued conflicts are stressors that weaken the immune system and can lead to health problems such as heart disease and chronic intestinal disorders.

2. **The aftermath of extreme conflict can have high financial, emotional, and social costs.** Incidents such as the beating of Rodney King, the RCMP handling of the OPEC protest in British Columbia, and other reported examples of questionable officer conduct have high costs that all police services pay for long after the precipitating incident. Financially, the service(s) involved may have to pay high costs for lawyers and other experts. Officers personally involved in the incident pay emotional costs that result from stress, demotion, suspension, and a ruined reputation, regardless of the outcome. When such incidents occur, public trust that has been hard-won may be lost and take years to restore.

3. **Conflict, even when it does not produce emotional or physical symptoms, is fatiguing for everyone.** Police officers who continually manage conflict after conflict, shift after shift, become tired and drained from their experiences. Fatigue may create more conflicts at home.

4. **During a conflict, people may be more concerned with winning and getting what they want than with preserving a relationship.** In other words, people can be more concerned with their interests to the detriment of the interests of their family, service, or society. So concerned with making an arrest, an officer may not follow procedure, and the suspect may be freed on a technicality.

5. **An extreme negative consequence of conflict is that a disgruntled person resorts to violence or even murder.** In the workplace, former employees have opened fire on co-workers. For example, in April 1999, Pierre Lebrun shot and killed four former colleagues in an Ottawa bus garage. When police intervene during a violent conflict, or during incidents such as the Lebrun example, officers themselves may become targets of the violence and aggression.

The all-too-frequent negative consequences of conflict illustrate the need for good conflict management skills to handle a spectrum of conflicts ranging from a person unhappy with a ticket to a man threatening you verbally or physically.

HOW THIS BOOK CAN HELP YOU

To more effectively manage conflict (both on and off the job), you need the skills to handle each type of situation. The skills used in one setting may be inappropriate for use in another setting. Good "conflict managers" can quickly assess a conflict and then choose the right "tools" to do the "job." This is the main focus of the text. What follows is a brief overview of the topics and the goals for each area.

This text will help you:

Understand the nature of conflict

By understanding the nature of conflict (its causes, its consequences, and its characteristics), you will more readily identify potential conflict or those conflicts that may escalate without immediate intervention.

Recognize the impact of personality on conflict

Who you are and who others are influence conflict in many ways, including the perception of conflict, comfort level with conflict, and basic conflict management styles.

Develop self-awareness

Dealing with your own reactions and paying attention to your own behaviour during a conflict will assist you in your personal development towards becoming an excellent police officer. Understanding your own reactions to conflict, anger, and stress will assist you in a wide variety of difficult situations, such as telling a family about the death of a loved one or managing your own reaction if you have to draw and fire your weapon.

Develop a set of skills to manage conflict

There are many alternative methods to handle conflicts with members of the public, other officers and professionals, and anyone else in your lives. Skills range from the apparently simple act of active listening, to the more complex skills of crisis intervention, which may require physical force. Also, paying attention to verbal and nonverbal communication will assist you in a wide range of conflicts.

Increase your knowledge of different populations that you will deal with as a police officer

This text includes information on a wide variety of mental disorders, mental challenges, and emotional problems. In several areas, we concentrate upon aggression, because angry and frustrated people are the subjects in many calls.

Manage conflict with difficult people or in difficult situations

Dealing with substance abusers, individuals with mental or emotional challenges, and domestic disputes can take a heavy toll on officers' patience and skills. Negotiating with subjects is a specialized skill, but as the first officer on a scene, you may need to be the initial contact with this person. A more thorough knowledge of negotiations and mediation will help you manage these people and their situations.

Manage the stress of police work

The final chapter of this text will assist you in managing the stress that results from many of the difficult situations that you will encounter on the job. A special section on post-traumatic stress disorder is included. Developing stress management techniques early in your career will help you manage the negative stress of policing.

This text is both knowledge- and skills-based, and upon completion of this text, you will have gained a more thorough understanding of conflict and the skills you will need as a new or current law enforcement officer.

SUMMARY

In this introductory chapter, conflict was defined as two sets of demands, goals, or motives that are incompatible. Conflict has four properties that are important to understand in the development and continuation of conflict. The continuum of conflict was introduced to demonstrate the stages in the escalation or de-escalation of conflict by identifying behaviours characteristic of each stage. Conflict has numerous causes that, for our purposes, can be classified into five categories: competition for limited resources; personality differences, including differing values, beliefs, and attitudes; cultural differences; policing styles; and the building of stone walls.

Conflict can be productive, with positive consequences, or it can be destructive, with negative consequences. Properly managed conflict can have many positive consequences, including the development of new ideas and new respect for the other party, as well as the realization and resolution of larger issues. It may also underscore the need for change, leading to the development of improved social relation skills. However, the many negative consequences of conflict underscore the need for development in this critical area of law enforcement. Negative consequences include detrimental effects on a person's physical and emotional well-being, high financial, emotional, and social costs, fatigue from long-term "battles," more concern about winning than other consequences or outcomes, and the possibility of extreme violence.

This text will help develop effective conflict management skills, including understanding the nature of conflict, recognizing the impact of personality on conflict, developing self-awareness, and developing a set of skills needed to manage people or situations specific to law enforcement.

CASE STUDY

The Irritable Partner

Cindy had been a police officer for ten years and spent nine of those years in a small town in northern Alberta. When her husband was transferred to work for his company in Toronto, Cindy applied to the Toronto Police Service, was accepted, and began working out of one of the downtown divisions. Working in a small town and usually without a partner, Cindy developed many ways of dealing with drunk and disorderly individuals and could usually talk a person out of any argument and get him or her to leave any situation and go home. In other words, she had "the gift of the gab." She would cajole, sympathize, and spend time talking to people, and she rarely had to use force in her previous position. In fact, some of the "town drunks" treated her like a long-lost friend and rarely gave her any trouble.

Her new partner, Joachim, seemed nice enough, and several shifts went by uneventfully. She found him to be a little "short" with people, and on several occasions he used some phrases that made Cindy a little uncomfortable, such as "welfare bums" and "leeches." When she commented on these labels, he told her to wait until she had been in the city for a year, to see what he had seen, then she would change her tune. He said that his job was "to arrest first and ask questions later and leave everything else to the bleeding-heart social workers." Cindy believed that an important part of policing is to help others, especially the disadvantaged of society.

One Friday night the two partners were dispatched to an unwanted visitor call at an address in a deteriorating area of the city. Upon arrival, the two partners found a very intoxicated man sitting on the couch in the living room. Although also intoxicated, the woman complained that she wanted the man to go home, but he had refused and threatened to "put her in her proper place." She wanted him to go home and leave her alone.

Cindy approached the man and said, "Hi there. How are you feeling tonight?"

"Just fine, Officer. Hey, you're awful pretty to be a cop!"

Cindy said, "Sir, the lady here has requested that you go home now. I think that might be a good idea, and maybe you can call her tomorrow when you're feeling better."

"Well, maybe you gotta point. I guess..."

Before he could finish his sentence, Joachim stormed over and shouted, "Look, you lousy drunk. Stand up before I have to come over there and help you!"

Suddenly, the man stood up from the couch and took a swing at Joachim, who sidestepped the lunge, and the intoxicated man fell down. Joachim immediately cuffed him and said, "I'm arresting you for assaulting a police officer."

Cindy could barely restrain her anger at the way the situation ended but prudently decided to wait until near the end of the shift when things were quieter to speak to Joachim.

Cindy said, "Look, I'm having a real problem here. Why did you go after that guy? I had the situation under control, and I think he was going to leave on his own. You just aggravated him and caused that confrontation!"

Joachim replied, "You don't know about big city policing. You have to subdue these guys right away or they take advantage or attack when you're not looking! Our job is to get these guys off the street, not play counsellor to them!"

Cindy responded, "I know that we're supposed to get the 'bad guys,' but he was just sad and drunk. You deliberately provoked him!"

"Obviously, you don't understand what real police work is all about. I'll do things my way and don't get in my way," Joachim retorted. With that, Joachim began to write in his report, leaving Cindy perplexed and angry.

Questions

1. What is the cause of the conflict between Cindy and Joachim?
2. Using the Continuum of Conflict, explain the escalation of the conflict at the call.
3. Should Cindy just drop the issue or continue to talk to Joachim about their differences? Why or why not?
4. If Cindy decides to continue this discussion, how should she approach the topic again?

KEY TERMS

Attitudes: Complex internal constructs that consist of feelings and thoughts that are perceived through an individual's behaviour.

Beliefs: Things or ideas that individuals hold as being true or false.

Conflict: A condition where two sets of demands, goals, or motives are incompatible. One person or party interferes or disrupts the actions or pursuits of another person or party.

Culture: A learned and shared system of knowledge, behaviour, beliefs, attitudes, values, and norms.

Ethnocentrism: A mistaken belief that one's cultural way of doing something is the most correct or preferred way.

Face-saving: An attempt to protect or repair our image to others.

Norms: Unwritten guidelines or rules about what constitutes acceptable or unacceptable behaviour within a group, team, or culture.

Personality clash: An antagonistic relationship between two people.

Values: Central and enduring goals in life that individuals feel are true and right.

WEB LINKS

www.statcan.ca
This is the site for Statistics Canada. Many of the statistics used in this textbook have been found using this comprehensive site.

www.eiconsortium.org.htm
This is the site for The Consortium for Research on Emotional Intelligence in Organizations. Visit this site to learn more about emotional intelligence, because emotional intelligence is linked heavily to the ability to manage self, including conflict.

www.gov.on.ca/opp
This is the site for the Ontario Provincial Police. The motto for the home page—Times change and so we change with them—illustrates the continued need for ongoing training for police and police recruits.

REFERENCES

J. E. Alcock, D. W. Carment, and S. W. Sadava (1998). *A textbook of social psychology* (4th ed.) Scarborough, ON: Prentice Hall.

Christopher Cooper (January 8, 2001). Mediation training to improve police social interaction skills. *Mediation Newsletter.* www.mediate.com/articles/police.htm

The Consortium for Research on Emotional Intelligence in Organizations (2000, March). "Conflict management for police." www.eiconsortium.org/conflict_management_police.htm

Andrew J. Dubrin (2001). *Human relations: Interpersonal, job-oriented skills.* Upper Saddle River, NJ: Prentice Hall.

Andrew J. Dubrin and Terri Geerinck (2001). *Human relations for career and personal success.* Scarborough, ON: Prentice Hall.

Joseph P. Folger, Marshall Scott Poole, and Randall K. Stutman (2001). *Working through conflict: Strategies for relationships, groups, and organizations.* New York: Addison Wesley Longman.

M. S. Greenberg and R. B. Ruback (1982). *Social psychology of the criminal justice system.* Belmont, CA: Wadsworth Publishing.

Richard J. Mayer (1990). *Conflict management: The courage to confront.* Columbus, OH: Batelle Press.

chapter two

The Process of Conflict

LEARNING OUTCOMES

After studying this chapter, you should be able to

- Identify the ways that you personally manage conflict.

- Identify the five major conflict management styles.

- Explain the three stages in a conflict.

- Understand the nature of emotions.

- Identify the emotions of frustration, anger and aggression, and sadness by checking verbal and nonverbal cues.

- Identify the influence of culture and gender on conflict.

Courtesy Peterborough Lakefield Community Police Service

On-the-Job Scenario

Ted, arriving a few minutes late for work, hastily drove into his assigned parking spot. He did not realize until too late that someone had parked a recumbent bicycle (which the rider drives with legs out in front) in his spot. Slamming on the brakes, he caught the rear of the bike, and it fell over. Ted put his car into park and jumped out to see if there was any damage to the obviously very expensive bike. As he was leaning over the bike, he heard a voice behind him.

"Hey, what did you do to my bike, you moron!" screamed Sonja, the bike owner.

Upset, Ted replied, "I'm really sorry. I didn't see the thing until I was already turning into the spot."

"You must have been really moving! Look at my bike! The paint is scratched, you've flattened the tire, you've dented the bumper, and it looks like you bent the wheel, too! You have to pay for this!"

"This is my spot. What are doing, parking here? And my car has damage too. Your bike scratched my front end. Do you even work here?"

"I'm calling the police, and then we'll see who the guilty person is. You're not getting away with this!"

"Fine, I have my cell phone right here! We'll see who is paying the damages!"

As we have already discovered, conflict is a complex process and not always easy to manage on many occasions. How the conflict continues in the above scenario will depend greatly on a number of factors. To develop a true understanding of conflict, it is important to discover how we deal with conflicts in our own lives. First, each person has a dominant style or way of conflict management. Our dominant style is the one that we use most often when confronted with a particular problem. Second, each person sizes up the other person and tries to calculate possible outcomes (if each person is thinking clearly). Third, other characteristics of the person and the situation come into play. For example, in this scenario one of the people is female and appears angrier, and the result may be continued escalation in this conflict. These other important characteristics of conflict include emotions, verbal and nonverbal behaviours, and the situation or the setting. This analysis of the situation is made from our personal viewpoints and perceptions. What do you think will happen in this scenario? Will they calmly wait for the police? Will they continue to argue? What will the police do upon arrival? And if you were the attending officer, what would you do?

In this chapter, we will explore conflict in more detail by exploring our own ways of managing conflict. First, conflict management styles will be explained. Then, we will examine some of the more complex components of conflict, including the stages in a conflict, emotions, verbal and nonverbal behaviours, and the influence of gender and culture.

CONFLICT MANAGEMENT STYLES AND APPROACHES TO CONFLICT

There is little doubt that we are all different from each other, and these very differences influence how we manage and deal with conflict. The family you were raised in has a great deal of impact upon how you deal with conflicts yourself. For example, did family members shout at each other and voice their differing opinions? Did they talk quietly about the problems they were having with each other? Or did your family not express any differences of opinion and avoid confrontation with each other? Your comfort level today around conflict was influenced by your family and predisposed you to the styles or methods you now use to manage conflict.

Conflicts are expressed in two major ways between people or parties. **Overt conflicts** are conflicts that are openly discussed. **Covert conflicts** are hidden. When there is conflict, people may hide their feelings and express them indirectly. People may play "games" or deliberately hurt the feelings of another person when they feel angry or hurt. You may have had the experience of someone not directly telling you what the problem is, but expressing discontent in more indirect ways such as picking fights about unimportant things. Although we do not have time to deal with all the ways that covert conflict occurs, be aware that they can and do happen. A classic book on interpersonal games was written by Eric Berne (1964) titled *The Games People Play*. To learn more about these games, you may want to read this book.

Conflict Management Styles

Regardless of the cause, we all manage conflict by relying on a particular style. A discussion of these five styles or orientations will help you to better understand the nature of conflict and the different ways that people handle conflict. Kenneth Thomas (1976) identified these styles as competitive, accommodative, compromising or sharing, collaborative, and avoidant. Each style is based on how concerned you are about satisfying your own needs and achieving your own goals, and how concerned you are about other people's needs and goals. In other words, the styles vary according to how concerned you are about yourself versus how concerned you are for the other. Refer to figure 2-1 where the five styles are plotted.

- **Competition** Competition is based on the idea of **win–lose**. One party has his or her needs and goals met, while the other party loses. There is very little concern about the other person's thoughts or feelings. People who rely on competition can be aggressive (verbally and/or physically) and extremely argumentative. How concerned were the two people in the opening scenario about each other's feelings? Much aggression is based on this style in which one or more people use physical violence or force to get what they want, with little or no concern about others. When members of the public have an "us versus them" view of police officers in the community, disputes are usually based on one side losing and one side winning.

- **Accommodation** When using accommodation, you are more concerned with satisfying the other's needs and goals than with taking care of your own. This person puts the other's needs ahead of his or her own and can be called self-sacrificing or generous. The person yields to the other person's needs or desires. For example, rather than fight, many victims of abuse give up and let the dominant person get his or her own way.

- **Compromising** When you compromise or share, both parties get at least part of what each wanted. When dealing with a domestic situation, a police officer may get both sides to arrive at a solution in which both partners get some of what each person wants. The officer suggests that one person leave for the remainder of the night while the other person stays. The officer may then suggest that the two people get together the next day when everyone is calmer and the effects of the alcohol have been "slept off." While the conflict may be far from over, the fight is over, the officer can leave, and disgruntled neighbours can go back to sleep.

- **Collaboration** Collaboration is based on the idea of **win–win**, where both parties can get what they want. When you use a win–win strategy, you are genuinely concerned with satisfying both your needs and the needs of the other party. Collaborators use persuasion, logic, and a problem-solving approach to find mutually satisfying solutions. Communities, working with the local police service, have formed many mutually beneficial services to reduce such problems as youth crime and bullying. With these services, areas of concern of both the community and the police have been addressed, to the satisfaction of both partners.

- **Avoidance** People who rely on avoidance can be both uncooperative and unassertive (they do not voice their needs). Such people may physically or mentally withdraw from the conflict and have little concern for their needs or the needs of the other person. They may adopt an attitude of "Who cares?" A police officer questioning a youth who witnessed a crime may receive responses from the youth that typify avoidance. The youth may be belligerent because he has little concern for the officer's needs and does not care about the incident. At times, this uncaring attitude surprises inexperienced officers. This type of conflict is **lose–lose**, because neither person gains anything from such a conflict.

FIGURE 2-1	Conflict Styles

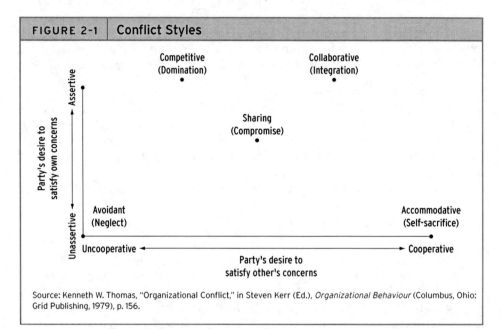

Source: Kenneth W. Thomas, "Organizational Conflict," in Steven Kerr (Ed.), *Organizational Behaviour* (Columbus, Ohio: Grid Publishing, 1979), p. 156.

None of these styles or orientations is correct or incorrect all of the time. Any style may be correct if it matches how important the goal is to you (satisfying your own concerns) and how important it is that you also satisfy the goals and concerns of the other person. The problem is that most of us rely on one style only, and the result of that approach is that we may react rigidly in a conflict. In our opening scenario, competition may be the immediate style that Sonja adopts in any type of conflict instead of thinking the situation through. She immediately becomes angry and looks for a way to "win" the fight. For example, if the relationship is very important (and therefore the goals of each party are also important), collaboration is the right strategy to choose. If your goals are not that important but those of the other person are, you might choose to use accommodation. We could re-label the X-axis of the above chart, "Importance of the Relationship," to assist you in your choice of strategy. In reality, we seldom make a conscious choice of style, and many of us rely on a preferred style that is not always appropriate. Below is a self-assessment that will give you the opportunity to assess your own style(s) of conflict management.

| Self-Assessment | *Conflict Style Questionnaire* |

For each of the following statements, choose which of the five reactions is most like you. Choose only one from each statement.

1. If I know I am right about a particular issue, I
   a. continue to defend my position, no matter what.
   b. state that I respect the other person's opinion and ask him or her to tell me more.
   c. change the topic of the conversation.
   d. listen to the other person and strive to get him or her to agree with at least some of what I am saying.
   e. agree with the other person's view to make the other person happy.

2. When someone makes me angry, I
   a. often shout so that I get heard.
   b. talk to the person about why I am angry, so that we can come up with a solution.
   c. leave immediately.
   d. try to calm down and try to get him or her to see at least some things my way.
   e. immediately give in and apologize.

3. In general, conflict makes me feel
   a. really angry.
   b. hopeful that an agreeable solution can be found.
   c. like I want to hide.
   d. uneasy, because I may have to settle for a solution that I only partially agree with.
   e. scared that I may hurt the other person's feelings.

4. When I suspect that someone is taking advantage of me, I
   a. get the person to stop immediately.
   b. rely on persuasion and facts so that the person can see how I feel.
   c. try to stay away from the person.
   d. change how I relate to the person.
   e. simply accept the situation and go along with it.

5. If I don't agree with another person about an issue, I typically
   a. try to get the person to see things my way.
   b. talk the issue out and try to see it more logically.
   c. let the issue resolve itself rather than get involved.
   d. search for something about the issue that we both agree with.
   e. let it lie.

6. When someone is openly hostile with me, I usually
   a. respond in kind.
   b. use persuasion to try to cool the person down.

    c. immediately walk away.

    d. let the person wind down and then try to make him or her feel better.

    e. try to find something positive in the exchange.

7. If I am having a conflict with a co-worker over how something should be done, I tend to

    a. get my way.

    b. discuss it with him or her and do it in a way that makes us both happy.

    c. don't let him or her know that I disagree.

    d. give up some points if he or she gives up some too.

    e. just let the co-worker do it his or her way.

8. In general, I

    a. like a good fight.

    b. approach conflicts as problems to solve.

    c. detour around conflicts.

    d. try to get some of what I want in a conflict.

    e. try not to hurt anyone's feelings, even if it means agreeing with something I am totally against.

Scoring

Count up the number of a's, b's, c's, d's, and e's that you answered for each of the eight questions. If you scored mostly a's, you tend to approach conflict in a more aggressive manner and like to get your way, sometimes to the detriment of relationships. If you scored mostly b's, you tend to use collaboration and often see conflicts as problems that need solving. If you scored mostly c's, conflict makes you very uncomfortable and you would rather avoid it, even if it means not voicing your thoughts and ideas. Scoring mostly d's, you prefer to negotiate in conflicts so that you can get at least some of what you want in the situation. If you scored mostly e's, you don't like to hurt other people's feelings and would rather give in than take a stand.

    If you did not score strongly in any one area, you may be a person who uses a variety of styles. If so, then you already have one good conflict management strategy, if you match your style with your goals in any situation. In the next chapter, matching style with goals and relationships will be discussed as one method of conflict management. An awareness of your style or preferences is the starting point for developing this important tool for conflict management.

Sources

Dawn M. Baskerville (1993). How do you manage conflict? *Black Enterprise, 23* (10), 62–66.

Andrew J. Dubrin (2001). *Human relations: Interpersonal, job-oriented skills.* Upper Saddle River, NJ: Prentice Hall.

THE THREE STAGES IN A CONFLICT

A helpful way to view conflict is to see conflict as consisting of three stages (Pondy, 1967). Although this research is several years old, it is an excellent frame for viewing conflict. Police officers may be present for all three phases, and officer behaviour will vary according to each stage and the intensity of the behaviour in each stage. The continuum of conflict and the four properties of conflict from chapter 1 mesh with these phases to give an overall and clear picture of the conflict process. These phases are loosely based on the work of Pondy (1967).

Stage One: Antecedent Conditions

The antecedent conditions are the factors that precipitate the conflict. They include the thoughts and emotions that pertain to the conflict. In the opening scenario, hitting the expensive bike is the antecedent to the conflict. Sonya's thoughts may have been that Ted was not looking or that he was going to try to drive away. She was angry and ready for a "fight." Also, her immediate combative approach may be regarded as an antecedent. If she had been calm and more rational, there may have been no continued conflict.

Stage Two: Conflict Behaviour

Conflict behaviour includes all of the behaviours that are produced during the conflict, ranging from nonverbal indicators to violence and murder, as illustrated on the Continuum of Conflict. Ted and Sonya begin shouting at each other and finally decide to phone for police to solve the conflict. Personality, disposition, and preferred conflict management styles will all influence the progress (and escalation or de-escalation) of a conflict. If officers can become involved early in a dispute, they can defuse the situation and prevent further escalation. If we were to speculate on our scenario, what will happen if the police do not arrive quickly? Do you think the conflict will escalate? Do you think it might de-escalate? What if the two disputants were male? Since emotions are such an integral part of conflict, we will explore them in greater depth later. In many situations, disputants will look to the officer to end the conflict, and the officer often becomes the third party or mediator.

Stage Three: Aftermath

At one point or another, a conflict is over (at least temporarily). It can end by one person walking away, one person injuring another, one person being arrested, or by the two parties coming to an agreement. On the negative side, after a conflict people may feel hurt, drained, stressed, angry, or even suicidal. After a particularly devastating conflict, police officers may call in specially trained personnel to talk with the person. On the positive side, people may feel happy, relieved, and unburdened after a conflict. How would the conflict have ended if Ted had stayed calm and said to Sonya, "I'm really sorry about the bike. I think my insurance will cover the damage to your bike and my car. I really did not see your bike until it was too late." Conflicts can end on positive notes. Unfortunately, in police work happy endings are not guaranteed. However, using good conflict management skills, police officers have a better chance of ending altercations safely and peacefully.

EMOTIONS AND CONFLICT

During a conflict, strong emotions may be present. You may have heard the phrase "carried away," such as when someone says, "I don't know what happened. I guess he just got carried away and started yelling." Emotions can be overwhelming and make a tense situation even worse. Therefore, it is in your best interest to understand the nature of emotions, because they are evident in most conflicts. Here we will examine emotions and how they are displayed. We will look at three in detail—frustration, anger and aggression, and sadness—and explore how to manage these very potent emotions.

What Are Emotions?

There are several theories of emotions ranging from the earlier explanations of Canon and Bard and James and Lange to the newer theories of Singer and Schacter. **Emotions** are reactions to the environment and consist of physiological reactions, subjective cognitive states, and behavioural reactions. Scientists generally agree on these three characteristics of emotions (Baron, et al., 1998). Let's examine each of these three characteristics more closely.

When we encounter a situation, our bodies respond. For example, you are walking home late at night and hear a noise behind you that sounds like footsteps. Your heart rate increases, the hair on the back of your neck stands up, and your mouth suddenly goes dry. These reactions are prompted by your **autonomic nervous system**—the part of your nervous system that connects internal organs, glands, and involuntary muscles to the central nervous system. Two parts of the autonomic nervous system are active in regulating the physiological reactions (bodily responses) that accompany emotion (Baron, et al., 1998). The activation of the *sympathetic nervous system* readies the body for vigorous action by performing such functions as increasing the heart rate, blood pressure, and respiration. The *parasympathetic nervous system* helps restore the body's resources through such actions as diverting blood from large muscles to the digestive organs for digestion. For the most part, you do not actively control this aspect of your nervous system, which includes such activities as maintaining your heart rate, breathing, swallowing, digestion, and other more "automatic" physiological functioning. Part of these automatic reactions to a stimulus is the **flight or fight response**, which prepares you for action in such situations as the example of being followed late at night. Since many of these physical reactions are also visible, such as "getting red in the face," it is important to learn to look for them when dealing with angry suspects or members of the public when you are on duty.

The second characteristic is the subjective experience of emotion based on the personality and characteristics of the person. If you are over six feet tall, weigh over 200 pounds, and have a black belt in karate, you may not even notice the sound of the footsteps, or if you do, you may think to yourself, "Hope this person does not want any trouble, because he is going to be messing with the wrong person." But if you are just over five feet tall, weigh 100 pounds, and are terrified of being mugged, you may well perceive this as a threatening situation and experience fear. In the first example, the increased heartbeat of the person is the thrill of a possible fight, whereas in the second example, the increased heartbeat is the fear of possibly being hurt. One person may be relieved that a police officer is on the scene, while another person may be angry at the officer's arrival. Our thoughts and cognitive processes greatly affect our emotions.

In many cases, we end up guessing how a person feels by watching his or her behaviour. This is the third component of emotions: the behavioural expression of the internal feeling or state. If someone starts shouting at you, waves his or her arms, and stomps his or her feet, you would hazard the guess that the person is angry or very upset about something. Police officers must continually assess situations based upon the behaviour of the people involved—not an easy task, especially in situations that are dangerous or even life-threatening to the participants, including the police officer.

Consider This...

One officer watches hands to determine if she is going to be attacked. "When I see those fists clench, I get ready. I know that the next move is going to be a bad one unless I can talk my way out of it."

How do you know if someone is about to lose control? How do you know if you are about to be attacked? Paying close attention to nonverbal behaviour and to other uncontrolled actions will become important skills and abilities for you to learn. Some of these nonverbal indicators will be covered in the next two chapters.

Research indicates that the expression of some emotions is universal, particularly facial expressions. Six different basic emotions are clearly expressed in the face: anger, happiness, sadness, disgust, fear, and surprise (Ekman, 1992). Two other emotional responses have recently been researched that may also be fundamental: contempt (Ekman and Heider, 1988) and pain (Prkachin, 1992).

Another interesting ability to develop is the ability to discover if someone is being honest. How can you tell if someone is lying? Two people are arguing with an officer about their whereabouts during a crime. The officer is sure that they committed the offence, but they swear they were somewhere else (and alone). They are earnest in their denial, pleading with the officer that they had nothing to do with the incident. Points for Pondering sheds a bit of light on the indicators of lying.

POINTS FOR PONDERING

How Can You Tell When a Suspect Is Lying?

How can you tell if someone is lying to you? Can you tell when someone is consciously deceiving you? Is it easier to identify lying when the person you are speaking to is someone you know, or if the liar is a stranger? People will lie to an officer to avoid trouble, to avoid turning in a friend, or to get someone else into trouble rather than themselves. Are lie detectors a valid means of determining whether someone is lying? Much research has been devoted to identifying deliberate deception and the accuracy of lie detector tests. It has also revealed several *external* cues that may indicate lying:

- Basic discrepancies between nonverbal channels. For example, a liar may manage to control facial expressions, but body language may betray nervousness or tell a different story (Baron et al., 1998).

- Variations in paralanguage, such as a rise in voice pitch, or lack of verbal fluency (Zuckerman et al., 1991).

- More sentence repairs (Stiff et al., 1989). A liar may start a sentence, interrupt it, and then start all over again.

- An unusually low or high level of eye contact (Kleinke, 1986).

- Averting of eyes before answering a question. This is often interpreted as an effort to hide something (Burgoon et al., 1989).

- Exaggerated facial expressions (Baron et al., 1998).

- Nervous mannerisms such as excessive self-touching and fidgeting. Touching, scratching, and rubbing suggest emotional arousal, which may be caused by lying to the officer.

- Short and recurrent pauses may signal that the liar has to be continually thinking about what he or she needs to say next (Anolli and Ciceri, 1997).

Internal responses from the autonomic nervous system that indicate deception are measured with polygraphs or lie detectors. Polygraphs record physiological reactions that occur during questioning. Results of research into the accuracy of polygraphs are mixed. While many professionals believe that polygraphs are accurate, some research has indicated otherwise (Baron et al., 1998). Under questioning, nervousness or embarrassment may also cause arousal similar to the arousal when lying. Also, people can intentionally change their level of physiological arousal (Zajonc and McIntosh, 1992). Accomplished con artists and other criminals may also be able to control their physiological responses in the same way as the subjects in research. However, polygraph testing can be one tool to detect lying and should not be ruled out as a method in crime investigation. In fact, one research report has pointed out that reviews of the reliability of polygraphs in texts on introductory psychology may be negatively biased (Devitt et al., 1997). Because of this question of reliability, the results of polygraphs have not been admissible in Canadian courts since a Supreme Court ruling in 1987.

So how can you tell when someone is lying? Police veterans often rely on the external indicators of lying and use these indicators to increase questioning efforts. Also, it may be that experience and using gut-level feelings help in the quest to find out the truth behind a crime.

Emotions During a Conflict

During a conflict, people may experience a wide range of emotions, including frustration, sadness, hopelessness, surprise, and anger. Here we will examine three of the more common emotions that a police officer is most likely to encounter: frustration, anger, and sadness. As well, we will briefly look at aggression within the topic of anger, because extreme anger or rage can easily result in aggression. Police officers must be especially vigilant when dealing with angry people.

Frustration

Frustration occurs when an individual is blocked from doing something he or she wants to do; behaviour towards a goal is thwarted. For example, if you are headed for an important appointment and have to drive behind a very slow driver, you may experience frustration, thinking you may be late. The experience of frustration may be the antecedent to conflict. For example, people who feel frustrated when driving may act out their frustration by tailgating or honking their horn, which may create conflict with the other driver.

Consider This...

"When I pull people over and I can tell that they were in a hurry, I know I'm going to be treated rudely. They want to blame me for the ticket. I put it right back where it belongs. I wouldn't have ticketed if they hadn't been speeding. I guess they feel better after they yell at me."

According to some research, frustration can lead to anger and subsequent aggression. The original **frustration-aggression hypothesis** (Dollard et al., 1939) proposed that frustration led to a tendency towards aggression. In other words, aggression was preceded by frustration. Later theories (such as Berkowitz, 1989, 1990) have included the cognitive component of appraisal. People think about the event, and based on their appraisal of it, decide whether or not the event is frustrating. If they appraise it as extremely frustrating, they may become angry and aggressive. In other words, how you perceive the event and the extent to which it arouses negative feelings influences how much aggression you will display, if any. For example, if the appointment is not that important to you or is perhaps distasteful (such as having a root canal), you may experience less frustration.

Anger and Aggression

Anger is a common experience during a conflict. We all know that feeling—anger. It can build slowly or suddenly ignite, and it can make it hard to maintain control of oneself. **Anger** is a feeling of extreme hostility, indignation, or exasperation. Anger is stimulated when appraisal indicates that others are responsible for the achievement of an individual's goal (Ellsworth and Smith, 1988). Anger creates stress and brings about a number of bodily changes that were discussed earlier. Internally, the heart rate increases, blood pressure increases, galvanic skin responses change, and breathing becomes shallower and quicker. But we cannot see these changes and need the help of other indicators that we can see when standing at a distance.

Recent research has shed some light on two types of maladaptive anger, termed anger-in and anger-out (Martin and Wan, 1999). According to Martin and Wan, people prone to anger-in responses suffer frequent, recurring angry feelings. These feelings do not go away and colour future judgments and appraisals. Those who experience anger-out lash out at others, doing such things as slamming doors, striking out at others, and being verbally abusive and threatening. Both types of anger contribute to the development of cardiovascular disease. Police officers are more likely to encounter individuals who are expressing their anger outwardly, and they need to be aware of the external signs of anger.

Outwardly, there may be several physical indicators of anger that you can see if you are close enough. If the person is breathing more rapidly, you may notice it if the individual is wearing tighter-fitting clothing around the chest. One noticeable indicator of anger is enlargement of the pupils, which creates the look known as "wide-eyed with rage" (Dubrin and Geerinck, 2001).

According to Ouellette (1996), there are three areas of nonverbal behaviour that can reveal anger. Gestures, including facial colour, can give many clues about anger. A person's face may redden if the person is light-skinned. However, when a person becomes extremely angry (rage), the face may drain of all colour—a sign of possible physical attack. Opening and closing fists and baring teeth are two other important gestures to examine.

Second, he recommends that the person's eyes be closely monitored. Eyes that dart from side to side or up and down may indicate that the person feels trapped. "Target glances" occur when a person looks at a target person before attack. For example, the person may look at the police officer's chin before trying to hit it. If the person is going to attempt to flee, he or she may glance at possible exits (Ouellette, 1993).

The third area that can reveal anger is the use of space. A person may try to close the distance just prior to attack. Ouellette recommends that officers not violate personal space, but if they must, they should approach a person on his or her weak side.

It is important that police officers learn to recognize the signs of anger prior to attack. As well, police officers need to learn about their own anger and learn to manage it. Being in control of such strong emotions will decrease the chances of doing or saying something that may have personal and/or professional repercussions. The Points for Pondering discusses some techniques to help manage anger.

POINTS FOR PONDERING   *Dealing with Your Anger*

There is no doubt about it: we all get angry both on and off the job. Your ability to manage your anger is crucial for a successful career in law enforcement. There will be plenty of opportunities for you to feel angry: the uncooperative suspect, the witness who calls you names, the person who wants to take you on physically. And these are just a few examples! So what can you do about all of this anger? Here are a few tips to manage it:

1. **Channel your anger.** Anger can be an energizing force, and this force can be used in positive ways. If you are still angry after an encounter with a hostile witness, use the energy to finish paperwork.

2. **Express your anger before it reaches a peak.** Sometimes people are unaware that you are angry. Discuss it right away rather than letting it simmer. If it simmers too long, it can boil over. If your partner insults someone you like, let him or her know right away about your feelings.

3. **Think before you act.** In recent years, a police officer, in the heat of a fight, called a black Canadian "nigger." You can imagine the long-term implications for this insult. The old standard of "counting to ten" may not be a bad idea. At times, when being attacked you may not have the luxury of ten seconds, but always keep reminding yourself that all actions have consequences.

4. **Recognize when you are angry.** This may sound simple to do, but some people are not aware that they are angry. By being sensitive to your own bodily signs, you can learn to recognize anger long before it overwhelms you.

5. **Realize that you are responsible for how you feel.** While such a suggestion can be difficult to believe, you do make yourself angry. By changing your perception, you can change the feeling. For example, when you are driving and someone pulls out in front of you, rather than feeling angry, say to yourself, "The person is not

aware of what he did, and it was not directed at me personally." By owning your feelings, you can change them. In police work, thinking about the person being drunk, upset, or mentally challenged can lessen your anger at his or her abusive language or behaviour.

Sources

Andrew J. Dubrin and Terri Geerinck (2001). *Human relations for career and personal success.* Scarborough, ON: Prentice Hall.

Sadness

While sadness may not be the first emotion that crosses your mind as being a part of conflict, during or after a heated argument many people display sadness. Other emotions in this range include anguish, helplessness, and confusion about the sequence of events. These emotions may be more common as part of the aftermath of a conflict. Sadness may also occur when one person realizes that there is no resolution to the conflict or that the chosen solution is not appropriate or has negative results: In the heat of conflict, one domestic partner stabs the other, and police entering the scene may see someone who is remorseful and sad. People may also cry or become "glassy-eyed" as the battle continues without resolution. In a crisis, people also may have moods that swing from sadness ("I can't believe I hurt her") to anger ("Look what she made me do"). A suspect who is sad is usually easier to manage than a suspect who is angry.

Other than these obvious signs, what are the nonverbal indicators of sadness? A person who is sad may "droop" with sloping shoulders and appear to be "hunched into himself or herself." The mouth is downturned, and the chin may wobble as if the person were about to cry. A sad person may have difficulty with eye contact, and any talk about the problem may evoke an outpour of crying. The person may breathe irregularly as he or she tries to maintain control and keep emotions in check.

One research study that focused on women found that sadness was an indicator in depression and was the dominant mood and emotion of the subjects (Breznitz, 1992). Other symptoms of depression include low mood, feelings of helplessness and hopelessness, negative attitudes about the self, and an inability to experience happiness or joy. Depression will be dealt with in greater detail in chapter 7. At this point, it is sufficient to realize that dealing with someone who is sad may also indicate that the person is depressed. If so, as a police officer, you want to make sure that the individual is referred for further psychological assistance.

INFLUENCE OF CULTURE AND GENDER IN CONFLICT

With such a diverse Canadian population, the influence of culture and gender deserves brief mention. First, we will briefly discuss the influence of culture, followed by the influence of gender in managing conflict.

Cultural Influences on Conflict

There is little doubt that Canada is a diverse nation made up of many cultures. To be effective in conflict management, police officers need to be aware of these many cultures and the differences between them. "As any human endeavour, conflict and its management take place within a cultural context" (Kozan and Ergin, 1998, p. 526). The culture of the parties involved plays a vital role in all three stages of conflict.

One difference in managing conflict is the difference between collectivistic and individualistic cultures. **Collectivistic cultures** are less confrontational when managing conflict as compared to those of the United States, Canada, and the more **individualistic cultures** (Hofstede, 1984). According to Hofstede, collectivistic cultures emphasize group or team goals rather than the individual goals of more individualistic cultures. An interesting research finding is that collectivistic cultures (this experiment compared U.S. and Turkish subjects) preferred third-party involvement to settle a conflict rather than direct negotiation (Kozan and Ergin, 1998). Many conflict resolution strategies focus on the use of a problem-solving approach by the two parties to come up with a **win–win solution**. However, in cultures that are more collectivistic, this may not be an appropriate strategy, and third-party mediation may be better received. According to these researchers, an interesting problem occurs when the conflict occurs between a member of an individualistic culture and a member of a collectivistic culture. Attempts at direct negotiation may be seen as too aggressive, and attempts at mediation may be viewed as being evasive. Police officers who use direct negotiation with members of a more collectivistic culture may not be successful and may need to use mediation in order to settle a dispute. This points to the need for officers to be trained in mediation skills as part of conflict management training, which will be discussed in the chapter 8.

Cultures also differ in how much emotions are expressed. Some cultures believe in and allow for great verbal and nonverbal expressions of emotion. People from **high-context** (sometimes referred to as high-contact) **cultures** rely heavily on the situation (context) and nonverbal cues to communicate their feelings. High-context cultures use space, gestures, and physical contact as important parts of communication. Typical cultures include Arab, southern Mediterranean, and Latin American (Pritchett, 1993). On the other hand, people from **low-context** (sometimes referred to as low-contact) **cultures** are uncomfortable around such overt displays and lean towards non-contact and highly verbalized interactions. Canadians, Americans, British, and North Europeans belong to the more low-context cultures.

In conflicts, people from different cultures bring different approaches. A person from one culture may misunderstand or be uncomfortable around overt displays of emotion, whereas the other party may see the first as cold or uncaring. Police officers, too, come from their own culture and bring that culture with them to a situation. By being aware of their own and other cultures, officers will be more sensitive to their own responses. "Police officers who understand the communicative patterns of specific cultures can more accurately interpret the nonverbal behaviour of the members of the groups" (Pritchett, 1993, p. 24).

Gender Differences and Conflict

In recent years, much research has focused on the differences between men and women and how each gender communicates differently. Men and women are also socialized in different cultures (Wood et al., 1998). When children are very young, their play is segregated, and girls and boys early on learn to favour different games (Maltz and Barker, 1982). Girls tend to prefer games that rely on cooperation, sensitivity, and negotiation such as "house," and "school." Boys' games tend to require less negotiation and talking because the rules are clearer, as in baseball and soccer, and these games are often more competitive. It appears that this early socialization stays with us. Research suggests that there are distinct differences in how the two genders communicate as adults, especially if raised in a family with traditional gender roles (Tannen, 1990). Here are just a few of the differences between the gender cultures.

Women use talk cooperatively to include others, to show interest, and to respond to others' needs. Men use talk more competitively to assert themselves, to show knowledge, to gain the upper hand, and to maintain attention on themselves. Men, more concerned with asserting dominance and control, use more space, use greater volume when speaking, and use more forceful gestures (Hall, 1987). Women's talk tends to focus more on feelings and personal ideas, and to discuss problems and maintain relationships. On the other hand, men use talk to accomplish goals such as solving a problem, giving advice, or establishing their position on an issue or idea. Women are more likely to share feelings and secrets, whereas men prefer less intimate topics.

These differences also appear in nonverbal behaviours and communication. Women tend to use more touching and require less personal space during a conversation with friends. Women also use more supportive verbal and nonverbal indicators of listening such as utterances like "um-hmm" and "uh-huh," and head nodding. Women also tend to use more eye contact (Tannen, 1990). Often women assume men are not listening, because men are less likely to ask personal questions, less likely to make comments, and do not use utterances (Tannen, 1990).

These differences may not cause conflict, but they may make a conflict worse. Both male and female officers need to be aware of these differences so that they do not hamper communicating, investigating, or interviewing efforts. For example, if a female officer is talking to a disgruntled male subject, she should not assume that he is not listening to her because he is not making eye contact or verbal utterances.

SUMMARY

In this chapter, conflict was further explored, adding details to the introductory information in chapter 1. All of us manage conflict in different ways that are based on our personalities, cultures, gender, and life experiences. Five conflict management styles are competition, collaboration, avoidance, accommodation, and compromise. Many people have a dominant style that they favour in a variety of conflicts. While no one style is the best, an over-reliance on one style can create problems.

Conflicts have three stages. The first stage is the antecedent conditions or the situations that lead to the conflict. During a conflict, people engage in behaviours such as arguing and becoming defensive, as well as feeling emotions such as anger, hurt, and frustration. After the conflict has ended, the aftermath is the third and final stage, during which people must deal with the results of the conflict.

Emotions and the experience of strong emotions occur during conflict and increase in strength as a conflict escalates. Emotions consist of three components: physiological reactions, subjective cognitive states, and behavioural reactions. While there are many emotions that may be experienced during a conflict, three emotions were discussed. The exploration of one emotion—frustration—included an examination of the frustration-aggression hypothesis. While frustration does not always lead to aggression, frustration can be the antecedent of a conflict. During a conflict, people may also become angry, and their anger may lead to aggression, which ranges from verbal threats to physical attack and murder. The third emotion—sadness—can occur when people find the conflict too difficult to deal with or they become overwhelmed by it. Police officers must also be aware of the signs of possible depression.

We ended the chapter with a brief discussion of the influence of gender and culture upon how conflict is managed. Police officers must be aware of and be trained in understanding these differences to be more successful on the job.

CASE STUDY

The Noisy Party

On Saturday, at 3:00 a.m., two patrol officers receive a noise complaint in a low-income housing unit. It has been a hectic shift, and both officers are feeling the stress of the long evening. The officers approach the unit and hear loud music. A person comes out of another unit and says, "It's about time you got here! The noise is unbelievable. On top of the music, I've heard screaming and loud crashes. They fight all the time, and this racket never stops. I'm sick of it and I'm sick of them. Do something!"

Karma, the female officer replies, "That's what we are here for, Ma'am. Do you have any idea of the number of people there?"

"I think it's just the two of them. They're always fighting and I can't..."

Eric, the male officer, interrupts, "Are you aware if there are any weapons? Have they been drinking or doing any drugs?"

"Look," the woman retorts, "I don't know, just get the damn racket to stop." At this point, the woman turns around and angrily marches back to her unit.

Eric looks at Karma, "I'm getting sick of this tonight. Let's get in there and tell them to shut up or we haul their butts out of there. Typical boozing bums!" With that he storms toward the door of the unit, with Karma running to keep up. Eric bangs on the door several times and shouts, "Police. Open the door now!"

After several minutes, the door opens and a man stands there swaying unsteadily on his feet with a half bottle of rye clutched in one hand.

"Hey, Officer. How's it hanging? Wanna come in and join me? Nice to have another man around instead of that silly witch over there." He points to a woman on the couch, who appears to be drunk also and about to pass out.

"No, we don't want to come in. Turn the stereo off, quit shouting, and go to bed. There has been a complaint about the noise level here," Eric shouts to get heard over the music.

When the man just stares at Eric, Karma can see that Eric is getting angry. She hurriedly says to him, "Take it easy, Eric, they're obviously drunk."

Eric ignores Karma and shouts even louder, "Look, I mean it. Walk over there and shut off the music. And I mean *now!*"

The man, sensing Eric's mood, challenges him. "What are you going to do? Make me?"

"You bet I am if I have to!" retorts Eric, "You're so drunk, you couldn't harm a fly."

At this final insult, the man takes a lunge at Eric. He falls over, and Eric follows through with an arrest for assaulting a police officer.

Questions

1. What conflict management style did Eric use in this incident?

2. Would a different style have been more appropriate? If so, which one? Explain your reasoning.

3. Eric quickly became angry during this call. What techniques for anger management would you suggest that Eric try so that he can be more in control of his anger in future calls like this one?

KEY TERMS

anger: a feeling of hostility, indignation, or exasperation.

autonomic nervous system: the part of the nervous system that connects internal organs, glands, and involuntary muscles to the central nervous system.

collectivistic culture: a set of norms, values, and beliefs that emphasize group or community rather than the individual.

covert conflict: a conflict that is hidden and not demonstrated openly.

emotions: Responses to events that include psychological, subjective, behavioural, and physiological components.

fight or flight response: an emotional and physiological state or readiness that prepares an organism to fight a stressor or flee the stressor.

frustration: the feeling that occurs when an individual is blocked from achieving a goal.

frustration-aggression hypothesis: the hypothesis that aggression occurs as a result of frustration.

high-context cultures: cultures that rely heavily on situational and nonverbal cues for communication of feelings.

individualistic culture: a set of norms, values, and beliefs that emphasize the individual rather than the group.

lose–lose: another term used to describe the avoidant style of conflict management whereby both sides in a conflict do not get what they want.

low-context cultures: cultures that rely more heavily on verbal cues rather than nonverbal cues for communication of feelings.

overt conflict: a conflict where issues and problems are dealt with openly.

win–win (solution): another term for referring to the outcome of collaboration as a style or goal of conflict resolution.

WEB LINKS

www.queendom.com
There is a more comprehensive conflict management style test at this site than the one at the beginning of this chapter.

www.members.aol.com/nonverbal2/diction1.htm
From A to Z, this is a complete dictionary of nonverbal terms and phrases.

REFERENCES

Luigi Anolli & Rita Ciceri (1979). The voice of deception: Vocal strategies of naïve and able liars. *Journal of Nonverbal Behaviour, 21*(4), 259–84.

E. Aries (1987). Gender and communication. In P. Shaver (Ed.), *Sex and gender*. Newbury Par, CA: Sage, 149–76.

Robert A. Baron, Bruce Earhard, and Marcia Ozier (1995). *Psychology.* Scarborough, ON: Allyn and Bacon Canada.

Dawn M. Baskerville (1993). How do you manage conflict? *Black Enterprise, 23*(10), 62–66.

Aaron Beck (1988). *Love is never enough.* New York: Harper and Row.

L. Berkowitz (1989). Frustration-aggression hypothesis: Examination and reformulation. *Psychological Bulletin, 106,* 93–106.

——— (1990). On the formation and regulation of anger and aggression. *American Psychologist, 45,* 494–503.

Zvia Breznitz (1992). Verbal indicators of depression. *Journal of General Psychology, 119*(4), 351–63.

J. K. Burgoon, D. B. Buller, and W. G. Woodall (1989). *Nonverbal communication: The unspoken dialogue* (p. 324). New York: Harper and Row.

Deborah Borisoff & David A. Victor (1998). *Conflict management: A communication skills approach.* Needham Heights, MA: Allyn and Bacon.

Mary K. Devitt, Charles R. Honts, and Lynelle Vondergreest (1997). Truth or just bias: The treatment of the psychophysiological detection of deception in introductory psychology textbooks. *The Journal of Credibility Assessment and Witness Psychology, 1*(1), 9–32.

Andrew J. Dubrin (2001). *Human relations: Interpersonal, job-oriented skills* (7th ed.). Upper Saddle River, NJ: Prentice Hall.

P. Ekman and K. G. Heider (1988). The universality of a contempt expression: A replication. *Motivation and Emotion, 12,* 303–8.

P. Ekman (1992). Facial expression of emotion: New findings, new question. *Psychological Science, 3,* 34–38.

Joseph P. Folger, Marshall Scott Poole, and Randall K. Stutman (2001). *Working through conflict: Strategies for relationships, groups, and organizations* (4th ed.). New York: Addison Wesley Longman Inc.

J. A. Hall (1987). On explaining gender differences: The case of nonverbal communication. In P. Shaver and C. Hendricks (Eds.), *Sex and Gender* (pp.177–200). Newbury Park, CA: Mayfield.

G. Hofstede (1984). *Culture's consequences: International differences in work-related attitudes.* Beverly Hills, CA: Sage.

C. L. Kleinke (1986). Gaze and eye contact: A research review. *Psychological Bulletin, 100,* 78–100.

Kamil M. Kozan & Canan Ergin (1998). Preference for third party help in conflict management in the United States and Turkey. *Journal of Cross-Cultural Studies, 29*(4), 525–40.

D. N. Maltz & R. Barker (1982). A cultural approach to male–female miscommunication. In J. J. Gumpertz (Ed.), *Language and Social Identity* (pp. 196–216). Cambridge: Cambridge University Press.

Rene Martin & Choi K. Wan (1999). The style of anger expression: Relation to expressivity, personality, and health. *Personality & Social Psychology Bulletin, 25*(10), 1196–1208.

Roland Ouellette (1993). *Management of aggressive behaviour.* Powers Lake, WI: Performance Dimensions Publishing.

——— (1996). Management of aggressive behaviour. In Ed Nowicki, *Total survival* (pp. 289–97). Powers Lake, WI: Performance Dimensions Publishing.

L. R. Pondy (1967). Organizational conflict: Concepts and models. *Administrative Science Quarterly, 12,* 296–320.

Garry L. Pritchett (1993). Interpersonal communication. *FBI Law Enforcement Bulletin, 62*(7), 22–26.

K. M. Prkachin (1992). The consistency of facial expressions of pain: A comparison across modalities. *Pain, 51*(3), 297–306.

D. Tannen (1990). *You just don't understand: Women and men in conversation.* New York: Morrow.

Julia Wood, Ron Sept, and Jane Duncan (1998). *Everyday encounters: An introduction to interpersonal communication.* Scarborough, ON: ITP Nelson.

R. B. Zajonc & D. N. McIntosh (1992). Emotions research: Some promising questions and some questionable promises. *Psychological Science, 3,* 70–4.

M. Zuckerman, R. F. Simons, and P. Como (1981). Verbal and nonverbal communication of deception. In L. Berkowitz (Ed.), *Advances in experimental psychology* (Vol. 14, pp. 1–59). New York: Academic Press.

chapter three

Nonverbal Strategies for Conflict Management

Courtesy Peterborough Lakefield Community Police Service

LEARNING OUTCOMES

After studying this chapter, you should be able to

- Recognize the signs of an impending conflict.
- Identify conflict starters that precipitate conflict.
- Explain the different types of nonverbal communication and how they influence conflict.
- Use nonverbal communication to assist in communication and conflict resolution.
- Set a supportive climate for conflict resolution.

On-the-Job Scenario

"Look, Roberto, I was not rude to the woman. She was drunk, swearing, and quite frankly she was trying to come on to me."

"As your platoon leader, I have to investigate this complaint. She states that you pushed her for no reason. She banged her head on the coffee table and claims that you did nothing to help her."

"Let me go over it one more time. Sam and I received the call to check out a noise complaint. When we got there, she answered the door. Her stereo was blasting and she was really drunk. And I mean drunk! She was swaying on her feet and slurring her words. Then she started licking her lips, and moving closer to me! I asked her to please turn her stereo down so that we could talk to her. She had a cigarette hanging out of her mouth, a bottle in one hand, and then she made a grab for me. It was just instinct. I just blocked her before she fell on me or something else. She was so drunk that she staggered off, tripped over some clothes on the floor, fell, and hit her head. We took her to the hospital, and I apologized several times. She came at me and now she says that I attacked her!"

"Well," said Roberto, "She claims that you pushed her with a lot of force. She also claims that she was not trying to hug or grab you."

"That's ridiculous. I'm surprised that she can remember anything. Have you talked to Sam? I'm sure that he will support everything that I have said."

Dealing with members of the public, co-workers, and other professionals is not always an easy task. This scenario is just one kind of situation that officers have to deal with: a person under the influence of alcohol attempts to become "physical." Later, a complaint is lodged against the officer who feels that he has done his job properly. A conflict with a member of the public can have repercussions later on. It is therefore important that you learn how to recognize an impending conflict, do your best to set up a supportive climate, and then choose a conflict management strategy or strategies that will help resolve the conflict. While you cannot always foresee the consequences, if you do your best at the time of the conflict, then you will have less to answer for later.

In this chapter, the first of two chapters, we will begin to learn the strategies that will assist you in becoming a good conflict manager. This chapter will be more generic, focusing on nonverbal communication. In other words, the material in this chapter can be applied to a wide variety of situations both on and off the job. First, we will examine the signs that can be spotted and assessed to indicate a potential for conflict. Of critical importance is the section on the types of nonverbal communication. Recognizing nonverbal cues and being able to interpret them is an essential skill. According to Garry Pritchett, a law enforcement officer in Idaho, being able to accurately read nonverbal communication allows officers to defuse potentially violent situations and to resolve them peacefully (Pritchett, 1993). People who are good at assessing possible conflicts are proficient in interpreting these nonverbal cues. Second, we will focus on strategies aimed at improving your ability to understand and use nonverbal communication in a wide variety of encounters. Last, developing a supportive climate for conflict resolution will be explored, so that you can learn how to change a defensive environment into a supportive environment to improve conflict resolution.

THE SIGNS OF CONFLICT

In this section, we will introduce nonverbal communication and types of nonverbal communication. Be aware that we cannot really separate the nonverbal and verbal components of a conflict and that we are doing so for learning purposes. A good example of the verbal and nonverbal components of conflict can be illustrated with conflict starters. Conflict starters are good examples of verbal communication that indicate that people are not happy with the current state of affairs (Devito et al., 2001). Conflict starters poke fun at the other person, are often sarcastic, may be highly insulting or stereotypical, or may question the character or integrity of the person they are aimed at. The tone of voice, eye contact, and gestures that accompany these verbalizations are classified as nonverbal communication. For example, you just arrive home on a Friday night after a particularly gruelling week. You flop down on the couch, and your significant other walks into the room and says, "Oh no, you don't. Don't even think about slouching around for the weekend. If you think I'm going to sit around and do nothing with you, think again!" Now what do you say? Your next words are important. If not managed properly, conflict starters do as the name implies: start a conflict.

Below are some examples of conflict starters for you to examine.

Skills Practice: Conflict Starters

All of us enter into conflicts. Many conflicts begin with a *conflict starter*. The conflict really begins when we answer the "starter" defensively or by simply getting angry and saying something that we later regret. For each conflict starter below, write out a response that would escalate the conflict or make matters worse. Then, try to write out a more productive response that you think would de-escalate the conflict. The first one is done for you.

1. "You're late again! Let me guess, you broke all your fingers so you couldn't use the phone."

   Unproductive response (conflict escalation): "Well, if that's the way you feel, I don't know why I bothered to come home at all!"

   Productive response (conflict de-escalation): "You're absolutely right. I should have called."

2. "Who made the reservations too early? Now we are going to be late!"

3. "If I have to talk to your mother and go over the plans once more, I'm going to scream."

4. "They don't make red lights any redder than the one you just ran, buddy."

5. "Well, isn't this interesting! Your license only expired three years ago."

Now we will more closely examine nonverbal communication, including the types of nonverbal communication.

Nonverbal Communication

To be a good conflict manager, you need to develop skills to read and interpret nonverbal cues. People indicate their feelings nonverbally in a number of ways. When people are angry, happy, sad, or ready to fight, they show these feelings nonverbally. Nonverbal cues may give you some idea about how a person is feeling or even about his or her next actions. However, a note of caution is in order. The interpretation of nonverbal communication is subjective and open to perceptual distortions. For example, having arms folded across the chest may be interpreted as being closed or angry. However, a person may have his or her arms crossed for another reason: perhaps the person is experiencing back pain or simply finds this arm position comfortable. While learning nonverbal indicators and paying attention to them, do not overestimate their validity. Nonverbal cues are simply tools that can help you interpret a situation. These cues can also be the starting point for perception checking, one of the skills in active listening that we will discuss later in this chapter.

A great amount of research has been done on nonverbal communication, although not enough from a cultural stance. Many of the following areas are based on North American research. Where possible, research from other cultures has been included to illustrate some of the cultural differences in expression. When examining nonverbal communication, also keep in mind cultural differences that can change your interpretation of the behaviour. Here we will briefly discuss six types of nonverbal communication and give examples for interpretation in potential conflict.

Types of Nonverbal Communication

Many nonverbal behaviours are classified as nonverbal communication. We may use several types of communication at once in interpersonal communication, or we may rely on a single mode or method of communication. According to Mehrabian (1972), in the communication of a message, only 7 per cent of the emotional or total meaning of a message is the actual verbal content. This means that 93 per cent of what we communicate to others is through nonverbal channels. Nonverbal behaviours account for 55 per cent of our meaning. Vocal cues, referred to as **paralanguage**, which include voice volume, tone, pitch, and intensity, make up the remaining 38 per cent of communication. Nonverbal behaviours include facial expressions, movement and gestures, use of territory and space, touch, and personal appearance, to name a few.

While we are dividing these types into discrete categories, be aware that these cues usually occur simultaneously. For example, an officer may feel that a suspect is lying because of lack of eye contact, stammered replies, fidgeting, and continuously arm-rubbing.

Paralanguage

Paralanguage includes communication that is vocal but does not include words. Voice volume (from whispering to shouting), tone, gasps, sighs, rhythm, pitch, inflection, accent, sentence complexity, and word pronunciation are all paralanguage. When we ask a question, we use inflection at the end of the sentence. Part of tactical communication relies on using loud volume and inflection. Our voices can communicate many feelings. Sarcasm is usually picked up through the use of paralanguage. For instance, to say, "Yeah, I really want to go," has just the opposite meaning when said with sarcasm.

During a conflict, the use of pauses and silence has received research attention. A short silence is categorized as an unfilled pause, whereas a long pause is categorized as an intended silence (Borisoff and Victor, 1998). When people speak with a lot of unfilled pauses, they are often perceived as contemptuous, angry, or even anxious (Lalljee, 1971). Silence can be a very powerful nonverbal tool, as anyone who has received the "silent treatment" can attest. Silence can be interpreted in a number of ways ranging from thinking or reflection to the expression of anger and disgust (Jensen, 1973). Because silence can be interpreted in a wide variety of ways, listeners can easily misinterpret its meaning. However, both pauses and silence should be given attention when talking with others.

Consider This...

Just prior to being attacked, a police officer noticed that the person became very quiet, although he had been shouting just seconds before. Having noticed the silence, the officer became more guarded. At that point the male lunged at the officer.

As a future law enforcement worker, practise speaking in a professional voice that sounds firm and certain. Correct use of grammar and appropriate vocabulary is also important. To appear frightened or unsure of what to do will undermine your credibility in the situation and could be dangerous. Also, examine your uses of silence and pauses. Do you pause frequently when you are anxious, or do you talk so quickly that you barely have time to breathe? You do not want to testify in court with too many pauses or long silences. You will be regarded as a "professional witness." If you have difficulty speaking in public, you may want to join a public speaking group such as Toastmasters to assist you in overcoming this fear or anxiety.

Facial Expressions and Eye Behaviours

If the face expresses 55 per cent of our communication when we speak to others, it deserves special consideration and a complete analysis. Your face can assume a vast number of expressions, and much research has been devoted to the expression of emotion. According to research, the face can engage in 46 unique actions using the forehead, eyebrows, eyelids, nose, and mouth (Ekman and Friesen, 1978). It appears, however, that facial emotional expressions can be categorized into six broad emotions. As we previously discussed in chapter 2, these six emotions are anger, fear, sadness, disgust, happiness, surprise, and possibly the expression of pain and contempt (Ekman, 1992). Obviously, we express more than these six emotions, because emotions occur in many combinations and at varying intensity. For instance, if someone cuts you off while driving, you can be slightly annoyed, or perhaps you experience road rage and erupt into a stream of loud curses to vent your extreme anger. You can be happy and surprised at the same time, if someone throws you a surprise birthday party! While there is some evidence that these six themes of expression are universal, we need to be cautious when interpreting emotional expression (Carroll and Russell, 1996). A smile may not always indicate happiness but can indicate other emotions, depending upon the situation. Some people smile when they are embarrassed or when they are caught in an illegal activity. We may smile because the social situation indicates that smiling is the appropriate behaviour, like clapping and smiling at the end of a play, even if we did not enjoy the production whatsoever!

As the proverb would have it, "Eyes are the window of the soul," and in some respects this may be true. Eye behaviours, especially eye contact, provide a great deal of information about how other people feel, what they perceive, and what they expect (Nolen, 1995). Whether we choose to look at someone or not, how long we spend maintaining eye contact, and how expressive our "eye area" is has a great impact on interaction and our relationship with that person.

Eye contact has four functions according to one text on interpersonal communication (Beebe et al., 1997). First, eye contact has a *cognitive* function. Through eye contact, you can gain an understanding of the other person's thought processes. When we are trying to remember a name or a place, we may glance slightly upwards to the right or left. To glance away indicates that the listener is not open to further communication at that time, while processing information. To make eye contact means that people are open to receiving more information. Conflict results when this making or breaking of eye contact is misread. If a person glances away, the speaker may erroneously think the person is not interested in any further information and may become defensive or stop speaking.

The second function of eye contact is to *monitor* the behaviour and reactions of others. When we are interacting with others, we try to decide whether they are receptive to our message by gauging their eye contact. Mistakes and conflicts arise when others do not look at the speaker, and the speaker assumes that the listeners have little or no interest. On the other hand, the speaker may assume interest or understanding when there is little or none by mistakenly reading the eye contact as interest or understanding.

Third, eye contact is a *regulator* in communication. We use eye contact to signal when we wish to speak and when we are finished speaking. Eye contact also regulates other interactions and behaviour, such as taking turns, and whether or not we want to participate in an activity. When a magician looks for a volunteer in an audience, those who do not want to be called upon avert their eyes and may also use posture to indicate "Please, leave me alone." During a heated conflict, people tend not to pay attention to regulative eye contact and often end up shouting at each other simultaneously. This is obviously very unproductive unless the goal of the conflict is to see who can scream the loudest. When a police officer has to deal with such conflict, he or she may have to make a noise that's even louder in order to get the attention of the warring parties. Learning how to whistle loudly may be a good tool to stop people from continuing to shout. They will often look at the police officer in shock, perhaps even unaware that he or she has been standing there for some time.

We can also learn what behaviour may occur next by observing the eyes and the direction in which they look. Many officers have noted that when suspects are about to flee, they first glance in the direction they will attempt to run. A suspect may glance at a place where weapons or other illegal goods are hidden. And when lying, a suspect may break eye contact more often or look at the officer not at all.

The fourth function of eye contact and the area around the eyes is *expressive*. The eyes and the area around them are very versatile and can express a number of emotions. Eyes blink, cry, open wide, close, and squint, and are an integral part of expressing the ways we feel and the intensity of that feeling. We express interest in what another person is saying by increasing eye contact, and by decreasing eye contact if we are not interested. When trying to talk about something that is difficult or embarrassing, we may decrease eye contact (Knapp, 1978).

Kinesics: Emblems, Illustrators, Affect Displays, Regulators, and Adaptors

Think back to a time when you were really happy. Maybe it was during the phone call that landed you a job you really wanted. What did you do after you hung up the phone? Some people literally jump and down with joy! Your **body language** reflected your mood and feelings at that moment. Your body language can also indicate how you feel about yourself. **Kinesics,** or the study of body language, has been extensively researched, including the cultural differences in use of body language. The following categories are based on the work by Ekman and Friesen who established five purposes of nonverbal communication that are particularly applicable to kinesics (Borisoff and Victor, 1998).

Emblems

Emblems replace verbal communication and are culturally determined. In North America, "thumbs-up" means "great" or "way to go," making an "O" with thumb and forefinger means "okay," nodding your head up and down means "yes," and displaying the middle finger up is a gesture of aggressive contempt. To illustrate the cultural determination of gestures, the North American gesture for okay means a big zero in Germany and a part of female or male anatomy in Russia (Axtell, 1989).

Illustrators

Illustrators are movements that complement verbal communication by describing, accenting, or reinforcing the words. For example, when describing how large something is, the speaker may outstretch his or her arms to illustrate the size.

Affect Displays

Affect displays are nonverbal messages of the body and face that carry an emotional meaning, including the strength of the emotional feeling. They can also include posture.

People who walk and stand erect, hold their heads up, and do not slouch, appear calm and self-assured. On the other hand, people who shuffle along, slouch, and keep their heads down appear to be unsure of themselves. As with eye contact, body posture may indicate whether or not we wish to be involved in interaction. Students who do not want to participate in a discussion often slouch over, look down, and avoid looking at the teacher. We also use posture to let others know whether or not we wish to interact. We may sit slightly forward and smile to invite interaction. Flirting signals our sexual or romantic interest to a prospective partner and involves postures and other nonverbal behaviours such as females swaying their hips and men swaying their pelvises (Rodgers, 1999). Specific postures and body movements may also be interpreted as threatening. Standing with legs apart and hands on hips, physically closing distance, suddenly standing up from a sitting position, making fists, and clenching teeth are all signals of a possible physical threat. Officers will watch for these indicators and also pay close attention to any sudden, unusual moves.

Regulators

Regulators are nonverbal messages that accompany speech to control or regulate what the speaker says. Earlier we discussed eye contact as being a critical regulator. Other parts of the body also help regulate communication. For example, periodic head nodding indicates that the person is listening to the speaker. Many cultures use this head nodding to indicate listening but vary as to whether or not eye contact is made at the same time (Borisoff and Victor, 1998).

"The use of regulators increases when communication becomes more difficult. Thus in conflict situations we would expect participants to use more regulators than in non-conflict situations" (Borisoff and Victor, 1998, p. 86). Participants in a conflict may not always be consciously aware of the use of negative regulators such as drooping eyes, small negative head movements, and impassive expression, but these regulators can give the impression to one or both participants the feeling that his or her position is not being well received.

Adaptors

Adaptors are movements that fulfill a personal need, and they occur at a very low level of awareness. Scratching your head, rubbing your hands together, and playing with your hair are all examples of adaptors that people use. Remember lying in the last chapter? One clue to look for is excessive self-touching. When people are anxious, angry, or nervous, they may use adaptors such as these. Other adaptors are classified as being more outward and involve the manipulation of objects. Examples include chewing on a pencil, playing with paper clips, and picking away at a Styrofoam cup. And last, some adaptors affect neither objects nor the body but include movements without a direct outcome such as swinging legs, shaking, or rocking.

Adaptors tend to increase with increased levels of anxiety. When questioning suspects, if officers note increased self-scratching and increased fiddling with such items as a can of pop, they press on with questioning. Often when questioned about the anxiety, the suspect will state that he or she is calm. Such a discrepancy leads the officer to think that the suspect is lying.

Haptics

Communication through touch or failing to touch or make body contact is referred to as **haptics.** Touch is the earliest sense to develop and is the primary way that babies learn about their world. Touch can communicate many emotions and feelings that we have about another person. Touch can express affection, sexual interest, caring, dominance, aggression, and power. Touch is an area in nonverbal communication that is filled with confusion. In the professions, touching is often an organizational taboo, and to touch another in any way can lead to charges of sexual harassment if the touch is unwanted or uninvited. In the opening scenario, the officer did not want to be hugged by this woman, or perhaps she could have been perceived as about to attack him.

Some people are more "touching" than others, and touching is often used to communicate intimacy. If you have been raised in a family where there was lots of touching, hugging, arm-holding, and kissing, you may be comfortable doing the same. However, some children were raised in families that were more restrained with physical affection, and as adults they may feel uncomfortable with overt displays of affection. Cultural rules for touching may also lead to differences in the types and comfort levels with touching. In some cultures, it is acceptable for male friends to greet each other with hugs and a kiss on the cheek—a display that most male college students in Canada would unlikely use when greeting a friend at the library. While North Americans use handshakes to greet each other, some Asian cultures do not like to shake hands right away, particularly with strangers. Few Asians engage in interpersonal touching, and in particular, frown upon cross-sex touching in public (McDaniel and Anderson, 1998).

While touching can convey intimacy or friendliness, it can also convey dominance and power differences. One researcher (Henley, 1977) asserts that those in power are more likely to touch those with less power than the opposite. Bosses are more likely to touch their subordinates, police their suspects, teachers their students, and so on. During a conflict, people may engage in unwanted touching such as poking the other person in the shoulder or chest, or slapping the other person's shoulder. Inevitably, these physical behaviours will escalate the conflict. When police officers see two people engaged in this way, they will attempt to increase the physical distance between the subjects to de-escalate the situation. Also, moving the two people so that they cannot look at each other is a useful strategy.

The Things around Us: Artifacts, Appearance, and Time

Artifacts are the personal objects that we display to announce who we are and to personalize our environments. Clothing is one of the most personal displays we use to make statements about ourselves. If you are a uniformed officer, the public will see and react to your uniform. This reaction will be positive, negative, or neutral, depending upon the perception of police at that time. Since you represent the whole police service, your officer in charge (commander) will insist that your uniform be clean, pressed, and presentable at all times. This perception also extends to criminals, who may make an assessment of an officer's capabilities that is based on appearance. Therefore, the officer's self-presentation becomes part of his or her margin of safety. Officer presence in uniform is the beginning of tactical communication, which continues throughout an encounter.

Artifacts also help to personalize and claim our space. Often personal areas are filled with objects that are important to us and reflect our values, ideas, and beliefs. If an individual values home and family, pictures of family members and pets may be on display. Religious individuals often decorate their homes and offices with religious symbols. One officer has his home office decorated with the "mug shots" of suspects he has personally helped to place behind bars. A doctor has her office decorated with pictures of all the babies she has delivered over several years. In residence, students decorate their rooms with objects that remind them of home, musical groups, and other items that are important to them, to personalize a room that is otherwise often drab. The next time you are in the office of a teacher or other professional, see what artifacts are in the room and try to determine what they say about the person.

We have less control over our physical appearance or physical traits than artifacts such as clothing. Serious conflict can arise when physical appearance is associated with stereotypes, prejudice, and discrimination based on gender, race, and ethnic classifications. For example, there are many examples of prejudice and discrimination against Native Canadians, black Canadians, and other visible minorities by police officers who hold negative stereotypes of these groups. Points for Pondering is just one example of prejudice by police officers.

POINTS FOR PONDERING   *Are Some Police Officers Racist?*

Despite all the training, all the warnings, and the knowledge that racism is politically incorrect behaviour, many police officers may be racist. But are they held accountable for such behaviour? Some would say yes, but many would say no. Here is just two examples of recent racist incidents:

- An officer in Toronto called a fellow officer whom he had never met to discuss a recent arrest. He referred to the suspect as a "nigger." He did not know he was talking to a black Canadian officer. The officer was reprimanded, but should he have been fired (Van Dyk, 1998)?

- Augustine Samuals, president of the Caribbean Community Council in Calgary, reported in 1996 that black teens driving their parents' cars were often stopped by the police (Sillars, 1996).

There are probably many other incidents that you can find in recent papers or magazines. What should be done to police officers who make racist remarks or treat individuals poorly because of their colour, sexual orientation, or other differences?

Sources

Les Sillars (1996). Race riot or just mayhem? *Alberta Report/Newsmagazine, 23*(47), 35–37.

Bill Van Dyk (Dec. 2, 1997). Our 99% perfect police. www.sentex.net/~bvandyk/police.htm

Besides space, another element surrounding us is time. **Chronemics** is the study of how we perceive and use time. We use time to define identities, interaction, and even status (Henley, 1977). In the fast-paced Western society, time appears to be valued and therefore so is speed. We often talk about the fast pace of life and look for ways to manage this pace. We want faster computers, faster highways, and faster food. Westerners who are used to this fast pace and the high value placed on time and speed can be frustrated by other cultures that do not give time and speed the same value. The pace and "need for speed" mentality may be one root cause for road rage, as discussed in chapter 1.

The Space around Us

All of us carry around an invisible bubble that is called our personal space. **Proxemics**, or the study of spatial communication, was pioneered by Edward T. Hall (1961). Often, we are unaware of our invisible bubble until someone gets too close or does not get close enough. In fact, many of our sayings use space to demonstrate feelings: "Get out of my face," "too close for comfort," and "get off my back" are just a few of the phrases we use when people are overstepping their boundaries in a relationship. When people whom we do not know get too close, we feel uncomfortable, and we will attempt to increase the distance in order to feel comfortable. During a conflict, one or both of the parties may decrease personal space to try to intimidate the other. The person who feels that he or she has the most power may also try to intimidate by touching, such as jabbing a finger in the other person's chest or arm. Inevitably, as stated previously in the section on touch, such invasive behaviours continue the escalation of the conflict and often lead to a physical confrontation unless one party backs down.

Many factors influence the distance between communicators (Borisoff and Victor, 1998). Culture and ethnicity affect comfort levels with closeness, some cultures being more comfortable than others with close proximity. Setting is another factor: in a setting that demands closeness between strangers, such as in elevators or airplanes, people are less uncomfortable than if strangers are close in places where there is ample space. The nature of the relationship also affects distance. Relationships vary from those between strangers, casual acquaintances, friends, and co-workers, to family and lovers. With friends and relatives, we may prefer to be closer than when interacting with superiors, strangers, or people we do not like. When an officer wears a uniform, the public treat the officer in a way that is different from how they would if he or she were wearing plain clothes. Many officers who work with victims of crime often prefer not to wear uniforms so that they can get physically and emotionally closer to the victim to assist in the investigation.

Several researchers have studied spatial distance and personal distance. According to one researcher (Hall, 1961), there are four interpersonal distances or circles that correspond to types of relationships: intimate, personal, social, and public, which are illustrated in figure 3-1. Be aware that these are general guidelines and can be influenced by many factors, including those discussed above.

| FIGURE 3-1 | Four Interpersonal Distances |

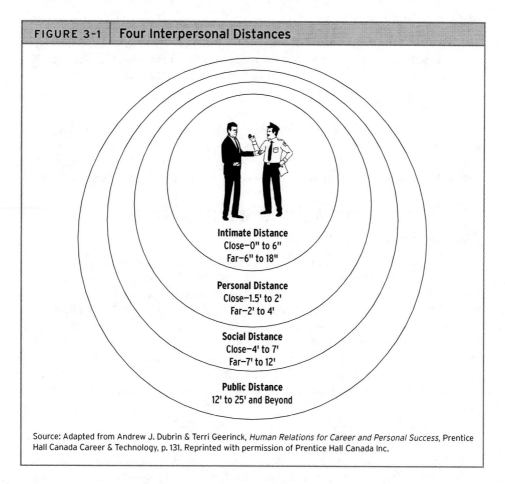

Intimate Distance
Close—0" to 6"
Far—6" to 18"

Personal Distance
Close—1.5' to 2'
Far—2' to 4'

Social Distance
Close—4' to 7'
Far—7' to 12'

Public Distance
12' to 25' and Beyond

Source: Adapted from Andrew J. Dubrin & Terri Geerinck, *Human Relations for Career and Personal Success*, Prentice Hall Canada Career & Technology, p. 131. Reprinted with permission of Prentice Hall Canada Inc.

Intimate Distance

Intimate distance ranges from actual touching to 18 inches. This distance is for close and intimate relationships, where touching is important. When strangers cross over into intimate distance, we feel threatened or very uncomfortable. For instance, in a crowded elevator, we do not look at each other and focus our eyes ahead on the floor numbers. To deliberately intimidate, we can invade this space, and such invasion can cause tempers to flare.

Personal Distance

Within **personal distance**, your comfort zone ranges from 18 inches to 4 feet. Many of our friendly relations stay within this zone. At 18 inches, you can still touch a person, as you do when you shake hands or pat someone's back, but the zone is less intimate. The area is still small enough that you can reach the person, and this is where the limits of physical control can be exerted. If you think someone may try to run, stay within this limit to maintain physical control without getting into the intimate area.

Social Distance

Ranging from 4 to 12 feet, **social distance** is the distance where we conduct impersonal business and have less personal interaction. Conducting business across a desk is usually in this zone and many office areas are designed to maintain this distance.

Public Distance

Public distance ranges from 12 to 25 feet and beyond, and is limited only when the speaker can no longer be heard. If someone is behaving bizarrely, you may choose this as your safe distance, because this is the distance within which you can more readily flee from a situation. Stage productions, lectures, and speeches are given within this distance.

USING NONVERBAL COMMUNICATION TO MANAGE CONFLICT

Now that you have gathered some knowledge about the complexity of nonverbal communication, you can use it in the field to assist with conflict management. Paying close attention to the rich data that can be accumulated from nonverbal language will assist you in de-escalating a conflict. Remember that nonverbal communication is heavily influenced by your personal perception, biases, and experiences. We all view the world differently, so when we view others' behaviour, we judge it by using our own personal yardsticks. It is important that you check out these perceptions so that you do not make errors in judgment or fail to fully comprehend a situation. Below are several methods for you to study to improve your use of nonverbal communication and to minimize inaccuracies created by the overuse of nonverbal cues.

Pay Close Attention to All Nonverbal Cues

As a police officer, you must always pay attention to the nonverbal language of the people that you are dealing with. Examine and explore all the cues that you register. While it may be easy to focus on the face, especially when the other person is talking, monitor the entire body. People can be good at "faking" facial expressions, but it may be more difficult for people to concentrate on their entire body to mask a feeling. Pay close attention to hands, feet, posture, use of personal space, fidgeting, eye movements, and body positioning. For example, if someone is about to attack you, he or she may bend slightly forward like a football player about to shoulder an opposing player. He or she may move into a more aggressive boxer's stance, with the dominant foot back and the opposite shoulder forward to protect his or her body. By paying attention to this *nonverbal leakage*, you will be a better skilled communicator and less open to surprise behaviour or movements.

Do Not Be Swayed by First Impressions

While it is important to pay attention to nonverbal cues, they are not always accurate and need to be used with care and discretion. Impressions and stereotypes (in the section below) rely heavily on nonverbal communication, but used incorrectly can lead to grave errors in assessing others. **Impressions** are collections of perceptions that we use and maintain to interpret the behaviours of others. Generally, these impressions are not specific, such as the impression that the person is nice, friendly, or unkind. Many of these impressions are based on nonverbal cues such as physical appearance, age, race, gender, and manner of dress. As in all perceptions, we select, organize, and interpret data to arrive at our own conclusions. Often we have a rich source of data for selection that is based on our own knowledge and conclusions, opinions, ideas from third parties, and repeated encounters with the person. These conclusions are an overall impression of the other person. Obviously, as we get to know another in more depth, the data collection is more accurate and the impression becomes more accurate.

However, if we look more closely at police work, there is often only one encounter, and judgments must be made quickly. **First impressions** are impressions made with very little information. The power and longevity of first impressions have been demonstrated in research (Asch, 1948) and replicated in more recent years. The first impressions we form about someone often affect our interpretation of subsequent perceptions of them. The major problem with first impressions is that they may be wrong. Police officers may deal with people who are not always at their best, and these impressions can affect further interactions with these people. People can be drunk or under the influence of drugs, they may be angry or out of control. Police officers need to realize that this first negative impression is not the sum total of the person. Rather than allowing these first impressions to colour subsequent treatment of the person, we need to see first impressions for what they are: initial and not always accurate perceptions of a person. However, on the other hand, as police officers, you must often respond to this first impression to ensure your personal safety.

The power of first impressions can also work the opposite way. We make negative judgments about people because of dress, and mental or emotional state. But people can also manipulate those impressions. Child molesters can be well-dressed business people. We should also not be swayed by an overly positive impression and should continue to seek more information.

Know Your Own Limits: Beware of Prejudice, Stereotypes, and Discrimination

As with impressions, many of our thoughts about others may be influenced by the quick assessment of nonverbal cues. Using these cues, we may group people together in a specific category. When we **stereotype**, we place people into categories or groups based on broad generalizations and assumptions that we hold about a particular group. The problem with stereotypes is that we "lump" large groups of people into the same category, often with minimal knowledge and experience about that particular category. Police officers, like all of us, use stereotypes, too. Some of these stereotypes are ones that include criminals

(Stansfield, 1996). Table 3-1 lists just a few of these common cultural and criminal stereotypes that can be found in the general public and in law enforcement personnel.

TABLE 3-1	Common Stereotypes
Common Cultural Stereotypes	**Common Criminal Stereotypes**
"Jews are good with money."	"All Italians belong to the Mafia."
"All women are soft."	"Young people are troublemakers."
"All cops are pigs."	"Native Canadians are drunks."
"Arabs are sneaky."	"Sikhs are terrorists."
"East Asian students are smart."	"Blacks and Jamaicans are drug dealers."
"Blacks have rhythm."	"Bikers are gang members."
"Mentally ill people are violent."	"White trash cause trouble."
"Gay men are effeminate."	

Adapted from Robert Stansfield (1996). *Issues in policing: A Canadian perspective* (p. 136). Toronto, ON: Thompson Educational Publishing.

Once we have stereotyped people, we tend to treat them according to the stereotype, so our responses become biased and limited. We also tend to seek information that fits the stereotype and ignore or dismiss information that does not (Philipchalk, 1995). For example, once a police officer has formed the stereotype that all black young people who drive expensive cars are drug dealers, the officer is more likely to treat these people differently. If we start to treat someone differently as a result of this stereotyping, we have developed a prejudicial attitude and may discriminate against members of this group. **Prejudice** is an unjustifiable negative attitude toward a group and its members; **discrimination** is the resulting unjustifiable negative behaviour based on this attitude (Philipchalk, 1995). If we do not like a particular group of people such as black Canadians, our attitude will affect our treatment of these people on the job. Our behaviours may include verbal expressions of dislike, avoidance of group members, actual discriminatory practices such as excluding group members from certain activities or rights, and physical attacks. At the furthest extreme is the extermination of this group, such as Hitler attempted during World War II (Allport, 1958).

The problem with stereotyping, prejudice, and discrimination is that they deny people's individuality. First, we often categorize on the basis of minimal information, and this information is often based on a minimum of nonverbal cues such as colour, accent, and style of dress. And once denied individuality, people may actually begin to behave and react according to these stereotypes. If the police hold true that the "typical criminal" is a young, black, or Native, urban male, then police no longer have to evaluate each individual upon individual characteristics and evidence (Stansfield, 1996).

In the United States, the same criminal stereotype exists; although the stereotype does not include "Native," it will often include "Hispanic" (Stansfield, 1996). So when police officers may hold onto these stereotypes, the public become aware of these stereotypes. Thus when the police deal with members of these groups, the members themselves become very aware of how they may be perceived by the police officers or other members of society. And as we know from recent cases in some of the larger cities, these groups have become very vocal about their mistreatment by law enforcement personnel.

When we judge others by the stereotypes we have of them, and then treat them in negative ways, or our treatment of them is the result of our perception of the group membership, we are building barriers to honest and open communication. Such lack of communication may lead to conflict. To treat someone differently because he or she is of another culture denies the uniqueness of this person. When police officers use their powers of discretion, they must be aware of the dangers of stereotyping, prejudice, and discrimination so that they do not treat people poorly because of a few nonverbal cues.

Seek Additional Information to Confirm or Refute Your Interpretation

One way to avoid the pitfalls of stereotyping and discrimination is to seek additional information in order to make more accurate assessments. This is a general strategy for improving communication and should be used to check out not only nonverbal communication but verbal communication as well. Now that you are aware of the number of errors that can be made in interpreting nonverbal communication, you need to learn ways to avoid them. Often, our nonverbal cues are more believable than what we say, because our nonverbal cues are under less personal control. In other words, we choose what we say but may be unaware of the nonverbal aspects of the communication.

So the first step to confirm your interpretation is to pay close attention to the entire body of the other person. Although facial expressions and eye contact are important, also pay attention to hands, feet, posture, space, and paralanguage. For example, I may say to a friend that I have time to chat, but taking peeks at my watch and increasing my distance may indicate otherwise. A person may say she has calmed down after a fight, but fidgeting and a tense posture may indicate that she may not be as calm as she says, and you need to remain very alert for the possibility of another altercation.

Once you have gathered your nonverbal "evidence," check that your perceptions are accurate. The better you know the person, the better the chance that your perception is more accurate. But as professionals, we may encounter someone only once, and this brief contact may lead to more inaccurate perceptions. After a car accident, the driver may say everything is fine. However, you notice that he is still shaking and rubbing his hands on his knees. At this point, you may want to re-check his statement that he feels fine. The most obvious way to check our perceptions is to ask the person about them in an unthreatening and non-confrontational way, and thus avoid conflict.

This **perception checking,** the third step in improving interpretation, is done by using "I" language. Using the previous accident example, the officer may say, "You say that you feel fine, but I see that you are still shaking."

After he hears such a statement, the victim now has a chance to respond. He may say, "You're right. I know I don't have any injuries. I guess it's all just sinking in."

With "I" language, the key is that you *own* what you perceive to be happening and that you are tentatively checking this impression. Using "I" language is a communication skill that we will revisit in the next chapter as an essential component of defusing a conflict and enhancing a supportive environment.

Sometimes, you may be wrong in your thinking or perceptions, and using this approach gives the other person an opportunity to tell you in a nonthreatening way that you are wrong. If you feel someone is giving you the nonverbal message that he or she does not have time to talk, try checking it out this way: "I see you glancing at your watch and I get the impression that you really don't have time talk to me." You may be pleasantly surprised. The reply may be, "I don't mean to give you that impression. I really want to talk to you, but I have a meeting in five minutes. Maybe we could meet later?"

Because we do not want to appear rude or uncaring, we often reply in socially acceptable ways rather than being honest. When given the opportunity, many of us would prefer to be honest! Therefore, this final step in interpreting or checking out nonverbal communication is to then use the corrected information to continue the interaction with the other person.

Be Aware of, and Monitor, Your Nonverbal Communication

What nonverbal "signals" are you "waving" at others around you? At times we may consciously control our movements, gestures, and other nonverbal messages. Often, however, we may be unaware of what we are nonverbally saying to others. By paying closer attention to our nonverbal messages, we may become more aware of what messages we are giving others.

Consider This...

"When I was first hired, my training officer noticed that I used a lot of 'ums' and 'ahs.' He said that it made me look unsure of myself and that it was important to look confident, even if I didn't feel that way. It took some work, but I got rid of them."

Once we are aware of the nonverbal messages we are transmitting, we can learn to better control them. In many encounters with people who are angry or upset, it is easy to become defensive. If a police officer shows this defensiveness or irritation, the subject will continue the tirade and the conflict may escalate. One strategy is to not take the abuse personally. It is the uniform and what it represents and not the person in the uniform that the abuse is aimed at. In other words, learn to be professional and let this professionalism guide your behaviour.

In other situations, emotions like horror, disgust, contempt, and sadness must also be held at bay. While it may difficult to control the outward display of these emotions, it is necessary to remain professional. For example, while arresting a suspect in a child molestation case you may feel disgust and anger towards a person who would hurt and abuse children. While you do not have to be nice to this person, you must behave according to a code of conduct. Below is a small activity to help you become more aware of your nonverbal communication habits.

Self-Assessment   *Nonverbal Communication Awareness*

For each of the following emotions, attempt to outline your personal nonverbal behaviours by finishing the sentence with at least two nonverbal indicators. If you are unsure, do this activity with someone you know well who has seen you in situations where you experienced these emotions. For example, the first emotion is anger. Describe how you nonverbally let others know that you are angry, such as by clenching your fists or raising your voice. (Remember that tone, volume, and pitch are classified as nonverbal communication.)

1. When I am angry, I...

2. When I am sad, I...

3. When I am disgusted, I...

4. When I am frightened, I...

5. When I am nervous or unsure of myself, I...

Were there any overlaps in your behaviours? For example, when nervous and angry do you wring your hands? Now that you are more aware of your nonverbal signs and "leakage," you will find it easier to control these signals when they are inappropriate for the situation.

Use Mirroring to Establish Rapport

When we like certain people and are getting along well with them, we tend to copy or "mirror" their nonverbal behaviours. Watch carefully when you view two people talking who like each other. If they are sitting, they lean towards each other. If one person has an excited expression, so does the other. Conversely, when people dislike each other or are experiencing conflict, this mirroring effect is absent (Kircshner and Brinkman, 1994). During a conflict, distinct and different patterns of nonverbal behaviours are often evident. For example, observe two people having an argument in a restaurant. One leans forward, talking quickly in a loud voice. The other person sits as far back in the seat as possible and refuses to speak.

Mirroring, as a strategy, is the subtle imitation of someone. Two effective mirroring strategies are to imitate the breathing pattern of another person and to adopt the rate of speech of another person (Dubrin, 2001). When we subtly imitate someone else, we are increasing "common ground" or a shared environment. Once we establish this common ground, conflict resolution is more likely (Kirschner and Brinkman, 1994).

CREATING A SUPPORTIVE CLIMATE

While creating a supportive climate is a skill that relies heavily on your ability to manipulate nonverbal communication, it is such an important facet of interpersonal communication and conflict resolution that it deserves to be put in a separate category. Police officers do not spend all of their time in the company of the "bad guys"; they also spend significant time and effort with people who need help and support. To be helpful and supportive, it is essential to promote and manage a climate that fosters these goals. This can be a difficult task when dealing with people who distrust police officers and other representatives of a variety of agencies. The officer may also have to deal with people with significant personal, emotional, or mental challenges. How well you manage these groups will be directly related to your ability to provide a supportive, rather than a defensive, climate.

Also, during a conflict, people may become defensive. When people are defensive, the conflict is more difficult to resolve and may lead to conflict escalation. As the continuum suggests, when frustration and anger increase, the conflict will likely escalate. What starts out as an argument turns into a screaming match. Once at this level, the issue becomes harder to resolve, tempers continue to flare, and the risk is that things will get out of hand.

How may times in your life did an argument turn into a serious conflict? One good way for a conflict to escalate is for one or both parties to become defensive. If a police officer uses a harsh tone when questioning someone or appears to be in a hurry, very little is likely to be accomplished. In fact, many crimes such as sexual assault go unreported because the victim is afraid of the treatment by police or other agencies.

In order to establish a supportive climate, we need to explore the differences between supportive and defensive climates. One researcher, Jack Gibb, has identified six types of communication that foster one climate or the other (adapted from Wood, 1998, pp. 193–98).

Evaluation versus Description

When we are called names or it is assumed that we are similar to another person, we feel that we are being evaluated. When others evaluate us, they often use sentences that begin with "You." Also, evaluation often groups or stereotypes people, such as when someone says, "You're just like my old man," or, " You're just like all the other cops I've talked to before." On the other hand, using description acquired from observations fosters a more supportive climate. If I describe what I see without passing any judgment, I can keep the climate supportive. Using statements that begin with "I" are less offensive and do not lead to such a defensive climate. For example, "I feel hurt when you don't call when you are going to be late," is much less defensive than saying, "You never call when you're going to be late." Describing behaviour rather than evaluating it will lead to a more supportive exchange. "You" versus "I" language will be discussed further in the next chapter as a method to improve communication and resolve conflict.

Certainty versus Provisionalism

The language of certainty allows things to be only one way, without room for other ideas or opinions. Have you ever tried to argue with someone whose mind is already made up? Banging your head against a wall may be less painful! On the other hand, stating your ideas as if they are not carved in stone keeps a discussion open. But beware, if you keep your discussion and your mind open, you run the risk of being changed! By stating your ideas provisionally, the climate is more supportive and open. For example, I might say, "The way I tend to view communication courses is that they are essential for learning good communication skills." By using provisional statements, I am stating that there are other views, other ideas, and other ways to approach problems. Your tone of voice and volume help ensure that what you say is provisional. You state your ideas as your ideas rather than as absolute facts. Such statements leave room for further discussion and other opinions. As a police officer, stating observations in this way allows the subject to answer without becoming defensive.

Strategy versus Spontaneity

When we think others are trying to manipulate us or are not being honest with us, we become defensive. If others appear to be "planning" what they are saying, we become suspicious of their motives. For instance, if I start off my conversation to you by saying, "Remember when I helped you with that essay you were having so much trouble with?" you may start to wonder what I am leading up to. People who are actively manipulating speak slowly and deliberately and may lack the enthusiasm we hear in others' voices when they are being spontaneous and open. On the other hand, spontaneous communication is just that: it feels open, honest, and unrehearsed.

Control versus Problem Orientation

When we attempt to control others, we do so by using communication that asserts our solutions or ideas are the only acceptable ones. When we attempt to control another this way, we are demonstrating that we are more superior, have more power, have more rights, have more intelligence and more abilities than the other person. We may try to control others by pointing out what it is that we control and what they do not. For example, "I'm the one paying the bills here. So we are going to buy the stereo that I want and not the one you want." What would be the tone of voice in this statement? The volume? Body language? Using many channels, this person would be essentially saying, "I am the one in control here, and you are not!"

The opposite of control is to use communication that is problem-oriented, to maintain a supportive climate. When we problem-solve, we attempt to find a solution that satisfies everyone involved. For example, "Why don't we take a look at both stereos and draw up a list of their respective features, then make our choice based on what we find?" Regardless of who is paying for the stereo, making joint decisions as co-members of a household demonstrates respect and fosters a supportive climate. We can view differences as opportunities to reach mutually satisfactory solutions.

Neutrality versus Empathy

According to Gibb (1970), when people react to us neutrally or with detachment, we become defensive about this lack of demonstration of care or concern. What do people look like when they are behaving neutrally? Do they demonstrate enthusiasm, make frequent eye contact, or lean forward to listen? Using empathy demonstrates concern for the other's thoughts and feelings. Empathy is demonstrated nonverbally in a number of ways, including nodding your head as the other person speaks, and leaning forward while sitting. Maintaining eye contact and making sounds such as "Mm-hm," or phrases like "I see," also demonstrate empathy. Empathy demonstrates acceptance of the other person, even if his or her opinion is contrary to your own.

Superiority versus Equality

When people act as if they are better than we are, communication deteriorates. A person fostering a defensive climate asserts superiority in a number of ways, such as trying to demonstrate superior knowledge, intelligence, and power. As we have seen, people can demonstrate their power and superiority nonverbally: invading another person's space, touching or poking the other person, or talking louder and more forcefully than the other person. A teacher who says, "What do you know? You're only a student," is trying to demonstrate superior knowledge. What are the chances that you will have a second discussion with this teacher?

When people treat us like equals, they create a climate of support and mutual respect. If the teacher were to say instead, "That is a very interesting observation. You have taken some time to think this issue through," he or she is demonstrating that your thoughts are valuable and deserve attention. We feel more comfortable to self-disclose in this more relaxed and supportive climate.

A supportive climate encourages communication, and building such a climate relies on verbal and nonverbal communication. To distinguish between nonverbal and verbal communication is artificial, because interpersonal communication involves both modes of language. However, with this increased knowledge of the nonverbal elements of communication and conflict, you are now ready to concentrate on conflict resolution strategies that involve a combination of verbal and nonverbal elements.

SUMMARY

This chapter focused on the nonverbal aspects of conflict and communication. Conflicts are often precipitated by a "conflict starter" that begins the conflict. Properly managed at this stage, many conflicts can be de-escalated. Nonverbal communication makes up a major portion of interpersonal communication, so it plays an important role in conflict. Eight types of nonverbal communication were discussed: paralanguage, facial expressions and eye behaviours, kinesics or body language, haptics or touch, artifacts, appearance, time, and proxemics or personal space.

By paying attention to and understanding the language of nonverbal behaviour, we can improve our communication and manage conflicts more effectively. Six strategies or suggestions were proposed for such assistance: pay attention to all nonverbal cues of others; do not be swayed by first impressions; know your own limits and be aware of your own prejudices, stereotypes, and ability to use discrimination; seek additional information to confirm or disconfirm your interpretation; be aware of and monitor your own nonverbal communication; and use mirroring to establish rapport.

In the last section of this chapter, we differentiated a supportive climate from one that was defensive or non-supportive. A supportive climate focuses on description rather than evaluation, is provisional rather than certain, is spontaneous rather than strategic, has a problem orientation rather than a control orientation, values empathy over neutrality, and fosters a climate of equality rather than superiority.

CASE STUDY

The Speeder

At 2:00 a.m. Constable Mike Jones turned and pulled up to a car that was speeding. He pulled the car over. He approached the car and knocked on the window. The driver was a white male, dressed in a suit, and appeared to be in his early twenties. As he rolled the window down, he smiled at Mike, giving Mike direct eye contact.

"Hello, Officer," he said in a pleasant voice. "I guess you caught me this time. But I didn't think that I was driving over the speed limit. Guess you better ticket me though, so I can get home. My mother never sleeps really well until she knows that I'm home and safe and sound. You know how mothers are!"

"I need to see your licence and registration, sir," Mike responded. He had a funny feeling about this guy. He was too nice and all smiles.

"Look, you don't have to really give me a ticket do you? I was out with my girlfriend. We had a great time, but I have my job to go to in the morning. Have to pay my way through college," the young man said.

Mike also noticed that he was extremely fidgety and kept rubbing his hands together. Although he was working hard on maintaining a friendly demeanour, he kept glancing around as if he found it too hard to meet Mike's eyes. However, he did not appear to have been drinking, but something was going on.

"Would you mind remaining in your car, while I check the registration?" said Mike. "No problem, Officer."

But as Mike started to return to his cruiser, the male suddenly left his vehicle and began running.

As Mike ran after the suspect, he shouted for backup in his two-way communicator. Fortunately for Mike, the suspect fell over a log in a field. Mike handcuffed him without incident, with backup immediately following. Later, Mike found out that the man had sexually assaulted his girlfriend and there was a Canada-wide warrant for his arrest.

Questions

1. What nonverbal behaviours led Mike to think that there was something "not quite right" in this situation?
2. What behaviours of the male would be classified as *nonverbal leakage?*
3. How was the man trying to fool Mike so that he might get away?

KEY TERMS

Adaptors: nonverbal movements that fulfill a personal need for a person, often performed without conscious awareness.

Affect displays: nonverbal messages that carry an emotional meaning and include the strength of the meaning.

Artifacts: personal objects that people display in their surroundings to personalize the environment.

Body language: postures, movements, and gestures that nonverbally communicate information to others.

Chronemics: the study of how people perceive and use time.

Defensive behaviour: protective actions people take when they feel that their self-esteem or "selves" are being threatened by another.

Discrimination: unjustifiable negative behaviour directed towards members of a group.

Emblems: gestures that are used to replace words.

First impressions: impressions that are quickly made, based on very little information about other people.

Haptics: the study of the use of touch and body contact in communication.

Illustrators: gestures that complement verbal communication by describing, accenting, or reinforcing the verbal content.

Intimate distance: a distance between people that ranges from touching to about 18 inches, reserved for intimate communication.

Impressions: collections of perceptions that we use to interpret the behaviour of others.

Kinesics: the study of body language.

Paralanguage: vocal communication that does not include words, including voice volume, pitch, tone, and intensity.

Perception-checking: soliciting feedback to confirm the accuracy of a perception.

Personal distance: a distance between people ranging from 18 inches to about four feet that is reserved for friendly relations.

Prejudice: an unjustifiable negative attitude toward a group and its members.

Proxemics: the study of the use of personal space.

Public distance: a distance between people ranging from about 12 to 25 feet and beyond that is maintained for very impersonal contact.

Regulators: nonverbal communication that accompanies speech, which assists in controlling the interaction between speaker and listener.

Social distance: a distance between people ranging from 4 to 12 feet that is used to conduct impersonal interaction.

Stereotypes: people or situations placed in separate and distinct categories based upon broad assumptions and generalizations.

 # WEB LINKS

www.mapnp.org.library
This is an interesting site devoted to business, but rich with material and links to various areas of interpersonal communication, including nonverbal behaviour and conflict.

http://pertinent.com/pertinfo/business/KareCom3.html
Read a fascinating article titled "Six Ways to Get Along Better" by an expert in the field. Note how much of this article involves nonverbal communication.

REFERENCES

Gordon W. Allport (1958). *The nature of prejudice.* New York: Doubleday.

Roger E. Axtell (1989). *Do's and taboos of hosting international visitors.* New York: John Wiley and Sons.

Steven Beebe, Susan J. Beebe, Mark V. Redmond, et al. (2000). *Interpersonal communication: Relating to others.* Scarborough, ON: Allyn and Bacon Canada.

Deborah Borisoff & David A. Victor (1998). *Conflict management: A communication skills approach.* Needham Heights, MA: Allyn and Bacon.

P. Ekman & W. V. Friesen. (1978). Facial action coding system (FACS): A technique for the measurement of facial action. *Journal of Personality and Social Psychology, 39,* 1125–34.

Andrew J. Dubrin (2001). *Human relations: Interpersonal, job-oriented skills.* Upper Saddle River, NJ: Prentice Hall.

P. Ekman. (1992). Facial expression of emotion: New findings, new question. *Psychological Science, 3,* 34–38.

Jack Gibb (1970). Sensitivity training as a medium for personal growth and improved interpersonal relationships. *Interpersonal Development, 1,* 6–31.

E. T. Hall (1961). *The silent language.* New York: Doubleday; Fawcett Publications.

J. A. Hall (1987). On explaining gender differences: The case of nonverbal communication. In P. Shaver and C. Hendricks (Eds.), *Sex and gender* (pp. 177–200). Newbury Park, CA: Mayfield.

Nancy Henley (1977). *Body politics: Power, sex and non-verbal communication.* Englewood Cliffs, NJ: Prentice-Hall.

Rick Kirschner & Rick Brinkman (1994). *Dealing with difficult people: How to bring out the best in people at their worst.* New York: McGraw-Hill.

C. L. Kleinke. (1986). Gaze and eye contact: A research review. *Psychological Bulletin, 100,* 78–100.

M. Knapp (1978). *Nonverbal communication in human interaction.* New York: Holt, Rinehart, and Winston.

M. C. Lalljee (1971). *Disfluencies in normal English speech.* Unpublished dissertation, Oxford University. Quoted in M. L. Knapp (1980). *Essentials of nonverbal communication.* New York: Holt, Rinehart, and Winston.

L. A. Malandro & L. L. Barker (1983). *Nonverbal communication.* Reading, MA: Addison Wesley.

Ed McDaniel & Peter A. Anderson (1998). International patterns of tactile communication: A field study. *Journal of Nonverbal Behaviour, 22*(1), 59–75.

Albert Mehrabian (1972). *Nonverbal communication.* Chicago: Aldine-Atherton.

Ronald P. Philipchalk (1995). *Invitation to social psychology.* Orlando, FL: Harcourt Brace and Company.

Garry L. Pritchett (1993). Interpersonal communication. *FBI Law Enforcement Bulletin, 62*(7), 22–26.

Joann Ellison Rodgers (1999). Flirting fascination. *Psychology Today* (Jan./Feb.), 36–41, 64, 65, 69, 70.

Robert Stansfield (1996). *Issues in policing: A Canadian perspective.* Toronto: Thompson Educational Publishing.

Julia Wood, Ron Sept, and Jane Duncan (1998). *Everyday encounters: An introduction to interpersonal communication.* Scarborough, ON: ITP Nelson.

chapter four

Verbal Strategies for Conflict Management

Courtesy Peterborough Lakefield Community Police Service

LEARNING OUTCOMES

After studying this chapter, you should be able to

- Choose an appropriate conflict management style to resolve a conflict.
- Assess aggressive, non-assertive, and assertive behaviour.
- Use a problem-solving approach to manage conflict.
- Choose from several conflict management strategies to effectively resolve a conflict.

On-the-Job Scenario

"I can't believe Tom these days. One shift he's great, and the next shift he's angry and jumps on every little thing that I do," complained Sitka to her husband. "I just don't get it!"

"Maybe Tom is dealing with some rough things at home. You've been partners for almost a year, maybe you should talk to him about this."

"I've tried. He just tells me to mind my own business. And if he is in a good mood, he tells me I'm imagining things! All I know is that I can't take it much longer. Even *my* patience has an end!"

In the last chapter, we examined the nonverbal aspects of conflict as well as how conflicts start and how they might escalate. As previously noted in the last chapter, the verbal and nonverbal aspects of conflict are not separated. For example, during a conflict, anger is often displayed verbally as we express our anger, and nonverbally by our frowns and raised voices. However, for the purposes of learning, we have done some separating of these two features. Conflicts are rich in verbal and nonverbal content, and understanding both these aspects and using them together to resolve the conflict will lead to the best solutions for both parties. Effective communication and a variety of conflict resolution strategies will help police officers to identify several alternative courses of action when responding to calls for service.

In this chapter we will explore several strategies to assist resolution in a wide variety of conflicts. However, most of these strategies presented here are for milder conflicts, where there is no initial threat of physical confrontation. These milder conflicts are most likely to occur with co-workers, superiors, other professionals, and members of the public who are irate with police service, or committee members with whom you come into contact. However, as illustrated in the opening scenario, these conflicts can be as disturbing as more major conflicts, especially if they have continued for some time. These strategies may also be suitable for dealing with more minor infractions and calls for service. Not all strategies are suitable for all types of conflict. Rather, view these strategies as tools, and each job requires the right tool. For example, if you are dealing with a belligerent co-worker, using empathy may not be the right choice. Instead, you will need to use assertiveness to end the tirade. When your co-worker has calmed down, you may want to use a different approach, such as problem solving and being open and honest your concerns about such unfair treatment. As you gain experience in managing a wide variety of conflicts, you will become adept at choosing the right strategy or combination of strategies.

First, we will examine the styles of conflict management and assess situations where each style would be an appropriate choice. Then we will look at the differences in passive, assertive, and aggressive responses and how assertiveness helps resolve conflict. The remaining strategies in this chapter include using a problem-solving orientation, managing criticism and using constructive feedback, exchanging image and using empathy, being open and honest, maintaining the focus on the present, and using active listening. Last, we will examine some techniques to help you deal with a difficult co-worker.

CHOOSING THE RIGHT CONFLICT MANAGEMENT STYLE

In chapter 2, we discussed the five different styles of conflict management. The styles are based on two dimensions: the concern for achieving your own goals (ranging from unassertive to assertive) and the concern for the other party and the goals of that party (ranging from uncooperative to cooperative). Many people rely heavily on one of the five styles, and that reliance then becomes the person's dominant style for conflict resolution. Research has indicated that the style you prefer to use (as measured by the Thomas-Kilmann Conflict MODE Instrument) will be related to your behaviour during a conflict (Volkema and Bergmann, 1995). But a dominant style may not be the correct style across all situations. Have you ever had a minor discussion with someone that ended up in a shouting match? People who use a competitive style may be argumentative over even trivial issues. This is a misuse of this style. However, good conflict managers change their style to suit the conflict by analyzing their own goals and the importance of the relationship. Here we examine each style and when it would be appropriate to use each. Refer to the styles and the chart of these styles in chapter 2 on page 20.

Competing

Anyone who uses the competitive style wants to dominate or win at the expense of the other party, with little concern for the goals of the other party. Competitors use arguing and other tactics to win. Competition is focused on power and is based on the notion that one person has more power than the other. While you may instantly feel that this style should never be used, there are instances when it should be the style of choice. There are many situations where police officers must assert that they have more power than those they are dealing with, and that power is the law. If you have been called to remove someone from the premises where there is a restraining order in effect, your goal is to get the person out of there. If the person becomes uncooperative and unwilling after you have explained your intent properly and assertively, you may be forced to use a competitive approach. If the confrontation becomes serious, police officers adhere to the use of force guidelines, which are discussed in more detail in chapter 5. Of interest is the fact that police presence is included in the first level of the use of force response options. Remember that you may use only as much force as necessary for the situation. While you may have to physically remove the person, you should try to do so with a minimum of physical force.

Another situation where competing is an appropriate strategy is where a decision must be reached immediately, when there is no time for consultation. Managers often make decisions without input from staff. At times, you may also use this strategy when you are absolutely correct about something, or when you must defend your rights. For example, if you are being sexually harassed at work, it is within your rights to state, "If you make another remark like that about my body, I have no choice but to report you immediately to the supervisor." A person can use this style to maintain an assertive response to aggressive and demeaning overtures.

Accommodating

This style is the opposite of competing. When accommodating, a person neglects personal concerns to satisfy the needs or concerns of the other party. Such a person is highly cooperative and unassertive and is often seen as self-sacrificing. This style can be used effectively in a variety of conflicts. For example, it is useful to be accommodating when you find out that you were wrong about something and the other person was right. At times, the issue may be important to the other person but not to you. By giving in to the other person, you will be seen as caring and fair. (You may also be in a position to exchange this favour later on.) Sometimes a conflict can cause serious damage in a relationship. If the relationship is a valued one, then accommodation may be the wisest strategy. It is important to know when to pick your battles.

For example, you are a police officer walking down a main street with your partner on foot patrol, and a teen shouts out while you walk past, "Oink, oink!" What would your response be? You might want to ask yourself, How important is this relationship to me? And how important is it that I step in and try to win? What would I prove by confronting this teen?

Many would conclude that the best recourse here is to keep walking and ignore the youth. Another accommodating strategy here would be to use humour if there are other members of the public around. The humour can be directed at the public rather than the teens. It shows that you are "bigger" than the teens, and you are not seen as compromising your authority.

Compromising

Compromising consists of giving up something to get something. The concern for getting what you want is somewhat balanced by your concern for the other person. Compromise is the strategy of choice in several types of conflict, such as when officers on the job need a temporary solution. If a couple are fighting and both are intoxicated, a temporary separation (one leaves and goes to another home such as friend's or sister's place) is often the best solution. It is compromise, as the solution is a temporary one, but both sides "get something." The fighting stops, the officers can now leave, and the couple are doing no further damage to their relationship (at least for now).

Avoiding

The avoidance style demonstrates both lack of cooperation and lack of assertiveness. Wrongly used, avoidance can be thought of as neglect, where the person cares little for personal concerns and does not care about the other person's concerns or interests, either. When someone withdraws from a conflict physically or emotionally (for example, refusing to talk about the issue), the person is withdrawing from the conflict. Such withdrawal can damage a relationship if the issue is important to one person. When the issue is important to a relationship, avoidance is not a good strategy.

However, as with the other styles, there are times when it is the best choice. When emotions get too intense and people are no longer thinking rationally, avoiding the conflict for a set period of time may be a good move. It is better to come back to the issues later, when both parties have cooled off and are better able to think rationally. Labour negotiators often call a temporary halt to proceedings in such circumstances. Also, the context may not be suitable for conflict—it may not be the right time or place. Avoiding is also appropriate when you are taken by surprise and are totally unprepared to deal with an issue. For example, if your teenage daughter announces she is pregnant, you may want to take time to think through your response carefully. It may be wise, then, in some potential conflicts to state, "I need time to think about what you have told me before I respond." Avoidance may also be a suitable tactic if there are other more important issues pressing and must be dealt with immediately. At times, we have to prioritize our conflicts! Managers must often put off one issue to deal with a more pressing one. A good response might be, "I know that a pay raise is a big issue for you. However, I must finish fighting for my budget concerns before I can discuss pay raises with anyone." In policing, you may have several people all shouting to get your attention during an altercation at a park concert. You may have to say to the loudest person, "I will be with you as soon as I finish talking with this person. He was closest to the incident." You have to temporarily "avoid" one person to deal with another.

Collaborating

Collaborating is a highly assertive approach that rates the concerns of both sides in the dispute highly. Highly cooperative, collaboration is based on **win–win** rather than the

win–lose orientation of the competitive approach. In relationships that are long-term, such as those with co-workers, superiors, and others, collaboration is the appropriate method. Conflicts between people who must see each other and work or live with each other need to be dealt with in such a way that both people come out "winners." If these important issues are not managed, the conflict may remain just beneath the surface and do damage to the relationship in the long-term. Also, conflicts that are not managed immediately become more difficult to bring up later on. If your goal is to maintain the relationship and you wish to have your goals met as well as the goals of the other party, then collaboration is the best choice.

Collaboration is also appropriate for handling conflicts that occur in teams where all members can become involved in searching for a team solution. Using the strengths of the team members, the team can search for the best solution. Community groups that include police personnel have arrived at unique solutions to community crime problems. Anti-bullying programs and neighbourhood watch programs are often the results of the collaboration of police and community members. To use collaboration effectively, there needs to be a high level of trust. If the two sides do not trust each other, collaboration may not be effective. Collaboration is also a technique that fosters commitment. If two sides have to work together to come up with a mutually satisfying resolution, there is likely more willingness to follow through with and implement the solution. When people are angry and hard feelings have developed, collaboration is also useful. In essence, collaboration says, "I value you and I want both of us to get along and be happy. How can we go about achieving this?"

Collaboration takes a great deal of energy and may be very time consuming. Also, arriving at solutions may take creative thinking and demand a great deal of empathy for the other side. Thus collaboration should be used only if there is enough time available for a prolonged meeting or discussion (Borisoff and Victor, 1998).

AGGRESSIVE, NON-ASSERTIVE, AND ASSERTIVE RESPONDING

Many of us have difficulty being open and honest with others, especially during conflicts—for any number of reasons. During a confrontation, many of us become hostile and indignant and end up defensively holding our ground, because we feel that our self-esteem has been threatened. What started as a minor dispute becomes a screaming match, with the winner being the one who can scream the loudest. We might be afraid that we are going to hurt the other's feelings, so we don't say what is actually on our minds. Maybe it is easier to give in rather than open ourselves up for a potential conflict. We may feel that someone has power over us and we are genuinely afraid to engage in any confrontation at all. Whatever the reasons, being honest and assertive can be difficult. And yet in intimate and close relations, such lack of honesty may eventually erode the relationship. In professional and work relations, aggression and non-assertiveness also take their tolls. In many professional situations, you will need to act aggressively and forcefully as an individual and as a unit. However, to do so in situations where such a response is unnecessary can have serious consequences. See the Points for Pondering for one example of an inappropriate aggressive response. On the other hand, being too passive or non-assertive can also have serious consequences. Let's examine each of three types of responses in relation to conflict.

POINTS FOR PONDERING   *Are Police Becoming Too Aggressive?*

Over the last couple of years, there have been some incidents that have been viewed as being too aggressive on the part of the police. What do you think? Here are two of those incidents:

- In 1997, a Chilliwack dad and his young son were strolling home after shooting at cans with an air gun. They were surrounded by six RCMP officers with weapons drawn. The RCMP forced the man to the ground and cuffed him while one of them pointed a shotgun at his head. Although an apology was demanded, none was given (Byfield, 1999).

- In March 2001, eight female university students staged a sit-in at the vice-president's office of Trent University to protest the closure of off-campus colleges. After two days, they were removed and arrested by a team of tactical police officers. There was much public protest about the way the removal was managed (Marchen, 2001).

However, some other issues must be addressed here. The first incident involved weapons, and police officers must deal with such calls carefully. How much information did the officers have prior to their response? In the second example, the university called police because the students had refused several requests to leave the premises. When examining reports from the press or other sources on use of force, use caution, because the whole story may not be in the coverage.

Some of us can become **aggressive** in conflicts. Aggressive people are overbearing and push for what they want, without concern for the feelings of others. During a conflict, aggressive people may bully, shout, and generally do their best to win, without thinking of the consequences. In the heat of a debate, aggressive people may become irrational and infringe upon the rights of others. Some people who are aggressive just stick dogmatically to their point of view, regardless of evidence to the contrary. They are argumentative and do not handle criticism well.

If we cannot assert ourselves, some of us become **non-assertive**. Non-assertive or more passive people let things happen to them without making their feelings known. They give in to another person's requests or point of view. Some people have **passive-aggressive** tendencies. These people give the impression of giving in to your side of the conflict, but then behave in ways to assure that you have no easy time enjoying the victory. They use such tactics as trying to induce guilt, making costly mistakes, sabotaging the project through inaction, or not making others aware of important problems or information. For example, you and your roommate cannot agree on which television show to watch. Finally, your roommate gives in to you and your favourite sitcom is on. While watching, your roommate sits there and makes sarcastic comments about the actors and makes noises of disgust. You won, but what have you won?

Responding to others using assertiveness is a technique that not only assists you in everyday communication but is also an essential skill for conflict management. **Assertive** people communicate in a direct and straightforward manner that does not infringe on the rights of the other person (Dubrin and Geerinck, 2001). Let's look at an example:

A fellow student continually borrows your notes. Twice, the notes were not returned very promptly when tests were pending. You have decided that you will not let this student have your notes again. It is the night before a major test and you are studying in the library when this student approaches you. "Oh, thank goodness you're here! I need your notes right away. I missed the last two classes. I need them right now!"

Non-assertive response: "Oh, okay. Here you go."

Aggressive response: "Forget it! Quit whining and complaining. You're an idiot and you're not touching any of my notes again."

Assertive response: "I won't be able to lend you my notes. I also need them to study for the test."

To assert yourself in a conversation, maintain a straight posture, have your body well-balanced, and use gestures that support your key words. Choose words that express your feelings and needs that do not insult the other person. For example, if a classmate asks you out, you can say no in an assertive manner that should not hurt the feelings of that person. You can say, "Thank you for the invitation, but I would prefer not to go out with you." This is better than being non-assertive or passive, by going when you do not want to, or by making the excuse of being busy that evening, which only leaves you open to being asked again. Telling the person to "get lost" or worse is aggressive and hurtful. By being open and assertive in your communication, you will maintain honesty in your relations with others and have your needs met in a more fair and non-manipulative way. Try the activity below to improve your skills in assertiveness.

Skills Practice: Assertive Responding

For each of the following situations, write out a response that would demonstrate assertiveness. You may also do this activity in class in pairs.

1. You work part-time at a doughnut shop to help make money for school expenses. For the last six weeks, you have worked every Thursday, Friday, and Saturday night. Two weeks ago, you asked the manager for this Saturday night off because you have tickets for a hockey playoff game in Ottawa. On Friday night just before closing, your manager approaches you and says, "Oh, by the way. You can't take tomorrow evening off after all. Shelley can't come in and you have to cover for her."

2. You are on foot patrol downtown. One of the downtown "regulars" who chats to you every shift starts talking to you. As usual, he rambles on and on, and you try to tell him several times that you must be on your way. How could you tell him in a more assertive manner that you need to move on?

3. After a particularly difficult shift, you are unwinding with a few friends by having a game of pool and a beer. One of the guys on your shift comes over and says, "Well, how about another one? That was a heck of a day wasn't it? Let's have a couple more and drown our sorrows." You want to finish this one drink and head home to your family. You know that he will harp about this. How can you be assertive here without becoming aggressive?

The remainder of this chapter will explore several other techniques for conflict resolution. When resolving a conflict, choose from a variety of techniques that suit the conflict and the outcome that you desire, and that match your personal style. As you master these strategies, you will find yourself becoming a better conflict manager.

USING PROBLEM SOLVING FOR CONFLICT RESOLUTION

Viewing a conflict as a problem to solve can be an excellent strategy. When people can view a conflict as a problem that requires collaboration, they will likely be less defensive and will make a greater effort to resolve the problem. Collaboration takes time, energy, follow-through, and follow-up if it is to be effective. If the two parties cannot sit down and remain calm, it will be doomed to failure. Both must be committed to finding a mutually satisfying solution. At times, a mediator can look after this process by taking information from both sides in the initial stages to demonstrate the commitment of both sides to resolve the issues at hand.

There are many models of problem solving that can be used to help arrive at a solution. Most rely on a set of defined steps. These models can be found in business texts and counselling texts, and are used by many organizations, including police services. For example, the Ontario Provincial Police use PARE Analysis, a step-by-step problem-solving model adapted for police work (OPP, 1997). Here, we will focus on a very straightforward model that can be used for interpersonal conflict: define the problem, analyze the problem, generate many possible solutions, select the best solution that achieves the goals of the conflicting parties, implement the solution, then evaluate the solution at a mutually agreed upon date. For each step of the process, additional strategies are suggested to help promote and maintain an atmosphere for collaboration. Figure 4-1 illustrates the steps in this model. Before attempting to use this model, it is recommended that you choose a location where everyone feels comfortable. Also, the atmosphere must be conducive to open and honest communication (Weeks, 1994). Without a location and atmosphere where people feel comfortable, this process may not be effective.

1. **Define the problem.** Most conflicts and problems boil down to something you want more or less of. You can think of a **problem** as a deviation from where you would like to be or what you want on a specific issue. Make sure that you define the "real" problem and not just the symptoms. At this stage it is important to clarify perceptions to get at the "real" problem or root of the conflict. For example, two people may argue about small issues when the root of the conflict is different values.

2. **Analyze the problem.** Next, analyze the problem to determine its cause. When we analyze something, we reduce it or break it down into smaller pieces. Sitting down with the other person, begin by describing the events that produced the conflict, in the order that you feel they have happened. Describe the events in an unbiased way, without evaluating the other person. You do not want to start an argument here. Remember that you are trying to get at the root of the conflict, not start a new one! Is the conflict centred on one major issue, or are there several issues? According to Weeks (1994), it is also important to understand what happened in the past, to avoid repeating prior mistakes. By carefully analyzing the conflict, you will have a greater understanding of what led up to the conflict and how past attempts at resolution have not been successful.

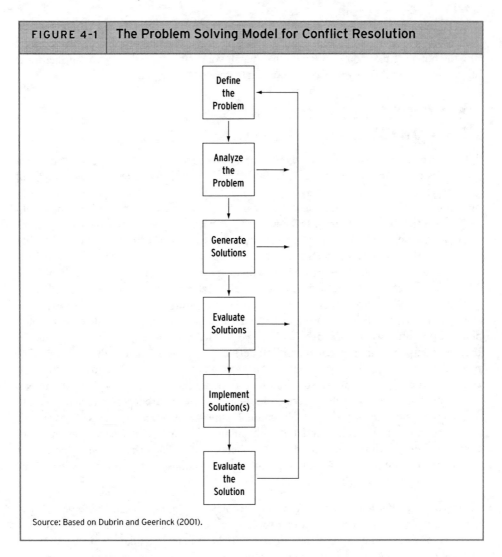

| FIGURE 4-1 | The Problem Solving Model for Conflict Resolution |

Source: Based on Dubrin and Geerinck (2001).

3. **Generate solutions**. For any problem, there may be multiple solutions. Part of resolving a conflict, using the problem-solving approach, is to list as many solutions as possible for the problem. The key at this stage is to generate solutions. Some of them may be strange, impossible, or highly improbable; just keep up the momentum. You may even want to write them down. **Creative thinking** should be encouraged. Creative thinking is an ability to process information that results in a product (or idea or solution) that is new, original, and meaningful. **Brainstorming** is an excellent method to foster creativity and can be done by individuals, pairs, and groups. The guidelines for brainstorming are presented in the Points for Pondering below.

4. **Evaluate the solutions.** Once you have a few solutions to end the conflict, you now need to evaluate them, based on the goals of the individuals. It is essential that the solution be accepted by everyone involved. If possible, the solutions should be evaluated using measurable criteria. For example, a couple decide that one problem in their

relationship is a lack of outside interests. A solution may be that they both take time to pursue individual hobby interests. The criterion for this hobby may be that it be pursued one night per week, the nights must be different to save on babysitting costs, and the activity cost less than $500 per year. With this criterion, golfing may be ruled out because of cost, but creative writing classes meet all the criteria and thus remain in the "solution pot."

5. **Implement the solution(s).** Once the solutions have been clearly defined, they can be implemented. Using the example in Step 4, each person enrols in an activity. One person does creative writing on Tuesday evenings and the other person joins a baseball league on Thursday evenings.

6. **Set a time to re-evaluate the chosen solution(s).** It is not enough to agree to a solution. Both parties must live up to their end of agreement. Once a solution has been agreed upon and implemented, many variables can get in the way of the intended goals. Therefore, particularly with long-term solutions, periodic checking is necessary to keep the parties focused and to discover if other problems are creeping into the solution. Again, using our previous example, after six weeks of going out, the couple sit down and talk about their enjoyment of their evenings out and decide whether to continue with the plan.

POINTS FOR PONDERING   *Using Brainstorming:*
It May Be Worth the Effort!

If you decide to use a problem-solving approach to resolve a conflict, brainstorming possible solutions is an integral part of the process. Brainstorming can be done in pairs or groups. **Brainwriting** is a type of brainstorming done by an individual in which the person writes down (or records in some way) all the ideas that he or she can generate. To use brainstorming correctly, there are four main rules or guidelines (Adams, 1979):

1. There is no criticism, defence, evaluation, or judgment of ideas. The focus is on generating as many solutions or ideas as possible.

2. Free association is encouraged. All ideas are to be voiced, no matter how "far out" the ideas are.

3. Quantity is the goal, not quality. The more ideas you can generate, the more solutions you will have more to evaluate in the next stages.

4. Building on previous ideas (piggybacking) is encouraged.

DEALING WITH CRITICISM

Has anyone ever verbally attacked you, launched into a long-winded critique about all the things you have done wrong? This may have happened on the job or at home. When you are in uniform, members of the public may feel it necessary to let you know what they think about police in general, and the media, ever vigilant, will also criticize police officers and policing in general.

Consider This...

"I like doing foot patrol at the free city concerts. However, there are always people who use your presence as an opportunity to air every beef they have about the police. It's like everything is your personal fault. Sometimes, I can feel myself start- ing to get really angry."

Whenever we are criticized, it can be an emotional experience that often leaves us angry, drained, and maybe even wanting a little bit of revenge. However, since you will likely be criticized again (especially by members of the public), it is necessary that you learn two skills: how to handle criticism, and how to give constructive feedback. While handling criticism and giving constructive feedback may not be thought of as conflict man- agement strategies, they are useful tools in avoiding conflict and ways of learning and improving yourself. First, we will examine handling criticism, then learn the conflict man- agement strategy of giving constructive feedback.

Managing Criticism

Criticism picks out the flaws and faults of another person. When criticism is harsh, it is invariably ineffective. One of three responses is likely when you criticize another. First, the person may become hostile and defensive, resenting and thus rejecting the criticism. Second, he or she may point out how your criticism is based on misunderstanding or errors in your way of thinking (Devito et al., 2001). For example, "You don't have the whole story," or, "That isn't how it went down." A third response may be a "non-response," and the person refuses to talk about the issue. Harsh criticism will not be accepted, and even if your intentions are good, there will be no or little change in behaviour. When criticism is delivered in this way, the climate is not supportive (chapter 3), and continued conflict is likely (criticism can be a conflict starter).

If someone criticizes you in an unconstructive manner, you can respond in several ways to avoid further conflict:

1. **Understand the goal of the criticism**. The intentions of the person may be good, just the delivery is poor. Sometimes we simply blurt out our ideas without taking the time to phrase them in a milder manner. The person's goal may be to belittle you. In this case, you can choose to ignore the criticism and not take the bait.

2. **Ask questions for clarification.** By asking questions, you may be able to defuse the situation. For example, your roommate accuses you of being a slob. You might say, "In what ways am I a slob?" However, take care with this one. Do not use it unless you honestly want a response.

3. **Do not respond defensively.** When being criticized, our immediate response may be to respond in kind. "If you think I'm a slob, you should take a look at your bedroom. I think some of that stuff could crawl away on its own!" Although such responses may give you some immediate satisfaction, they do not really solve the problem.

4. **Smile or try humour.** Depending upon the situation, smiling or joking can defuse the criticism. For example, "You're right, I am an absolute slob. Only you could tolerate me. Thank you," might calm your roommate down, and then you can discuss how both of you can work to keep the apartment clean (or learn to accept each other's ways).

5. **Accept the criticism and reword it for further understanding.** If you believe the intentions of the other party are good, or that the criticism is justified (you are a slob and need to learn some housekeeping skills), you can accept it and reword it for clarification: "Okay. You say I'm a slob. I can't change overnight. What is one thing that I can do that will help?"

Constructive Feedback

Criticism delivered properly will lead to more positive outcomes (Devito et al., 2001). This type of criticism is often referred to as "constructive criticism." One positive outcome is that the person agrees with you. Such agreement may open up the door for change and conflict resolution. Second, the person may accept your criticism as something to think about or as something that he or she never thought of and will consider. One method of delivering criticism effectively is to use *constructive feedback*. Constructive criticism or feedback is given within a supportive environment. The goal of such feedback is to help the other person develop new behaviours or to change less productive or inappropriate behaviours. For example, if you become a training officer, you will want to assist new officers in developing skills. Part of learning is trying something new, obtaining feedback about performance, and then trying again. As well, if someone is doing something that may lead to conflict (such as an annoying co-worker who continually chews gum loudly), engaging in constructive feedback may help you confront the person. There are nine basic steps in constructive feedback. You may not use all nine steps, depending upon the situation (based upon Engleberg and Wynn, 1997, Geerinck, 2000, and Lumsden and Lumsden, 1997).

1. **Feedback focuses on the behaviour, not the person.** People become defensive when they feel their self-esteem is being threatened. Focus on the behaviour that needs correcting, not the person.

2. **Feedback must be clear, specific, and descriptive.** Blanket labels like *slob, inconsiderate, lazy,* and *rude* do not clearly explain the troublesome behaviour. For example, rather than stating that the new officer looks nervous, the training officer wants to focus on specific behaviours that may be seen as demonstrating nervousness such a playing with his or pen or laughing nervously.

3. **Try to lead your feedback with a positive statement first or a demonstrated strength of the person.** You can soften the blow by first telling a person the things he or she has done right. For example, you can point out how polite the new officer was, then move on to the issue of nervousness.

4. **If the person solicits the criticism or feedback, try to understand why.** In formal performance evaluations, this is not an issue. However, in informal situations, the goal in mind may be something other than improvement. The person may be fishing for a compliment or for increased attention. The "compliment fisher" may just want reassurance that he or she is a valuable team member. It is appropriate to ask the individual what the purpose of the feedback is. For example, "I'm curious about why you would be asking me about your target shooting skills."

5. **Feedback should occur in a timely fashion and in an appropriate place.** When issuing feedback, be aware of the environment. No one likes to be confronted in front of others, because that can be embarrassing. The training officer would not criticize a new officer in front of members of the public. Also, feedback has more impact if it is

given immediately after the incident. Most of us do not like being told we did something wrong if it took place weeks ago. People can become defensive, wondering why they were not told earlier.

6. **Use "I" statements if the feedback is about your impression of performance.** It is your perception, you own it, not the other person. For example, "I think that your writing has improved considerably. There are still several grammatical errors that I would like to go over with you, but I saw only a couple of spelling errors." Statements that start with "you" connote that there is something wrong with the person, such as, "You are a slob."

7. **Feedback should include specific ideas or alternatives about how to improve or where to go to access information for improvement.** The problem-solving process can be used as one method to develop ideas or alternatives. Brainstorming can also work to develop a set of alternatives for improvement. For example, "Since it appears that grammar is the problem, may I suggest the on-line grammar course at the Learning Centre. You can try it when you have time and work at your own speed."

8. **For ongoing development, such as field training, set a goal for improvement, a period for completion, and a specific time for further feedback.** For example, "You still have three weeks before the paper is due. Why don't you use the program to correct the errors that I have underlined, then come and see me at the same time next week?"

9. **The feedback session should end on a positive note.** For example, "Thanks for letting me help you with this. I think that with a bit of work, you will be a very competent writer," or, "With more practice with the public, you will be less nervous and present a very professional image."

   Criticism does not have to be negative. When it is used wisely, we can experience criticism as the beginnings of a change or a method to bring conflict into the open so that a solution can be realized.

COGNITIVE RESTRUCTURING

Cognitive restructuring is not so much a tactic or strategy, as a way to view the conflict differently so that it can be lessened. Using this technique, you mentally convert negative aspects of the conflict into positive ones by identifying the positive elements in the conflict (Kaye, 1994). For example, an experienced and respected officer is being continually pestered by a recruit who continually asks her questions about police procedures. Instead of viewing this negatively ("This person is a pest"), by reframing the behaviour, she can see this as an opportunity to review procedures so that she does not forget them in the future. In this more positive light, the experienced officer may say to the recruit, "I appreciate how keen you are to learn the ropes. However, I would prefer if we could set up appointments to go over your queries when it is convenient for both of us." While this strategy may seem a weak one, it is an excellent choice for minor annoyances.

EMPATHY AND IMAGE-EXCHANGING

During a conflict, we often get caught up in our points of view and may have some difficulty understanding the other side. According to Devito (1997, p. 389), a "frequently used fight strategy is to blame someone." When there is conflict in a relationship, we try to find out whose fault it is and may attribute motives to the other person. Blaming and fault-finding do not resolve conflicts and may actually escalate the conflict from arguing to shouting and verbal aggression. These motives and attributes are not necessarily true and may further remove the two parties from trying to resolve the real problem at the root of the conflict.

Instead of blaming the other person, use empathy. **Empathy** is an attempt to see the conflict from the other's point of view; to walk in the other person's shoes. Try to understand what the other person is really feeling, what the thoughts and motives could be from the other perspective. Verbally express your empathy: "I can understand your being angry. I really should not have called you a 'bleeding-heart liberal.' It was an unkind thing to say." Practising empathy does not mean that you agree with the other person; it forms a basis for further understanding and further interpersonal communication.

Consider This...

"When I get involved with a domestic and the place is filthy and everyone is drunk, I try to remember that these people may not have the skills that I have in life. Like, maybe, they never had great parents like I do or money to do things. I find that I stay calmer and can be little more understanding that way."

A strategy that relies on the use of empathy is image-exchanging. **Image-exchanging** involves temporarily exchanging roles with the other person in the conflict. A convenient method to do this is to have each person exchange roles and then list all the reasons for the other person's side in the argument. For example, you may think a teacher is being harsh and unreasonable for not accepting your late paper. To more fully understand the teacher's point of view, you would list all the reasons that would influence this refusal. For example, your list might include the fact that deadlines to submit marks are too tight, that this is the second late paper, that if one student can be late, more students may ask for this privilege and lead to a deluge of requests, and that the instructor wants to teach the student to be more responsible. The teacher would then list your side of the argument, which might include the fact that a part-time job consumes many hours, that a noisy residence makes it difficult to concentrate, and that the subject is boring. When this exercise is finished, the increased empathy that results may help resolve the conflict. We do not have to agree with the other side, but with a little bit of empathy, tempers may not be as likely to flare, and rational people make better decisions!

BE OPEN AND HONEST

At times, we are reluctant to engage in conflict for many reasons. We may lack assertiveness, fear that we may hurt another's feelings, or be afraid of possible retaliation. When we are reluctant to manage a conflict, we may not be open or honest about the issues and about our feelings. Instead, we do not tell the truth. We say nothing is wrong and keep our feelings to ourselves, refuse to talk about what is troubling us, talk about irrelevant concerns, or downplay the conflict. A consequence of not dealing with the conflict may be the building of stone walls, and it may become more difficult to manage the conflict as feelings become hardened and anger develops.

If the issue is important and maintaining the relationship is important (whether it is a personal or professional relationship), conflict needs to be dealt with honestly and openly. Referring to conflict management styles, use collaboration, or depending upon the level of importance, consider compromise. Both strategies rely on expressing what you want.

MAINTAIN YOUR FOCUS ON THE PRESENT

Have you ever had the experience during a conflict of suddenly having someone bring up everything that you did wrong in the past? You have been late picking up your partner, but now a grievance from last summer is suddenly being discussed.

During a conflict, it important to stay in the present and discuss the current conflict. Bringing up past issues or "sore spots" is referred to as **gunnysacking.** If there are other issues, now is not the time to discuss them. You may want to say something like, "I understand that last summer is still bothering you, but let's continue with what the current problem is. We can discuss last summer at another time if you wish."

ACTIVE LISTENING

In *listening*, the listener tries to understand exactly what the other person is saying and feeling. In *active listening*, we give feedback to the speaker that demonstrates that we truly understand what is being said to us. Active listening involves reflecting back to the listener the content and the feelings of the message (Devito, 1996). In some texts, active listening is also termed reflective listening. Active listening is useful in conflicts where you truly wish to understand the other person's ideas and feelings. For example, if you are experiencing a conflict with a significant person in your life, active listening will help you further understand his or her point of view. Active listening also encourages empathy.

Active listening relies on three sets of distinct strategies. First, you must demonstrate that you are listening intently to the speaker. You can do this by maintaining eye contact. Other nonverbal methods to indicate that you are listening are for you to nod your head in agreement from time to time or lean forward. Also, saying "Mm-hm," or "Uh-huh" occasionally also signifies that you are listening.

Second, active listening relies on **paraphrasing** (Devito, 1996). Paraphrasing is expressing what the speaker has just said in different words. Often when people are upset, we want to launch into advice about how they should manage the situation. In conflict, we get so involved with our side of things that we literally stop listening to the other person. Have you had a conflict where you and the other person kept interrupting each other as you attempted to get your points in? Instead, paraphrasing reflects back to the speaker what we understand to be his or her thoughts and feelings. These paraphrases are worded tentatively so that the speaker can correct them if necessary. When we paraphrase, we can reflect back the feeling content of the message as well. For example, your significant other is angry because you are late coming home from work. You can paraphrase the feeling, the message, or both.

The third step of active listening is to ask questions to make sure that you understand the person's thoughts and feelings, and to get additional information. The questions should be open-ended to encourage the person to talk so that the whole issue is out in the open. These questions give the speaker the opportunity to express his or her side of the conflict.

You may discover that it is not being late that is irritating, but that you fail to notify your partner, who feels that this is disrespectful and inconsiderate. Lateness is not the issue, the failure to notify is at the root of the conflict.

If you decide to use active listening, remember that it takes time, energy, and effort. A front-line officer may not always find active listening appropriate. But you may branch out into other areas of enforcement such as victim's services and crisis intervention, or you may work in a community with few other support services, and you may be the only officer on the scene. Try the activity below to enhance your active listening skills.

Skills Practice: Active Listening

Below are three situations. With a partner, take turns as listener and speaker for each situation. This is an opportunity for the speaker to practise acting skills, while the listener practises active listening. Try to incorporate at least two active listening responses to each situation.

1. A friend in his last semester of police education is failing an essential course in the program: "I can't fail this course. If I fail, I can't do my placement. My parents will be absolutely furious with me!"

2. Your best friend has just broken up with a long-time lover (Sam can be male or female): "Out of the blue! No warning, no discussion, just a phone call. I had no idea that Sam was so unhappy."

3. You receive a call to attend a residence that has been broken into, and several items are reported missing. When you arrive, the occupant is in tears. You need to take down what is missing and file your report so that the missing items can be put on the list of stolen items at headquarters: *"Just look at this mess! My stereo, VCR, and I don't know what all. Everything trashed!"*

When you are finished, discuss with each other what was easy and what was difficult when using active listening. In what situations is it appropriate to use active listening? In what situations would active listening be inappropriate?

SUMMARY

In this chapter, we presented strategies of conflict management that rely on the ability to discuss the issues within the conflict. Building on material from chapter 2, we reviewed each of the five conflict styles to find when each style would be most appropriate to use. We then examined three styles of responding: passive or non-assertive, aggressive, and assertive. While at times aggressive responses may be necessary, assertive responses allow you to state your needs and rights without imposing upon the needs and rights of others. By behaving assertively, you may be able to end many conflicts.

Using a problem-solving approach was explored as a method of conflict resolution. By using this method, the parties define the problem, analyze the problem, generate possible solutions, evaluate the solutions, implement the solution, and set a time to re-evaluate their success. Viewing the conflict as a problem to be solved de-personalizes the conflict and leads to a step-by-step method of resolution.

Learning how to deal with criticism is an important tool for conflict management. However, if you must criticize another person's behaviour or performance, using constructive feedback is recommended. Cognitive restructuring, image-exchanging and empathy, being open and honest, and maintaining your focus on the present were also recommended strategies. Active listening, a major tool for effective interpersonal communication, is also suitable for many types of conflict.

CASE STUDY

Committee Woes

Miguel, a police officer of 13 years, is the service's committee representative for a new school-community initiative to reduce bullying in the schools. He firmly believes that intervening in this type of behaviour when children are young will go a long way in reducing later aggression and possible run-ins with the law when the children are older. The program is based on a curriculum that has been developed by a committee of teachers around the notion of problem solving and expressing anger in more appropriate ways, such as walking away or talking to somebody. The committee has recommended a policy of "zero tolerance" for bullying or other aggression at school. The penalty for any aggression against other students or staff is an immediate three-day suspension, including an interview with parents and an additional meeting with the student and parents with the principal upon return to school.

At the final meeting to tie up loose ends, a committee member states, "I think that this system is a little too harsh. After all, kids are going to fight. Suspension is just too much. I think there should be a warning system so that kids get put on notice first, and then if they fight or bully again, they're suspended."

Miguel was exasperated. "Look, we have done everything. We went through this. Look at the violence that we are dealing with regularly, including school shootings! You're in the wrong era—get with the present!"

There was a retort from the committee member. "Just because you're a cop doesn't mean that you're the authority on aggression around here. I have been a teacher for almost 30 years, and I have never had to suspend a student. And I don't want to start now. You just look for reasons to get kids into trouble. Kids are kids."

"They are not just kids anymore. They come to school with guns and knives. They pick on others, steal money, and think it's okay to beat up the weaker kids. This program is about teaching what is acceptable and unacceptable. You just don't get it. You have your head in the sand."

Finally, the chairperson intervened. "Hey, we're all adults here. Now you two calm down."

Questions

1. What is the cause of the conflict between Miguel and the committee member?
2. Do they have any goals in common?
3. Suggest two different methods that Miguel could use to resolve this conflict. Support your strategies.
4. If the chairperson must continue to intervene, what strategy would be most appropriate to use? Why?

KEY TERMS

Aggressive: A characteristic of a person that includes being overbearing, pushy, and hostile towards others.

Assertive: A characteristic of a person that includes making needs and feelings known in an open and honest manner that does not infringe upon the rights of others.

Brainstorming: A process for encouraging creative thinking by generating "free-wheeling" ideas and alternatives, usually done in a group.

Brainwriting: An exercise similar to brainstorming, except that participants write ideas down.

Cognitive restructuring: A method of mentally converting the negative aspects of a conflict into positive ones by identifying positive elements of the conflict.

Creative thinking: An ability to process information that results in a product (or idea or solution) that is new, meaningful, and original.

Criticism: Picking out the flaws and faults in another person.

Empathy: An ability to put yourself in another's "shoes," to feel how the other person feels.

Gunnysacking: Bringing up past hurts, issues, or transgressions into a current conflict.

Image exchanging: Exchanging roles in a conflict in order to more fully understand the other side.

Mediation: A formal process of third-party intervention.

Negotiation: Conferring with others to come up with a mutually agreeable solution or decision.

Non-assertive: A characteristic of not defending one's rights or letting one's feelings be known.

Paraphrasing: Expressing what a speaker has just said in your own words. Used for clarification of feelings and/or content.

Passive-aggressive: A tendency to give the impression of agreeing or supporting a decision, then sabotaging the decision.

Problem: A gap between what currently exists and a desired state; a deviation from where you are and where you would like to be.

Third-party intervention: Use of a person not involved in a conflict, to help the two parties negotiate a mutually acceptable resolution.

Win–win: A strategy for resolving conflict that meets the needs of both parties.

Win–lose: A strategy for resolving conflict in which one party has needs satisfied while the other party does not.

WEB LINKS

www.qvctc.commnet.edu/classes/ssci121/weeks.html
A summary of Dudley Week's book *The Eight Essential Steps to Conflict Resolution: Preserving Relationships at Work, Home, and in the Community.*

www.rbenjamin.com/manual.htm
This link is a complete manual, "The Effective Negotiation and Mediation of Conflict: Applied Theory and Practice Handbook." It is very thorough, with many ideas and strategies for conflict resolution.

http://hr2.hr.arizona.edu/tools.htm
This site has a table of contents that lists "tools" for managing and resolving conflicts.

REFERENCES

J. L. Adams (1979). *Conceptual blockbusting: A guide to better ideas* (2nd ed.). New York: Norton.

Link Byfield (1999). I don't know about you, but I'm starting to dislike the policing in this country. *Alberta Report/Newsmagazine*, 26(41), 4.

Joseph A. Devito, Rena Shimoni, and Dawne Clark (2001). *Messages: Building interpersonal communication skills*. Toronto, ON: Addison Wesley Longman.

Andrew J. Dubrin (2001). *Human relations: Interpersonal, job-oriented skills*. Upper Saddle River, NJ: Prentice Hall.

Andrew J. Dubrin and Terri Geerinck (2001). *Human relations for personal and career success*. Toronto, ON: Pearson Education Canada.

Isa N. Engleberg and Dianna R. Wynn (1997) *Working in groups: Communication principles and strategies*. New York: Houghton Mifflin.

Terri M. Geerinck (2000). *Interpersonal and group skills for law enforcement*. Scarborough, ON: Prentice-Hall Canada.

Kenneth Kaye (1994). *Workplace wars and how to end them: Turning personal conflicts into productive teamwork*. New York: Amacom.

Gay Lumsden & Donald Lumsden (1997). *Communicating in groups and teams: Sharing leadership*. Belmont, CA: Wadsworth Publishing.

Jack Marchen (2001). Trent defends actions, responds to protesters' parents. *Peterborough Examiner*, March 20, pp. B1, B2.

The OPP (Ontario Provincial Police) Community Policing Development Centre (1997). How do we do it. www.gov.ca/opp/english/howto/index.htm

Charles R. Swanson, Leonard Territo, and Robert W. Taylor (2001). *Police administration: Structures, processes, and behavior*. Upper Saddle River, NJ: Prentice Hall.

Roger J. Volkema & Thomas J. Bergmann (1995). Conflict styles as indicators of behavioural patterns in interpersonal conflicts. *Journal of Social Psychology*, 135(1), 5–15.

Dudley Weeks (1994). *The eight essential steps to conflict resolution: Preserving relationships at work, home, and in the community*. New York: Putnam.

chapter five

Managing Aggressive Behaviour and Crises

LEARNING OUTCOMES

After studying this chapter, you should be able to

- Explain the causes of aggression.

- Recognize the various types of aggressive behaviour.

- Prevent escalation to further aggression.

- Choose and use a variety of strategies to assist in managing aggressive behaviour.

- Identify when a person is in crisis.

- Identify the stages in a crisis.

- Explain the role of the Use of Force Continuum in policing.

- Identify when the use of force may be legally used.

Courtesy Peterborough Lakefield Community Police Service

On-the-Job Scenario

"Look at the place! It's completely torn apart! We had better be careful with this one, Jenna. It doesn't feel right."

"Well, whatever the fight was about, the caller was right. They must have produced a lot of noise tearing this apart. Even the TV is smashed."

"I don't think anybody is here."

"Shhh! I just heard something."

"Look out. She has a knife!"

As one author (a police officer) of this text states, "Policing is 99 per cent routine and 1 per cent fear." Situations like the one above are not routine, but police officers must be ready to react in such situations and must react appropriately, using only what force is required to subdue the person. Dealing with members of the public who are angry, frustrated, drunk, and mentally ill is not an easy task. After all, police officers are human, too!

Aggression is part of everyday life, displayed by bullies in schoolyards and the person who "gives you the finger" from his car. Every year in Canada, between 500 and 700 people are murdered, including 50 to 60 children (Alcock et al., 1998). Aggression ranges from acts of murder to screaming at another person. At times, aggression is well planned, but often it is elicited suddenly during a heated exchange between people who never initially intended to hurt each other. In this chapter, we will focus on knowledge and strategies to help you deal with these situations on the furthest right of the Continuum of Conflict. First, we will explore the causes of aggression from a more theoretical (although not impractical!) viewpoint. Next, we will focus on the types of aggression and the general effects that aggression has on people.

CAUSES OF AGGRESSION

Why are some people aggressive? This question has been asked for centuries and the debates are still ongoing. Why are some people aggressive and competitive all the time, where everything they say or do leads to some sort of altercation? Why do some people suddenly explode and commit unbelievable acts of violence against the ones they are supposed to love? And why do others direct their aggression inward, hurting or killing themselves? How is it that some people are always calm, no matter what the circumstances? You have probably asked yourself some (if not all) of these questions at one time or another. The profession of policing would be very different if people were rarely aggressive. In fact, some police officers might suddenly find the profession unexciting or even boring!

Here we will examine some of the recent theories and ideas about the causes of aggression. If you understand some of the underlying causes, your responses can also be more understanding. For example, if a police officer erroneously thinks that aggressive young offenders are violent because they were raised that way, he or she may discriminate against their parents. Such thinking can lead to poor investigation and can miss the real causes: they may have witnessed spousal abuse in the home, have low intelligence, or be the victim of repeated and long-term bullying. And there is a host of other causes and mitigating circumstances.

THEORIES OF AGGRESSION

There are many theories of aggression. Whole books have been written about violence and aggression, so be warned: this is a very brief sketch and does not include all of the variables. For more information on aggression, the Web sites at the back of this chapter are more detailed. First, let's define aggression to ensure that the meaning is clear. **Aggression** can be simply defined as behaviour that is intended to harm or destroy another person (Alcock et al., 1998). For the purposes of this text, contemporary theories will be stressed, and each theory will be presented in its simplest terms. After several theories have been discussed, a multi-dimensional theory will be presented to unify these theories into a clear picture of the complexity of the causation of aggression.

Instinct Theory

Although it is not a new theory, many believers hold that aggression is instinctual and an integral part of being a human "animal." From this theory, the frustration-aggression theory was developed, which was discussed in chapter 2. The basic notion is that when people are blocked from doing what they want, they experience frustration. And when people become frustrated, they become angry, and aggression of some sort is likely to follow. However, this theory does not always account for aggressive behaviour. When frustrated, there are many people who do not lash out. So while this theory may explain some components of aggression, it does not provide a comprehensive explanation.

Aggression as a Learned Response (Social Developmental Theories)

One cluster of hypotheses centre on the theory that aggression is developed during childhood when aggressive responses get reinforced (rewarded). For example, two young boys start fighting on a playground. A group of children gather round, cheering the fight on. The victor (the one without the bloody nose) gets pats on the back and praise for "winning." This behaviourist approach is very simple. If a child (or adult) gets reinforced for aggressive behaviour, the probability increases that the person will behave this way again. If individuals get their desired reinforcers from aggression, likely they will continue to do so in the future.

Aggression can also be learned by modelling after or imitating others. This **social learning theory** is based on behaviourist theory and on our capability of imitating others. We are more likely to imitate others if we see that the behaviour was successful: the person achieved a desired goal or end using the aggression. Children learn much of their behaviour by modelling after others, even when we do not think they are watching or paying attention. Most research has shown that the early years are the critical time for learning aggression (Olweus, 1972). Children, therefore, learn how to be aggressive during their early years and are more likely to use aggression if it is rewarded and used by others around them.

Let's briefly look at two sources of modelling that children have available from which they can learn aggression. These controversial areas in social developmental influences on aggression are child-rearing styles and family violence, including child abuse. If we examine child-rearing from a social development perspective, parents play a critical role in determining whether a child will grow up to be aggressive (Alcock et al., 1998). According to several research studies, parents or caregivers who use a punitive style of child-rearing tend to have highly aggressive children. Punitive parents rely on physical punishment and are often emotionally cold and rejecting. These parents often condone the use of aggression during conflict and directly and indirectly reinforce their children when they use aggression to manage conflicts. However, it is not only the punitive style of parenting, but lack of involvement with children in this type of home that may produce the aggressive tendencies in the children. The parents spend little time with the children, so they also fail to teach appropriate ways to resolve interpersonal difficulties. Some research has illustrated that neglected children may actually show higher rates of violence and aggression as adults (Widom, 1989).

In recent years, much attention has been focused on family violence. Since family violence is the focus of chapter 9, here we will examine it very briefly as a cause of aggression.

Several studies (Jaffe et al., 1986; Moore et al., 1989) show that experiencing or observing violence regularly tends to put children at risk of continuing the cycle of violence and aggression in adulthood. Each new generation of parents tend to repeat the same child-rearing techniques they experienced as children. However, the link between child abuse and violence is not as straightforward as it seems. For example, child abuse often produces depression, withdrawal, and self-destructive tendencies rather than violence. Some children also appear to be able to distance themselves from the violence and remain relatively unaffected by it. In other words, while some abused children or children who witness violence become aggressive, some do not. Therefore, we cannot say with certainty that children who come from violent homes will use aggression to manage conflicts or violence to solve problems.

Aggression as a Personality Trait

You may have heard people blame aggressive tendencies on personality: "Well, he can't help it. It's just part of his personality." Our personalities are affected by genetic factors and learning. Each theory of personality has its own ideas about how personality and associated traits are developed. Rather than reviewing each theory and its contribution to aggression, we will focus on the areas that relate directly to aggression as part of personality.

Regardless of the theory or approach to personality development, the desired outcome is that individuals have a relatively integrated sense of self, are able to cope with the demands and stresses of life, and can maintain balance after coping with difficult situations (Roy, 2000). It is clear that not all people develop proper skills for coping, and genetic and biological influences (such as attention deficit disorders, depression) may also predispose people to lack these skills. The parts of personality and personality traits that we are concerned with are clustered around the ability to handle frustration and anger. If people cannot cope with anger, anger can get out of hand; it can build up to dangerous levels or be expressed in violent and aggressive ways. Here we will examine several personal characteristics that contribute to aggression.

Intelligence

Interestingly, lower intelligence has been correlated with aggression. (Remember that correlation is not causation. We cannot say that low intelligence causes aggression.) As children grow older, aggression tends to decrease as they learn other methods of coping. However, the lower the child's IQ, the harder it may be to learn these other methods (Alcock et al., 1998). In other words, lower intelligence results in fewer options or responses for coping with life's frustrations. With less complex skills, these individuals may rely on simpler and earlier methods of coping, including aggression.

Self-esteem

Recent evidence suggests that aggressive individuals often possess inflated self-esteem. These individuals believe they are "better" than they really are and may view feedback from others as inadequate in light of their self-importance. They react to this apparent injustice with aggression and anger (Baumeister et al., 1996).

Masculinity

In many parts of the world, most males are concerned with being "masculine," that is acting "like a man." In North America, this concept of masculinity is associated with many personality traits including courage, loyalty, dominance, assertiveness, competitiveness, and of course, aggression. Teaching boys that being masculine is important means teaching and reinforcing all of these traits. Several Canadian studies have noted the teaching of aggression in hockey (Weinstein et al., 1995).

Authoritarianism

Authoritarianism is a personality syndrome characterized by rigid thinking, prejudice, and excessive concern about power. People high in authoritarianism give poor treatment to those they perceive as less powerful, which can include open hostility. They tend to better treat those they perceive as more powerful, and they defer to superiors. Authoritarianism can be accompanied by authoritarian aggression, which is aggression directed at individuals that they feel is sanctioned by authority (Altmeyer, 1988).

Self-Control

The ability to control aggression or other impulses varies from person to person. Self-control is part of **emotional intelligence** (Goleman, 1995), which is made up of qualities or abilities to control and regulate emotional expression such as understanding your own feelings, having empathy for others, and regulating emotions to enhance well-being. An important component of emotional intelligence is *self-regulation* or self-control, the ability to control impulsiveness, calm down when anxious, and react to situations with appropriate anger. People who lack self-control do not manage frustration well and anger easily. They may respond to frustration or provocation with aggression.

Cultural Influences and Aggression

Societies and cultures view and value aggression differently. Some societies may value aggression, while others discourage any acts of violence. While conflicts are inevitable, culture plays a large role in how these conflicts will manifest themselves. For example, Canadian children are often taught the importance of winning and that aggression is thus a means to an end, whereas children in Japan are discouraged from quarrelling. Japanese children learn that yielding is part of being honourable, as is giving in rather than fighting (Azuma, 1984).

While Canada may report lower numbers of murders and assaults than the United States, violence is a growing problem. For example, according to a recent report by the International Labour Organization, Canada ranked fourth in the rate of assaults and sexual harassment in the workplace (ILO, 1998). The dominant cultures in Canada and the United States are seen as more aggressive when comparing these cultures to others such as the Inuit, Amish, and several First Nations in Canada (Alcock et al., 1998).

The Media and Aggression

You do not have to spend much time flipping television channels on any night of the week to find a program with violence. Although many studies have indicated that watching violence on television is associated with increased aggression, caution must be used when interpreting these studies (Alcock et al., 1998). For example, many studies done on children demonstrate that aggression may be caused by other factors such as excitement after seeing a violent film. Also, many studies have been conducted in laboratory settings, and the relationship is unclear when we try to generalize these findings outside of the artificial lab settings. It is interesting that longitudinal studies (research that spans several years) with children generally find a positive relationship between viewing television violence and increased levels of aggression, including convictions as adults for serious criminal acts (Huesman, 1986).

Despite this evidence, not all children are affected the same way. Children have many models for their behaviour, and the media serve as only one source for learning. Peace-loving home environments, church membership, and membership in other non-violent groups may offset the impact of television. Also, many children watch very little television, and many parents carefully police their children's shows for violent and other unsuitable content. Therefore, we can say that watching television violence may be related to later aggression, but other factors may inhibit such effects.

Firearms and Weapons Presence

While this is not the forum to discuss gun control and gun registration, there is little doubt that the presence of weaponry, especially guns, increases the chances of violence if confrontation occurs.

POINTS FOR PONDERING   *Firearms in Canada*

While the expression "Guns don't kill people, people kill people" may be true, there is little doubt that the presence of firearms increases the chances of a violent ending to many conflicts. According to Statistics Canada (1999), in 1998 firearms were involved in 27 percent of all homicides. Guns are still the most popular method of killing someone. One woman is shot dead in Canada every six days, and most are killed by a current or former partner. Gunshot wounds are two to fifteen times more lethal than knife wounds. While the presence of firearms may not increase aggression (although research has been done on the possibility—called the *weapons effect* —that the presence of weapons can escalate a confrontation), having firearms present does increase the level of violence.

Aggression and Gender

Statistics reveal that men are more likely to commit homicide than women. Two-thirds of homicide victims are male, and one-third are female. This might lead you to ask, Why are men so much more violent than women? Are males naturally more aggressive? Watch any school playground at recess to see who the aggressors are, and you will probably discover what research has demonstrated over and over again (Hutt, 1974; Reinsch and Sanders, 1986; Roy, 2000).

One reason that males are more aggressive than females centres on the adoption of behaviours and characteristics of the appropriate **gender**. Gender refers to the roles, characteristics, and expectancies associated with being male or female. **Gender identity** is the sex (male or female) that a person identifies as his or her own. Our gender identity is acquired through learning. Displaying the appropriate sexual stereotypical behaviours is encouraged and rewarded, while inappropriate gender behaviours are discouraged (Baron et al., 2001). We learn the behaviours of our gender in much the same ways as we learn the correct behaviours of our cultures. According to Sandra Bem (1974), a researcher in the area of gender identity, there are male and female stereotypes that have associated characteristics. Several of the characteristics of the male stereotype include more aggressive traits than the female stereotype. Male characteristics include leadership, ambition, assertiveness, dominance, forcefulness, and defence of personal beliefs. Thus males are encouraged to be more aggressive, while females are discouraged from such behaviour.

Heightened Arousal

When we are angry, frustrated, or upset, we experience physiological arousal. If you recall from chapter 2, emotional experiences are accompanied by physiological changes in the body such as increased heart rate, respiration, and blood pressure. This arousal prepares the body for "fight or flight," even though neither behaviour may be required. For example, you are rushing in your car to meet a friend at a bar. On the way, you are narrowly missed by a driver who swerves into your lane and barely misses you. Your heart pounds, your mouth goes dry, and your hands clench the steering wheel. If you are like many of us, you may also utter a few choice words! As you continue to drive, you feel less stressed. When you get to the bar ten minutes late, your friend is not there. You wait another ten minutes. You finally order a coffee and are still waiting. As your friend approaches, you say angrily, "It's about time that you got here! What took you so long?"

A growing body of research indicates that emotional arousal lasts long after an incident and is very slow to dissipate (Zillman, 1988, 1994). It also appears that under some conditions, heightened arousal can enhance aggressive responses, regardless of the source of the arousal. According to **excitation transfer theory**, because physiological arousal takes time to dissipate, this arousal can be transferred to other situations. Instead of becoming merely annoyed (a small increase in arousal) at a further small incident (your friend's being late), you become enraged (Zillman, 1988). You are unaware of the *residual arousal* from the car experience and therefore attribute the arousal to your friend's being late: even when you are aware of this arousal, you attribute it to the current situation.

If we apply this theory to a different example, we can see that an officer's presence can increase arousal and intensify the possibility of aggression. Officers receive a call about suspected spousal abuse. Although the man is quiet when he first answers the door, the very presence of uniformed officers enrages him to the point where he must be physically subdued. The man may be unaware of the residual arousal from the earlier altercation and attributes his rage to the officers' being there.

Which Theory Is Best?

When examining all of the previous possible causes of aggression, it is safe to say that not one theory or idea accounts for the cause of aggressive behaviour. All of us have the capacity to be violent, and we all get angry. The major differences lie in how that anger is expressed. In October 1999, a conference about violent behaviour among youth, sponsored by the National Institute of Mental Health, concluded that no single variable or situation caused someone to be violent (Roy, 2000). It appears, then, that the complexity of violence is caused by a host of variables that come into play in various situations and then are precipitated by the actual situation.

One way to use these theories is to recognize the complexity of aggression and violence rather than to see it in simple black and white. Often, when we are too close to something or see it too often, we make generalizations that are oversimplified and often erroneous. For example, we cannot solely blame the parents of a young offender or the presence of poverty or a quirk in personality or the media.

A second way to use aggression theories is to put the theories together to get the whole picture and to develop a more in-depth understanding of causation. Figure 5.1 puts the theory together. Although not a complete picture, it clearly illustrates the complexity of aggression. The chances that someone will be aggressive with someone else increase if the aggressor has one or more of the personal characteristics related to aggression, has a high male gender identity (whether the aggressor is male or female), does not handle frustration well, learned to cope with problems by using aggression, and watched a great deal of violence on television as a child. However, even when all these factors are considered, a person may not behave as aggressively (if at all) if that person belongs to a culture in which violence and aggressive displays are discouraged and punished. But include a culture that values aggression and competition, and fuel may be added to the fire.

A precipitating event is required for the person to behave aggressively, such as being cut off in traffic or denied enrolment in a school (such as Marc Lepine, who was denied admission to engineering at École Polytechnique). The precipitating event heightens arousal and is often perceived as its cause (anger, frustration). The precipitating event may not begin as an aggressive situation, but escalates into aggression if people are already aroused or predisposed to using aggression. The presence of weapons may escalate the violence. When these factors are combined at various levels, then aggression is directed at a target. Note that the target may not be the source of the frustration. For example, a man who has had a bad day at work may come home and displace this anger onto his wife. A person who has just been assaulted may direct his or her arousal onto the attending officers. The use of mind-altering substances such as alcohol may also increase aggression. However, the use of alcohol will be discussed in more detail in chapter 7, so it is deliberately left out of discussion here.

Now that you have some understanding about the causes of aggression, let's move on to examining the types of aggression. As police officers, you will deal with all types of aggression ranging from someone calling you names to someone attempting to hurt or even kill you.

TYPES OF AGGRESSION

In chapter 2, we discussed three emotions: frustration, anger, and sadness. When we discussed frustration and anger, you may recall that both of these emotions can lead to aggression. Sadness can also lead to aggression, especially if the person is depressed, as in cases of murder followed by the suicide of the murderer.

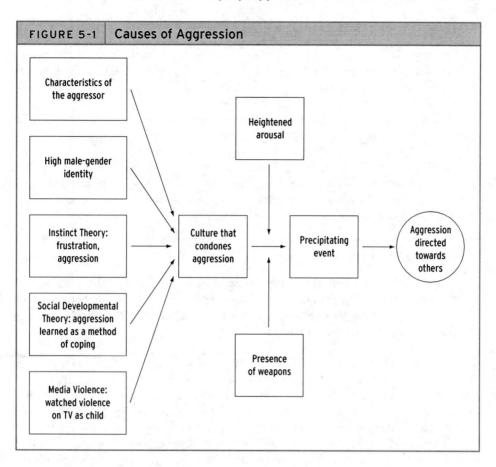

FIGURE 5-1 | Causes of Aggression

Instrumental versus Hostile Aggression

One useful way to look at aggression is to look at the purpose of the aggression. **Instrumental aggression** is aggression used to achieve a desired goal. For example, a bully may use aggression to get another child's lunch. Wartime aggression is viewed as instrumental aggression: killing the enemy to reclaim lost territory or defending territory from hostile forces. **Hostile aggression** is motivated by anger, and its goal is to hurt the other person. Hostile aggression may not be thought out or planned and may simply involve lashing out at the other person. For example, a hockey player elbows another player in the heat of the moment during a game. Verbal and physical aggression may be instrumental or hostile, depending upon the context. For example, during a heated argument, you call someone "stupid." This may be hostile aggression. However, if you taunt someone and call the person "stupid," knowing the person will blow up and then get into trouble, this may be instrumental aggression, because your goal was to get the person into trouble.

Verbal Aggression

While physical aggression may leave obvious damage, the "wounds" from verbal aggression are not as readily observed, with the result that many people feel that verbal aggression or aggressive communication is not as harmful as physical aggression. **Aggressive communication** is any behaviour that conveys dislike for another in an attempt to cause harm (Infante and Wigley, 1986, p. 61). Verbal aggression informs others that they are bad, worthless, have negative qualities, or do not live up to some sort of standard (Kinney, 1994). In other words, verbal aggression attacks the self-concept of someone else. It is noteworthy that several research studies point out that verbal aggression causes as much psychological damage as physical abuse, or even more (Ney, 1987; Hoffman, 1984). For example, verbal sexual harassment in the workplace has produced such effects as high blood pressure and headaches (Hadjifotiou, 1983).

Consider This...

"I really hate calls where you see adults screaming at children. You can just tell that the kids get yelled at all the time. Some are cowering while others dish it right back. Those are the ones I hate to see, because you just know that they're learning that this is how you deal with people."

The effects of verbal aggression include physical reactions (stress symptoms such as headaches, ulcers, sleep problems, and high blood pressure), emotional reactions (anger, sadness), psychological states (depression, low self-esteem), and relational and behavioural consequences (divorce, murder) (Kinney, 1994). If we examine the recent murders committed by adolescents, we find that they were often the victims of bullying, much of which was verbal taunting. The common link with all of the effects of verbal aggression is that the result of verbal aggression is some sort of distress, which ranges from mild distress such as annoyance or upset, to major distress such as the development of physical illness or of mental illness such as depression. Major distress is more likely to occur when the verbal aggression has been long-term.

A recent study developed a typology (list of types) of aggressive communication that outlined three main categories of aggressive messages and differentiated some of the emotional responses to each type (Kinney, 1994). Attacks on group membership (voluntary membership such as police officer and involuntary membership such as being male) did not evoke as much negative affect as did attacks on personal failings (lack of skill, appearance, and other personal characteristics) or on relational failings (inability to maintain a relationship or meet expectations in a relationship). Attacks on personal failings elicited more sadness and more fear than on group membership or relational failings. What this study discovered is that the type of aggressive communication can change the emotions that the receiver experienced. Verbally attacking who you are or your personal problems within a relationship leads to feelings of anger, sadness, depression, and fear. Attacking group membership leads to feelings of anger and annoyance but not to feelings of sadness or depression.

But what happens when the verbal aggression is continuous, unlike the many daily encounters that we have? When the verbal aggression is frequent and consistent, the behaviour is termed **verbal abuse**. Long-term verbal abuse not only has its physiological effects, but it also leads the receiver to change his or her view of self and the world (Kinney, 1994). As a result, verbally abused people tend to develop low self-regard, and they are often cynical, unhappy, and troubled (Hoffman, 1984).

Since verbal aggression and verbal abuse leave no outward marks, it can be easy to dismiss as unimportant or irrelevant. When a couple are screaming at each other, we might think that this is not severe and requires no intervention (unless the screaming is disturbing the peace). The research also points out that verbal aggression can be categorized as threats, and when threatened, people react. According to Lazarus (well known for his research on aggression), threats often exceed one's ability to meet the demand imposed by the event. This elicits distress. And when distressed by threats, one reacts. This reaction manifests in one of—or a combination of—three ways. The person can react cognitively, for example, thinking about what can be done about the threat. A second way to react is physiologically, such as becoming physiologically aroused with an increase in blood pressure. The third way is to react affectively and to feel aroused by emotions such as anger or sadness (Lazarus, 1993).

However, if the results of many research studies are as reliable as they appear to be, then verbal aggression and verbal abuse cannot be taken lightly or be easily dismissed. Police officers and other professionals should pay close attention when verbal aggression has occurred or continues to occur. Long-term threats to physical and emotional well-being may result in sudden acts of violence that police officers must be prepared to handle. A history of violence, however, is not always a good indicator of how someone may react. We have all read stories of people who have never been violent, and suddenly they erupt, killing or harming the people around them.

Physical Aggression

While aggression may be verbal, it can also be physical. Two topics—child abuse and spousal abuse—will be discussed in later chapters. Here we will examine physical aggression in a more generic way. While physical aggression may be well planned, usually physical aggression is an impulsive action or reaction to perceived or real threats to an individual's well-being. This well-being also includes self-esteem, and someone may be aggressive in order to save face or to display expected or required behaviours, as a gang might. Most physical aggression (as well as other types of aggression) is often the result of **provocation**—actions that are perceived as acts of aggression that arise from hostile intentions. It is important to include the word *perceived,* because it the perception of the other's intentions that is important. Often, people will say that they did nothing to provoke an attack, yet the other party does feel that a comment, a glare or stare, or even body posturing, *was* provocative.

On the continuum of conflict, physical aggression can range from jabbing fingers into the shoulder of another person, to action intended to maim or kill. If possible, intervening at the outset of a conflict is preferred. However, the reality is that officers are seldom called to a scene until the confrontation is well underway. Officers are then faced with having to use enough force to subdue the opponents or the person, without using excessive force. According to one author and trainer in law enforcement, a conflict can consist of three stages (Ouellette, 1993). The first stage is anxiety, and could also include frustration and anger. If anxiety and other emotions are not dealt with, they can result in loss of verbal control. This is the second stage, where people become defensive, belligerent, challenging, screaming and shouting. If the conflict is unresolved at this stage, a person may lose control physically. Thus physical aggression may be seen as the last stage on the continuum. Before examining crises and the use of force, let's turn attention to managing aggressive behaviours.

MANAGING AGGRESSIVE BEHAVIOUR

Many of the techniques we are about to discuss will be familiar from earlier chapters. The strategies you use to manage aggressive behaviour overlap and rely upon the techniques used for other types of conflicts. These strategies are also used to manage crises that are discussed after this section. The techniques here rely on three areas or sets of appraisal: analyzing and responding to the client, analyzing and managing the situation, and analyzing and managing yourself. At all times, you need to be aware of these three areas. Your edge will often be that the clients will be unaware of all of three because they are focused on only one area: themselves. Each of these areas overlap, but for ease of discussion, they have been divided up.

Managing Verbal Aggression by Analyzing and Responding to the Client

Many injuries occur on the job because officers were not fully aware of the state of the client during the event. For example, in the opening scenario, one officer knows that "something does not feel right." This gut-level appraisal of the situation and knowing that someone is present and hiding, may save the officer. In other words, be prepared for the unexpected. Even during routine traffic stops, it is essential to appraise the state of the client and respond appropriately.

Focus on Goals

When dealing with someone who is being verbally abusive and using verbal aggression, it can be difficult to "keep your cool." However, by focusing on your goals in the interaction, you can reduce the level of aggression and complete the required transaction. Let's illustrate with an example. As an officer you stop a Cadillac STS for doing 140 kilometres per hour in a 100 kilometre per hour speed zone. The driver is an expensively dressed 50-year-old woman. You are trying to tell her why you have stopped her, while she loudly denies that she has done anything wrong. As you attempt to continue your side of the conversation, she interjects, "Look, why don't you go and get the real bad guys and stop harassing important citizens. I know some very important people in this town, and you are going to regret this. You're going to know just who I am, and you won't ever forget my name, because I could be the one who ends your career."

So what are you going to do here? According to one source (adapted from Anderson et al., 1995), there are five steps to follow and think about that will assist you in reacting appropriately.

1. **What is the surface problem?** In other words, what is going on here on the surface? On the surface, for this example, this woman is threatening your job.

2. **What is the real problem?** In reality, what is the real issue or the real problem? The real problem is that this woman does not want a speeding ticket, and she is attempting to avoid receiving one.

3. **What is your goal?** What do you want to do with this transaction? Here, the obvious goal is to follow through and give her the ticket, politely and assertively.

4. **Respond in order to achieve your goal.** Give her the ticket. For example, you might want to say, "I am afraid I will have to issue you this ticket, no matter who you are. It's my job."

5. **Keep in mind consequences or how you would have reacted to a different person or situation.** What if the woman were wearing blue jeans? What if the car were old and rusty? Would you have acted differently? Will she follow through with her threats? And if she does, are you going to lose your job? Chances are that if she launches a complaint, you have done what you were supposed to do. Public complaints can be a hassle and even stressful, but the implications for treating people differently as a result of perceived class differences also has consequences.

This technique is very useful for managing verbal aggression directed at an officer who is attempting to complete a transaction, such as issuing tickets or dealing with other minor infractions. By being assertive and focusing on the goal, you will not be sidetracked by anyone trying to make an issue of who you are or anything about your job. When people see that they cannot get you upset, they will often let you do your job and stop complaining or being verbally abusive. However, some people will continue to behave aggressively and escalate in their demands and communication. The next strategy will assist you with continued verbal aggression.

Use Assertive Language

Although using assertive language to communicate tactically is not at the same level as the use of force, you will use officer presence and pair it with assertive communication. If you recall from chapter 2, assertive communication is based on meeting your needs while also respecting the rights and needs of the other person. Police officers, therefore, must maintain their professional image while others around them do not and act in hostile ways. For example, using the above case, what do you do if she continues her tirade, calls you "pig" and throws the ticket back at you? If you speak quietly, you may just become background noise as the shouting escalates. Or in another situation, how do you get the attention of two males brawling outside a bar? Your recourse in both instances is to talk loudly to get attention.

Two researchers and facilitators label these kinds of people as "tanks." Tanks are so involved with their argument or tirade that they will run you over if given the chance. Their goal is to get attention and to get their way, to avoid getting ticketed or to beat the other person senseless (Kirschner and Brinkman, 1994).

Consider This...

"I learned over 20 years ago that if two people are screaming at each other, the only way to get them to stop is to be louder than they are. I whistle, and then I shout for everyone to be quiet. Sometime, everyone stops and just looks like I'm the one that's losing it, but they stop shouting!"

You can be quite creative in how you get the attention of tanks. Loudly clapping or whistling is sometimes effective with the "brawlers." When both parties look at you, this is your chance to try to break up the fight verbally with an order: "You over there and you over there, now." If this does not work, then you will need to move on to the use of force, which will soon be discussed.

In the situation where you are dealing with one person who is getting louder and more abusive, you also need to raise your level of assertiveness while maintaining your goals of the interaction. For example, "Ma'am, you can throw the ticket away, but it is still recorded as issued. Please refrain from further language and drive safely." At this point and with no further problems (such as her getting out of the car), you may return to your car and continue with your shift. Again, if this situation escalates, you would now move along the continuum to the use of force.

Let the Person "Run Down"

When you let a toy run for long enough, the battery drains. Sometimes, given enough space and time, the person will shout, scream, rant, and rave into exhaustion. In one instance, officers responded to a call of a drunken male standing in front of a house of an ex-girlfriend. The male was dressed in a T-shirt and shorts and did not have a visible weapon. He was not harming himself or making moves to enter the residence or come after the officers, so the officers let him scream and shout at the house and them until he was done. He sank down on the grass and passed out. This was a wiser strategy than trying to subdue the male by using other methods while he was angry, which may have ended in physical confrontation. It should be noted that both officers maintained extreme vigilance in case there was a weapon. Although this method can be time-consuming and perhaps irritating to onlookers and neighbours (not to mention the attending police officers), it can be effective.

Try the Buddy Approach (Empathy)

An unexpected way to gain co-operation is to actually agree or empathize with the person about his or her feelings. For example, "I'm sure you are an upstanding citizen, Ma'am, and I can relate to how mad you are, but I have to ticket all speeders that I come across on patrol." Some may criticize this approach as being "soft" or self-deprecating, but if it prevents further conflict escalation, it is worth a try.

Use Deflection (It's Not My Fault)

Using deflection puts the blame on a third party for the intervention. In this way, both you and the other person can agree that it is too bad that the officer has to do his or her job and follow through with the necessary actions. For example, if you are called to a loud party, you can blame the call on city bylaws on noise after 11 p.m. Many platoon commanders or police chiefs do not mind being blamed as well! "I'm sorry I have to give you this ticket, but the captain is very clear about all speeders, and that includes you." Again, you are engaging in these behaviours to achieve a goal, whether it is issuing a ticket, quieting a noisy party, or getting an unwelcome guest out of a residence. The same strategy may not work with everyone, and your assessment of the situation is critical. An unwelcome and drunk guest may respond to a statement about "all women being alike," while another one may not. An offer of a ride home might work or it might not. The key is to select and use the appropriate strategy with the least amount of force. The final section deals with the use of force, which may be required for situations where people do not respond to regular conflict management strategies or are so out of control that use of force must be the first response to ensure public and officer safety. Use of force is to be used when people have gone beyond verbal aggression and are about to be or are being physically aggressive.

Be Aware of All Nonverbal Behaviours of the Individual

How does the person look to you? How does the person sound to you? Is she or he glaring at you, staring at you, or using appropriate eye contact? As the Points for Pondering below indicate, eye contact as well as use of space and gestures are powerful tools to use for assessing potential aggression. Before physically attacking, people prepare for the attack in several ways, from positioning the body to closing personal space in order to obtain striking distance. If the person is agitated, giving the person a little more space may help to calm the person down. Also, a careful nonverbal assessment may indicate whether or not the person is drunk or under the influence of drugs. Assessing voice tone and clarity is also important. Is she or he slurring words, rambling incoherently (a possible indication of mental illness), talking to someone who is not there, babbling happily and then being tearful? Voice volume is also crucial. A person who is becoming more anxious, angry, or agitated may start to talk more loudly or start to shout.

POINTS FOR PONDERING   *Watch the Space, Eyes, and Gestures*

One leading trainer in law enforcement and security writes that monitoring three areas of nonverbal communication can help officers decrease their chances of being assaulted. The three areas are space, gestures, and eye contact. Here are just a few of his suggestions:

Space
- Allow enough space for control, but do not violate personal space.

- Approach the person's weak side. Remember that nine out of ten people are right-handed and that we gesture with our strong hand.

Eyes
- If the person's eyes focus their attention of the officers' eyes, chest, and hands, this may indicate that the person is sizing the officers up.

- If the person's eyes dart from side to side or up and down, this may indicate agitation and that the person feels cornered by the officers.

- If the person's eyes are glazed or empty, or appear to be "looking through the officers," this may indicate that the person is drugged, drunk, deranged, or has other medical problems. This may mean there is a higher potential for aggression.

- Target glances occur when a person looks at his or her target before attacking. For example, a person may look at an officer's chin before trying to hit it. According to this author, there is usually a pause of at least four-tenths of a second between the target glance and the behaviour. This gives the officer a good advantage to react.

Gestures

- If the face turns from red (displaying anger) to white (displaying rage), attack is imminent.

- Hands that are open and then become clenched into fists indicate that there is a good chance of attack.

- Lips pushed forward, baring the teeth, mean anger. Lips pulled tightly over the teeth indicate possible attack.

- If the aggressor is beyond the officer's reach, the final gesture may be the individual's lowering of the body to push off for an attack.

Source

Roland Ouellette. Management of aggressive behaviour. In Ed Nowicki (1996). *Total Survival* (pp. 289–97). Powers Lake, WI: Performance Dimensions Publishing. Printed with permission of the author and publisher.

Obtain Knowledge of the Client Prior to Meeting (If Possible)

While it is not always possible, gaining a little knowledge of the person may assist you in the situation. The person may have a record that you are aware of, or there may be other history available. When you arrive at the scene, witnesses or onlookers may also have valuable knowledge. For example, a neighbour who has called about a loud dispute may be able to tell an officer how long the fight has been going on, how many are in the dwelling, and whether the person is often loud and aggressive. Realize, however, that this report may not be accurate. However, it does provide additional information. For example, a man is by himself in his residence, threatening to shoot himself. The neighbour's information of a recent separation may be of great assistance in getting the man to surrender his weapon and to come out peacefully. An important piece of information to get is the person's name, to personalize upcoming interaction.

Use Other Verbal and Nonverbal Communication Skills to Defuse the Person

Here you have many tools to choose from, depending upon the situation and the level of aggression. Several strategies are included here.

Use active listening. You may decide to use active listening, which was discussed in the previous chapter. Remember that active listening relies on empathy, paralanguage, and nonverbal communication—all of which emphasize rapport and support. When people feel they are being listened to, their anxiety may be reduced, and further escalation of aggression may be prevented. Active listening is most effective in the early stages of verbal aggression when the person is not harming himself/herself or others. For example, a man who is visibly upset at his spouse may respond to such statements as, "I can tell that you are really mad, Bob. Why don't we sit down so we can talk about it." Using the person's name is also important here. Also, the term *we* indicates togetherness and makes the request less of an order and more of an invitation.

Introduce yourself and display etiquette. Most of us were taught manners as children and often respond in kind (and almost unconsciously) when others place us in a position where we should use our manners. For example, if you introduce yourself, the other person may respond in kind. This takes the focus off the situation and gets the other person talking. It is a kind of deflection. For example, "Excuse me, Sir, my name is Officer John Smith. Could I have a word with you?" By starting the intervention in a positive tone, you are more likely to maintain this tone than if you start off with, "What's the problem here?" Other ways to use etiquette are to ask the person his or her name or to make a polite verbal gesture such asking if the person would like to sit down.

Use conversational tone to your advantage. A person who is really angry may not notice or respond to you unless you match his or her level of assertiveness. For example, if someone is shouting incoherently, you will have to shout as well to get attention. Loudly saying a person's name will usually get you attention. At this point, make a request in a loud voice (but not as loud as the original shout) for the person to talk to you. As the conversation continues, slowly lower the tone. People often unconsciously mirror others when they are getting along with them. This will also give you feedback on whether or not you are getting anywhere with the person. Remember that the longer you can keep a person talking, the less chance there will be of physical confrontation (Ouellette, 1993). Talking in a lower tone of voice also calms the body and returns it to a more relaxed state. Once relaxed, a person who has been in a heightened state of arousal for a long period of time may feel tired, and tired people rarely attack.

Use short sentences. People who are upset and out-of-control have a hard time focusing. Short and simple sentences work best. "Let's sit and talk," will be better received than, "You look like you need to talk to someone. Why don't we sit over here where it's more comfortable and have a chat?" You have probably lost the person by the fifth word. If people don't know what you are saying, you may escalate the conflict.

Analyzing and Managing the Situation

Calls take place in different settings, from bars and streets to private dwellings. Each setting has its own unique makeup, as does each situation. It is important that you analyze each situation carefully. If you have been attending a number of calls in bars, it may be easy to be less aware of the setting than you should be. Other situations such as a crisis (see below) or situations with physical aggression will be dealt with differently. Physical aggression may call for use of force, which is dealt with as the last section in this chapter.

Analyzing and Managing Yourself

Part of managing any situation is to manage yourself. By managing yourself, we mean understanding who you are and how events affect you. For example, in what kinds of situations do you experience anger? What kinds of interactions with others create stress for you? There are many cases that you can read about in which police officers "lost their cool" and used excessive force or called the person names or failed to respond appropriately. How do you cope with the stress of dealing with aggressive people? Because policing is a stressful profession, the final chapter in this text is about stress management.

MANAGING CRISES

At times, a conflict can become a **crisis**. As many police officers and other law enforcement officers can verify, routine calls can quickly become or already are in the stages of crisis. There are several definitions of crisis. In some situations, the person becomes aggressive against others or against himself or herself or threatens to be so. The common thread running through the definitions is that a crisis is a reaction to an event that goes beyond the individual's capability to cope with at that time (Arnold, 1980; Golan, 1978). A crisis can be a sudden change or turn in behaviour, and often a crisis has the potential to become violent or may already be violent when officers arrive at the scene. A crisis overrides an individual's normal psychological and biological means of coping. People in a heightened state of anxiety with reduced self-esteem often react recklessly to crises, and that is how they come into contact with law enforcement personnel (Noesner and Webster, 1997). These reckless situations include hostage-taking and barricading, often with weapons. Officers can precipitate or escalate just by showing up. Therefore, it is important that you learn some techniques that will defuse the situation slightly, not increase the escalation, and be able to do something until the situation is taken over by specialized units (if available). This section will examine the stages of a crisis, discuss preventive strategies to avoid a crisis, and offer crisis intervention techniques. A very brief look at use of force will conclude the chapter.

Stages of a Crisis

Crises appear to go through a set of identifiable stages (for instance, see Arnold, 1980; Golan 1978). It should be noted that these four stages are also used to define the stages in hostage negotiations and other police negotiations (McMains and Mullens, 1996). First, there is the *hazardous event,* which may be one event or a series of events that trigger stress. Second, the impact of this event throws a person off balance and places him or her in a *vulnerable state.* If the problem continues, tension continues to rise, and a *precipitating factor* (sometimes called a turning point) can occur that no longer allows for the individual to use his or her current coping mechanisms. This is the third state of *active crisis*. During an active crisis an individual may act out aggressively or turn inward and withdraw. The fourth phase is *adaptation,* where an individual adapts and changes to cope with the crisis.

Crisis Indicators—Before a Crisis

How can you tell if a conflict or intervention is about to turn into a crisis? There are many signs that an officer needs to be aware of that will help gauge if an attack or other crisis is imminent (Ouellette, 1996; Jurasz, 1996; McKenna, 1998). First, the *nonverbal language* of the attacker will change. The person may move into a defensive stance, with the feet moving to shoulder distance apart and the strong foot moving back. The eyes may shift to an escape route or glance at a target such as the chin of the officer or the officer's gun. The person may appear more agitated, using more gestures and engaging in more fidgeting. The person may begin to talk louder or begin shouting. Personal space may change as he or she tries to get closer for an attack or tries to get further away for flight.

  The verbal content may also change. The person may start to swear, engage in name-calling, threaten, and attempt to verbally aggravate the officer: "What kind of a man are you?" "Throw down your gun and I'll show you who's the boss." There may be talk about weapons or acts of violence. At this point, you want to engage in **crisis prevention** to avoid a continued escalation and possible physical intervention. Below are ten tips for preventing a crisis from the Crisis Prevention Institute.

Ten Tips for Crisis Prevention

1. **Be empathic.** Try not to be judgmental of the other person's feelings. They are real, even if they are not based on reality, and they must be attended to.

2. **Clarify messages.** Listen to what is really being said. Ask reflective questions, and use both silence and restatements (paraphrasing).

3. **Respect personal space.** Stand at least one and a half to three feet from the person who is acting out. Encroaching on personal space tends to arouse and escalate an individual.

4. **Be aware of body position.** Standing eye-to-eye, toe-to-toe with the person sends a challenging message. Standing at arm's length and at an angle rather than toe-to-toe is less likely to escalate the individual.

5. **Permit verbal venting when possible.** Allow the individual to release as much energy as possible by venting verbally. If this cannot be allowed, give directives and set reasonable limits during lulls in the venting.

6. **Set and enforce reasonable limits.** If the individual becomes belligerent, defensive, or disruptive, state limits and directives clearly and concisely.

7. **Avoid overreacting.** Remain calm, rational, and professional. How you, the officer or other personnel, respond will directly affect the individual.

8. **Use physical techniques as a last resort.** Use the least restrictive method of intervention possible. Employing physical techniques on an individual who is only acting out verbally can escalate the situation.

9. **Ignore challenge.** When the client challenges your position, training, etc., redirect the individual's attention to the issue at hand. Answering these questions often fuels a power struggle.

10. **Keep your nonverbal cues non-threatening.** Be aware of your body language, movement, and tone of voice. The more an individual loses control, the less attention is paid to your actual words. More attention is given to your nonverbal cues.

From Crisis Prevention Institute Inc. (1986). Ten tips for crisis prevention, www.crisisprevention.com ©1986. Reprinted with permission.

Crisis Intervention Strategies

Often, no matter how hard you try, a situation can escalate into a crisis. As an officer, you may enter into a crisis that is already taking place, such as a domestic incident or other violent crime scene. There may be little difference between an active crisis and preventing a crisis; the real difference may be more a matter of degree than anything else. Other courses taken at police colleges will go into more detail about tactics and strategies to defuse active violence. Also, many different and specialized units manage the types of crises that police may encounter, such as emergency task forces, hostage rescue teams, hostage negotiation specialists, and officers trained in managing and defusing domestic violence (McKenna, 1998). However, as first officer on the scene, you will need some knowledge in this important conflict management area. In this text, we want to concentrate on the interpersonal components of managing a crisis that may occur during regular patrol.

First, you need to quickly assess the situation. If the person is an immediate danger to himself or herself or others, you may need to react quickly with physical force. You may need to immediately call for other emergency assistance such as backup, specialized force units, Children's Aid Society, or ambulance. If no other assistance is required, you can apply the strategies listed here that rely on the ability to communicate effectively. Here we have divided the skills into verbal and nonverbal, but be aware that there is a great deal of overlap and you will use a combination of these skills.

Nonverbal Skills

Be Aware of Personal Space

In a crisis, people may need more personal space if they are agitated or hostile. You can allow as much as six feet, unless you feel the person may attempt to flee.

Use Eye Contact Appropriately

Proper use of your eye contact is an important nonverbal strategy. Eye contact by the officer can convey concern, support, confidence, and authority. By reducing eye contact, the power role is lessened and the helper role is increased. Maintain eye contact, but break it occasionally when the other person is speaking (Ouellette, 1996).

Use Non-threatening Body Positions

Do not stand directly in front of the other person. If both the person and the officer sit, this is not aggressive and can help open the door to verbal interaction (Ouellette, 1996). Not only is the probability of aggression reduced, people who have been victimized are more approachable if you let them sit down. Sitting has a calming effect, because we usually relate sitting with relaxing activities such as eating and watching television.

Monitor Other Nonverbal Behaviour

What are your hands doing? Are they clenched into fists, resting on your hips? Are your arms crossed? During a crisis, it may be easy to forget many of the nonverbal communicators and what they may appear to be saying to the other person. Gestures should be natural, as if you were speaking to a friend. This does not mean that you are not wary of the individual, but you do not want to give any signs of aggression.

Demonstrate That You Are Listening

Nonverbal indicators of listening include nodding your head and saying things like "Mm-hm," "I hear you," and "I see." If talking over the phone, you would use words or sounds to communicate listening. People in a crisis may feel let down by others and want someone to listen to them, even during such situations as hostage-taking or barricading. Pauses can also be useful. By pausing, you can let the person in the crisis think and calm down. Use the strategies from chapter 4 to demonstrate listening. Listening is a sign that you care on a professional and personal level.

Verbal Skills

What you say is also important and will demonstrate your relationship with the person. Officers need to remain courteous, although this may difficult to achieve if being verbally assaulted.

Use Paraphrasing of Content and/or Feelings (Active Listening)

Many crises can be handled more effectively if officers use paraphrasing along with active listening. Paraphrasing is part of active listening. It's noteworthy that the FBI and a growing number of law enforcement agencies are using active listening to resolve volatile situations (Noesner and Webster, 1997). If you recall from chapter 4, active listening includes paraphrasing, responding, and labelling the person's feelings, using open-ended questions and "I" messages.

Use Direct and Simple Language

During a crisis, people may not be thinking clearly. It is best to use direct, clear, and simple language. Keep your sentences short. If you need to issue a directive, state it firmly and clearly. Most tactical communication follows this simple rule.

Use Verbal Instructions to Remove Onlookers

If people are watching what is going on, their curiosity may add fuel to the person who has lost or is about to lose control. If it is possible, firmly ask onlookers to leave the immediate area.

Use Humour If Appropriate

Sometimes laughter is the "best medicine." Make sure, however, that the humour does not include laughing at the person in crisis. For instance, a victim of domestic violence who was in a lot of pain was lying on the floor, waiting for an ambulance. The officers did not want to move her because she might have had a back injury. One officer kept her company. The woman on the floor suddenly noticed from her position that there was dirt on her ceiling and she made a funny comment to the officer. This small bit of humour helped reduce the emotional level of the incident for both her and the officer.

USE OF FORCE

Often crises or physically aggressive or threatening behaviours do require that police officers use force. What starts as a conflict, may lead to a crisis, and even further, require the police to use force. Police officers must constantly assess situations and identify and act upon a plan in response to the behaviours of individuals. Police are authorized to use force by the provisions of the Criminal Code of Canada (section 25(1) and section 27). However, excessive use of force can be challenged by criminal and civil action (Dantzker and Mitchell, 1998). In essence, police officers may use force with discretion, but only as much force as the situation requires. Using force is a method of obtaining compliance to an officer's request, such as to lower a weapon or get out of a vehicle. Proper use of force can result in no injury to either the officer or the individual.

Dantzker and Mitchell (1998) developed a continuum of coercion that extends across four levels. The first level is verbal, which includes promises and threats. The second level is physical, which includes using various techniques of physical restraint. The third level includes the use of a non-lethal weapon such as a baton or pepper spray. The fourth level is the use of a lethal weapon, which would normally be a firearm. Police are supposed to assess the level of force that the individual is using and then respond with only a slightly higher use of force (Stansfield, 1996). The Ontario Use of Force Response Options are provided for you to examine, because you may be trained in the use of force (or you may have already received this training in your current career). This model is used for training because the "proper use of force is a critical concern in contemporary law enforcement" (Province of Ontario, 1993). Note that this model is under revision, with a federal use of force model being proposed.

FIGURE 5-2	Use of Force Response Options

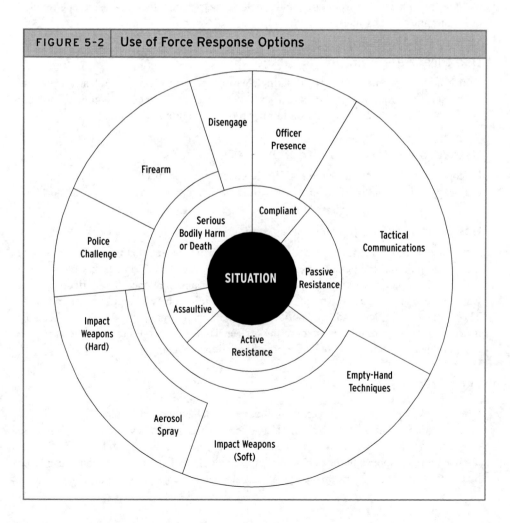

FIGURE 5-2	Use of Force Response Options (continued)

Profiled Behaviours

Use of Force Response Options

I. **Compliance** is "a cooperative and willing compliance in response to lawful police officer's request or direction."

II. **Passive Resistance** is "non-compliance to a lawful request or direction through verbal defiance but with little or no physical response (e.g., refusal to leave the scene, failure to follow directive, taunting officers, advising others to disregard officer's lawful requests, etc.)."

III. **Active Resistance** is an "increased scope and intensity of resistance beyond verbal defiance" that includes pushing or pulling away with intent to escape, or verbal refusal to respond to lawful commands.

IV. **Assaultive** is an "active, hostile resistance exhibited whether an actual assault has occurred or is about to occur on an officer or a citizen in response to the officer's attempt to gain lawful compliance or in an unprovoked assault (e.g., kicking, punching, spitting, etc.)."

V. **Serious Bodily Harm/Death** is a "behaviour likely to cause death or serious bodily harm to an officer or a citizen (e.g., choking, holding at gunpoint, brandishing an edged weapon, threatening and approaching with a weapon."

I. **Officer Presence** includes manner of arrival (e.g., foot, cruiser), number of officers at scene, etc.

II. **Tactical Communications** includes both verbal (i.e., crisis intervention skills) and nonverbal (i.e., proxemics) behaviours (idid., 4).

III. **Empty Hand Techniques** include "soft control" (i.e., restraining techniques and joint locks) and hard strikes (i.e., punches, and elbow, leg, and knee strikes).

IV. **Impact Weapons** when used for "soft control" include the use of batons in restraining techniques and joint locks.

V. **Aerosol Spray** includes oleoresin capsicum, orthochlorbenzalmalononitrite, and chloroacetophenone.

VI. **Impact Weapon** when used for hard control includes baton strikes and blocks.

VII. **Police Challenge** includes verbal commands such as, "Police, don't move!"

VIII. **Firearm** includes the drawing and discharging of service revolvers and pistols or the use of supplementary weapons such as shotguns and rifles.

IX. **Disengage** includes calling for backup and creating time and distance.

Source: Reprinted with permission from: Ronald T. Stansfield, *Issues in Policing: A Canadian Perspective* (1996). Toronto, ON: Thompson Educational Publishing, pp. 112, 113.

Training in Canada and in the United States emphasizes the use of the least intrusive measure of force to gain compliance. According to one defensive tactics instructor (Klugiewicz, 1996, p. 204), "Any use of force has to be based on a system of verbalization skills coupled with physical alternatives." The officer's physical presence, the words he or she says, and tone of voice are critical verbalization skills for defensive tactics. These skills must be used before, during, and after the use of force. Many police services require offi-cers to engage in specialized training to handle the challenges of dangerous situations where force may have to be used. For example, Metropolitan Toronto police officers in the Public Safety Unit take intensive training in several areas of crisis resolution including training in stages of crisis development, verbal interventions, appropriate use of force, and officer response to crisis stages (McKenna, 1998).

SUMMARY

This chapter concentrated on managing conflicts that included some form of aggression. First, the possible causes of aggression were discussed, including those proposed by instinct theory, social development theories, aggression as a personality trait, cultural influences, media influences, presence of weapons, gender, and heightened arousal. While no one theory of aggression can explain causation, it can be concluded that aggression has multiple causes finally perpetuated by a circumstance or event.

Aggression can be instrumental or hostile and can be further divided into verbal or physical aggression, with different levels of escalation such as verbal abuse. Managing aggression is focused upon de-escalating the aggression to a more manageable level and helping the person regain control and behave more appropriately. There are many different strategies for handling aggression, and police officers can make a choice from them based upon their analysis of the client and the situation. Verbal aggression can be managed by focusing on interaction goals, using assertive language, letting the person "run down," try-ing a "buddy approach," and using deflection. It is important that the officer be continually aware of the nonverbal behaviours of the other person, because they provide important clues about the person's emotional state. Obtaining knowledge of the client is also helpful if this can be arranged. A variety of verbal and nonverbal skills can also be used, such as active lis-tening, displaying etiquette, using a conversational tone, and using short sentences. Officers also need to manage themselves to assist in maintaining personal control in situations.

Crises can be difficult for officers to handle. During a crisis, there are identifiable stages as well as indicators that may give warning that a crisis may occur very soon. Intervening in a crisis involves many of the same strategies as managing aggression, including being aware of personal space, using appropriate eye contact, using non-threatening body positions, monitoring other nonverbal behaviours, and demonstrating that you are listening. Verbal skills include paraphrasing (active listening), using simple direct language, removing onlookers, and using humour.

Some situations may involve the use of force when behaviours get out of control and the aggression becomes threatening and physical. Police officers use a continuum of force to help ensure that excessive force does not occur. Training in use of force is provided after individuals are hired by a police service in Ontario.

CASE STUDY

The Eager Partner

Angelo and his partner, Rick, were on patrol when they received a call at 10 p.m. to check out a couple of "suspicious characters" in a neighbourhood park. The person who called would not give her name, just that she thought there was some kind of drug deal going down. By the time the partners reached the park, there was only one male left. They decided to approach the male with caution, because they were not sure that he was one of the reported males. Getting out of the car, the pair walked over to the male.

"Hey, how's it going, Buddy? Mind if we talk to you for a minute?" called Angelo as he approached the male carefully. Angelo noted that the male looked "jumpy," with eyes darting everywhere. The man's nose was runny and he was dirty. His clothes were old and he was unshaven. On the bench behind him, Angelo noticed an old brown shopping bag that looked as if it had clothes in it. The man's eyes continued to dart from Angelo to Rick and back to Angelo again.

The male replied, "I didn't do nothing. What you bugging me for?"

Rick, who only been with the service for six months, really hated this type of call, which he thought should be left for the social workers, not police officers. He said sarcastically, "Look, we got a call to come check out this park. You have a problem with this? Got something to hide?"

"Hey, I just got here a couple of minutes ago. Leave me alone!" the male retorted.

Angelo said, "Hey, we don't want to cause you any trouble. Did you happen to see ...?"

At this point, Rick jumped in and closed the distance between the male and himself, oblivious to the fact that the male was getting more agitated and had his hands clenched into fists.

With his hands on his hips, he shouted, "Don't start talking back to me! We want to know what you have been doing here, and we want it fast!"

Suddenly the male grunted and lunged at Rick. Angelo quickly stepped in and helped subdue the male, who was arrested for assaulting a police officer. Later that shift, Rick and Angelo found out that he was homeless and frequented the park every night. The neighbourhood was used to him and often gave him food. He was definitely not one of the "suspicious characters" reported earlier.

Questions

1. What indicators can be identified that the male was distressed?
2. What did Rick do wrong?
3. If you were one of the officers responding, how would you approach this situation? List some of the skills that you would have used to ensure a better ending than this one.

KEY TERMS

Aggression: Behaviour aimed at another person that is intended to harm or destroy the other.

Aggressive communication: Aggressive verbal behaviour that conveys dislike for another person that is intended to hurt the other person.

Authoritarianism: A personality syndrome characterized by rigid thinking, prejudice, and excessive concern about power.

Crisis: A reaction to an event that goes beyond the individual's capability to cope.

Emotional intelligence: A type of intelligence characterized by self-insight and the ability to regulate and control emotional expression.

Excitation transfer theory: Aggression may be the product of heightened arousal that a person may be unaware of, because emotional arousal takes time to dissipate.

Gender identity: The sex (male or female) that a person identifies as her or his own.

Hostile aggression: Aggression that is motivated by anger with the goal of hurting the other person.

Instinct theory: The theory that humans are aggressive because aggression is an inborn tendency.

Instrumental aggression: Aggression that is used to achieve a goal.

Provocation: Actions by others that are perceived as acts of aggression that arise from hostile intentions.

Social learning theory: The theory that humans are aggressive as a result of learning to be aggressive by watching and imitating others.

Verbal abuse: Verbal aggression that is persistent and continuous.

 # WEB LINKS

www.general.monash.edu.au/MUARC/rptsum/escr81.htm
Read "Driver aggression: The role of personality, social characteristics, risk, and motivation" from the Accident Research Centre, Monash University (a global university with eight campuses, including one in South Africa).

www.learnerl.org/exhibits/personality/human_nature.html
A site about human nature, including aggression.

www.athealth.com/Consumer/newsletter/FPN_4_22.html
This issue of a newsletter from athealth.com features anger and aggression.

REFERENCES

J. E. Alcock, D. W. Carment, and S. W. Sadava (1998). *A textbook of social psychology.* Scarborough, ON: Prentice Hall Ally and Bacon Canada.

William Arnold (1980). *Crisis communication.* Dubuque, IO: Gorsuch Scarisbrick Publishers.

Robert A. Baron, Donn Byrne, and Gillian Watson (2001). *Exploring social psychology.* Scarborough, ON: Allyn and Bacon.

R. F. Baumeister, L. Smart, and J. M. Boden (1996). Relation of threatened egoism to violence and aggression: The dark side of high self-esteem. *Psychological Review 103,* 5–33.

Sandra Bem (1974). The measurement of psychological androgyny. *Journal of Consulting and Clinical Psychology, 42,* 155–62.

Naomi Golan (1978). *Treatment in crisis situations.* New York: The Free Press.

Daniel Goleman (1995). *Emotional intelligence.* New York: Bantam Books.

B. A. Hadjifotiou (1983). *Women and sexual harassment at work.* London: Pluto.

P. Hoffman (1984). Psychological abuse of women by spouses and live-in lovers. *Women & Therapy, 3*(1), 37–47.

L. R. Huesman (1986). Psychological processes promoting the relation between exposure to media violence and aggressive behavior by the receiver. *Journal of Social Issues, 42,* 125–39.

Rick Kirschner & Rick Brinkman (1994). *Dealing with difficult people: How to bring out the best in people at their worst.* New York: McGraw-Hill.

International Labour Organization (July 20, 1998). Violence on the job: A global problem. http://us.ilo.org/news/prsrls/violence.html

P. Jaffe, D. Wolfe, S. Wilson, et al. (1986). Similarities in behavioral and social adjustment among child victims and witnesses to family violence. *American Journal of Orthopsychiatry, 56,* 142–46.

Terry A. Kinney (1994). An inductively derived typology of verbal aggression and its association to distress. *Human Communication Research, 21*(2), 183–223.

R. S. Larazus (1993). From psychological stress to the emotions: A history of changing outlooks. *Annual Review of Psychology, 44,* 1–21.

T. E. Moore, D. J. Pepler, R. Mae, et al. (1989). Child witnesses to family violence: New directions for research and intervention. In B. Pressman, G. Cameron, and M. Rothery (Eds.). *Intervening with assaulted women: Current theory, research, and practice.* Hillsdale, NJ: Lawrence Erlbaum Assoc.

P. G. Ney (1987). Does verbal abuse leave deeper scars: A study of children and parents. *Canadian Journal of Psychiatry, 32,* 371–78.

Gary W. Noesner & Mike Webster (1997). Crisis intervention. *FBI Law Enforcement Bulletin, 66*(8), 13–21.

D. Olweus (1972). Personality and aggression. *Nebraska Symposium on Motivation, 1972,* 261–323. Lincoln, NB: University of Nebraska Press.

Roland Ouellette (1993). *Management of aggressive behavior.* Powers Lake, WI: Performance Dimensions Publishing.

Robert Stansfield (1996). *Issues in policing: A Canadian perspective.* Toronto: Thompson Educational Publishing.

Statistics Canada (1999). Homicide statistics, *The Daily*, October 7, 1999. www.statcan.ca/Daily/English/991007/d991007b.htm

Kenneth G. Roy (2000). The systemic conditions leading to violent human behavior. *Journal of Applied Behavioral Science, 361*(4), 389–408.

M. D. Weinstein, M. E. Smith, and D. L. Wiesenthal (1995). Masculinity and hockey violence. *Sex Roles, 33,* 831–47.

C. S. Widom (1989). Does violence beget violence? A critical examination of the literature. *Psychological Bulletin, 106,* 3–28.

D. Zillman (1994). Cognition-excitation interdependencies I: The escalation of anger and angry aggression. In M. Potegal and J. F. Knutson (Eds.). *The dynamics of aggression.* Hillsdale, NJ: Erlbaum.

——— (1998). Cognition-excitation interdependencies in aggressive behavior. *Aggressive Behavior, 14,* 51–64.

chapter six

Dealing with Alcohol Abusers

Courtesy Peterborough Lakefield Community Police Service

LEARNING OUTCOMES

After studying this chapter, you should be able to

- Define the major reasons for alcohol use and abuse in our society.
- Understand the basic physiological and pharmacological effects of alcohol.
- Identify the stages of intoxication.
- Describe the basics of alcoholism.
- Understand the indicators of violent behaviour.
- Understand the role of alcohol in crime and violence.
- Describe techniques to de-escalate violence when dealing with alcohol abusers.

On-the-Job Scenario

You are working your fifth day of night shift. Most of the day was spent in court, so you're very tired. You and your partner are responding to a call for a domestic dispute. You have attended that address three times this month alone. As you knock on the door, you are not a happy camper. You know that there will be a report to write, and you know that they'll be drunk again.

There is no response at the door, so you enter to find the husband unconscious on the couch, as usual. The wife staggers out of the kitchen, and pointing at her husband, begins to talk to you unintelligibly. The couple's 16-year-old daughter walks in the front door, reeking of liquor and crying. Her clothes are a mess and she has a bloody nose. When you ask her what happened, she tells you to do something anatomically impossible and storms by you. The mother takes up her daughter's cause and begins to curse and swear at you (her words now much more understandable).

You determine that your presence is no longer required. You both shake your heads as you leave, your partner muttering something about "these" people and night shifts.

Dealing with substance abuse is a substantial component of policing. The use of illicit drugs is widespread and exacts a terrible toll. Not only are lives taken and wasted by drug use, but heavy users are frequently involved in crimes, including break-and-entry, robberies, and thefts. The user steals to support the addiction, and organized crime groups take that money and channel it into other lucrative endeavours. As pervasive as drug use is in crime today, the frontline police officer deals with alcohol abusers far more frequently than with drug abusers.

The above scenario is a little too convenient educationally, but it is very representative of the daily grind of police work. "Booze in, brains out," is an unscientific but relatively accurate description of the situation and similar scenes that law enforcement officers view everywhere. In 2000, one author experienced night shifts during which every call for service involved the use or abuse of alcohol to some extent. While many policing resources are utilized to deal with alcohol abuse and its fallout, little formalized training has been given to frontline officers. Further, officers are given little information about the abusers themselves. In the scenario above, the officers did nothing fundamentally wrong, but they reacted with indifference to a situation that they didn't fully comprehend. Chances are that they viewed the three people as lost causes, and chances are that they will be back to that house again.

Policing is, at times, a physical job. Of course the Criminal Code and provincial statutes give officers the right to use as much force as is necessary to do their job, but most officers do not want to create more trouble for themselves. At the end of the shift, most officers would rather go home to their family or think about that date tomorrow night. They do not want to spend their days off at the doctor, or worse still, the lawyer's office. In this chapter, we will offer an overview of alcohol and its abuse, with the goal of helping the reader comprehend the issues surrounding alcohol use in a police environment.

ALCOHOL USE: AN OVERVIEW

The use, and subsequent abuse, of alcohol is as old as humankind itself. The origins of alcohol likely date as far back as the Neolithic Age (Kinney, 1982). Much the same as with Dom Perignon's accidental creation of champagne, the first examples of alcohol were likely mistakes, in this case involving fermentation. The results of these "mistakes" had pleasurable outcomes and were therefore duplicated.

Alcohol is cited in literature going as far back as ancient times, the Bible being no exception. In fact, alcohol had such a prominent position in society that the ancients assigned their own gods of wine: the Egyptians had Osiris, the Greeks had Dionysus, and the Romans had Bacchus (Kinney, 1982).

Alcohol use has become part of the fabric of Western society. Sharing food, "breaking bread together," is integral to virtually all celebrations in our society, and if an occasion is really important, alcohol is introduced. Virtually no adult social gathering is complete without the presence of alcohol.

The cycle of alcohol consumption waxes and wanes despite the enormous financial and personal costs to society. The Canadian Centre on Substance Abuse has broken down the societal costs of substance abuse into six areas: workplace associative losses, administrative and transfer costs, prevention and research costs, law enforcement costs, health care costs, and other costs. There are also indirect costs to productivity. In a 1992 study, the total cost of substance abuse in Canada was a staggering $18.45 billion, 40.8 per cent of which was attributed to alcohol use (Canadian Centre on Substance Abuse, 1993). The costs relating to alcohol amount to 1.09 per cent of the gross domestic product of Canada and $265 per capita, and the authors of the study add that this is a conservative estimate (Canadian Centre on Substance Abuse, 1993).

We must be mindful that the costs listed so far are economic, and that alcohol exacts a greater toll in human terms. According to the 1993 General Social Survey, 9.2 per cent of Canadians reported having problems relating to their drinking, and 43.9 per cent reported having problems related to others' drinking (Canadian Centre on Substance Abuse, 1999). A 1995 study found that one-third of Ontario university students consume alcohol "at a level that puts them at risk of health and other problems." Male, first-year students living in residence were determined to be the heaviest drinkers. A 1999 press release by the Centre for Addiction and Mental Health indicates that since 1993, drinking involving students from Grades 7 to 13 has increased from an already high 56.5 per cent to a substantially higher 65.7 per cent. Significantly, 11 per cent of Ontario students reported hazardous drinking, a number higher than the national percentage of problem drinkers (Centre for Addiction and Mental Health, 1999).

POINTS FOR PONDERING   *Alcohol Use within Police Circles*

One would think that with all of their experience with the effects of alcohol abuse, police officers would not even touch it, let alone become abusers themselves. The myth of the heavy-drinking cop has been portrayed in literature in books such as *The Choirboys,* by Joseph Wambaugh, himself a former Los Angeles Police Department officer. Hollywood has likewise gotten much mileage out of the hard-living, heavy-drinking cop.

How much of this is reality? According to a 1989 study, more than one-third of all Royal Canadian Mounted Police employees drank at a daily level described by the World Health Organisation as damaging to health. The study added that as many as 17 per cent of RCMP members drank "heavily" on working days, and 29 per cent drank "heavily" on their off days (Corelli & MacAndrew, 1994).

Even on-the-job drinking has had its impact on policing. Part of the common jargon used in the New York City Police Department includes the terms, "The Thirsty Third," a nickname for the third squad of a particular precinct that is infamous for drinking on the job, and "four to four," which refers to the 4 p.m. to midnight shift with four hours of drinking at the end of the shift (Thibault, Lynch, and McBride, 2001). This problem is by no means limited to one or two departments.

The truth is that law enforcement personnel all too often themselves battle the substance that they spend so many working hours cleaning up after. Among the most publicized examples are accounts of motor vehicle accidents involving officers impaired by alcohol. Damage ranges from marked police cruisers being parked where bus shelters had been moments earlier, to much more tragic events involving the death of officers and innocent civilians.

REASONS FOR ALCOHOL USE

The reasons for alcohol use are as many and varied as there are people. We have spoken briefly of the place alcohol has in our society, and cultural aspects can be added here as well. While it is difficult to summarize all of the reasons that people consume alcohol, several factors are not only predominant, but also likewise factor into the field of law enforcement:

1. **The relief of anxiety.** That de-stressing drink after a hard day. Many people cope with the pressure of work, a difficult exam, or bad news by drinking.

2. **The need to have control over oneself and one's environment.** This is the illusion of increased power. Having to be subordinate at work or home can result in lowered self-esteem. Alcohol consumption often offers temporary relief.

3. **The desire to reach towards a "larger" experience.** This can be simple experimentation or an attempt to push one's limits.

4. **Peer pressure, the desire to conform and be cool.** This reason is most prominent with youth (Kinney, 1982).

ALCOHOL: A DRUG

Alcohol and pharmaceutical drugs, licit and illicit, are generally placed in separate categories. For our purposes, this practice will be maintained, because it makes it easier to differentiate between the two substances. However, make no mistake, alcohol is a drug.

According to the *Bantam Medical Dictionary,* a drug is "any substance that affects the structure or functioning of a living organism" (1982). Alcohol is a drug, and the abuse of it as well as of other substances is included within the realm of mental health disorders.

Alcohol is described as a depressant because of its effect on the body's central nervous system. When alcohol is taken in, small amounts are absorbed in the mouth through small blood vessels. Some 20 per cent is absorbed in the stomach, and the remaining 80 per cent is absorbed in the small intestine.

The first effect is expansion of the surface blood vessels of the skin. You experience a warm feeling and a flushed colour in your skin. Next comes a feeling of euphoria, that pleasant "buzz" associated with the first drink. Feelings of intoxication begin as the alcohol starts to act on the central nervous system.

TABLE 6-1	Alcohol and Its Effects	
Drinks per half hour	Effects	Blood alcohol level at one hour's end
1	The drinker feels more relaxed, minor mood changes Little discernible behaviour change	.02 mg. per ml.
2½	The drinker feels less inhibited Judgment sections of the brain are affected	.05 mg. per ml
5	Blood alcohol level exceeds the legal limit of .08 mg. per ml. Muscle co-ordination is depressed, a stagger and a slurring of speech begins The pupils become dilated and the eyes glassy Judgment is greatly affected, limitations are ignored	.10 mg. per ml
10	Judgment and motor control are significantly impaired, pain sensors diminished Control of emotions is affected, behaviour may be erratic	.20 mg. per ml
+ 10	Reflexes greatly diminished Consciousness reduced Anaesthetic type effects Alcohol poisoning to possible death	.30 mg. per ml to .50 mg. per ml

1 drink is based on 1/2 oz. of pure alcohol, 1 oz. of spirits, 12 oz. of beer

Table 6-1 provides some physical indicators that can help assess degrees of intoxication. The "Over 80" section of the Criminal Code prescribes the legal limit of alcohol while operating a motor vehicle at .08 mg per ml. It is worth noting that impairment actually begins before the legal limit and that the Impaired Driving section assigns no such limit.

As previously mentioned, most alcohol is absorbed by the small intestine. It is, however, the liver that processes approximately 95 per cent of the alcohol in the body, while excretions, through sweat and urine, process the remainder. The liver metabolizes alcohol at half an ounce of pure alcohol per hour. This rate, with minor variances, is a set rate. Contrary to popular belief, force-feeding coffee will not sober up the intoxicated drinker. Caffeine, which is a stimulant, may have a small immediate effect on the depressant qualities of alcohol; the would-be sober person may feel more energetic and in control, but is no less intoxicated.

The intoxicating effect of alcohol is based on two major factors: the quantity of alcohol consumed, and the rate at which the alcohol is absorbed into the body. Of the two, the rate of absorption has the greater effect on the feeling of intoxication. The rate of absorption is based on several factors including the size and body type of the drinker; the gender of the drinker (women tend to absorb alcohol more quickly); how much food is present in the stomach, thereby affecting the rate of absorption; and the degree to which the body's central nervous system has adapted to alcohol consumption. The first-time drinker will likely have a faster absorption rate and therefore become intoxicated with lower quantities of alcohol than the seasoned drinker. Another factor is that of the alcohol content of the drink. The greater the percentage of alcohol, the greater the rate of absorption. Therefore, quickly downing those shooters, or starting off with a double or two, will lead to a quicker "buzz."

The level of impairment is greater during the absorption phase than in the elimination phase, even though blood alcohol levels are comparable. Therefore when patrons down those last couple of drinks at last call and head out to the street and their cars, their impairment is at its highest.

ALCOHOL ADDICTION

Almost as old as the use of alcohol is the problem of **addiction** to alcohol. Alcohol addiction takes on many forms and has varied root causes. Current research cites a chemical substance called dopamine as a major link to addiction. Dopamine is a **neurotransmitter** present in the brain that is associated with pleasure and euphoria. Dopamine levels are increased by common addictive substances, including alcohol, as well as by such seemingly harmless acts as hugging or playing video games. Dopamine is so significant that it has been dubbed "the master molecule of addiction" (Nash, 1997). So alcohol abusers are not only abusing the substance, but they are using alcohol as means to get the "fix" of dopamine (Dubrin and Geerinck, 2001). This text will not attempt to exhaust the topic of alcohol addiction. The field is much too vast and is better left to scientists and addiction research specialists. However, it is useful for a police officer to have a basic comprehension of alcohol addiction and its related complications.

During antiquity, abuse of or addiction to alcohol was often attributed to the gods. The use of the word *spirits* to describe alcohol did not happen by chance. As time passed, psychological or moral weakness was often cited as the reason for poor behaviour resulting from alcohol consumption. During the days of early settlement, a misbehaver may have been publicly humiliated or punished in order to be made an example. Another reaction to alcohol abuse was banishment from social or religious circles, because the abuser just didn't measure up to standard.

There have been largescale responses to widespread alcohol abuse, which range from temperance movements, usually with a religious foundation, and their teetotallers (total abstainers of alcoholic consumption), to the Prohibition period of the United States. Social pressures, and in the second case, contraband liquor from Canada, ultimately contributed to the end of these movements as a means of alcohol reform.

Today, the issue of alcohol abuse and addiction is a science. Abusers are seen more as victims who require help.

ALCOHOLISM

The term *alcoholic* conjures up many visions. Alcoholics are long-term abusers of alcohol. They come in all types and from all backgrounds. If you look far back enough in most Western families, you are likely to uncover an alcoholic, or at least someone who abused alcohol sufficiently to cause misery to himself or herself, or to those who were close. Statistically, you'll find about as many professionals who are substance abusers as you will people who are much further down the socio-economic ladder. However, police officers are more likely to deal with drug and alcohol addicts who live closer to the margins. The more affluent substance abusers commonly have more space between themselves and their neighbours, are better able to ride out financial storms, and are less likely to call the police.

Police officers will make conclusions about substance abusers and the reasons for such abuse, based upon their observations. They may not, however, see the complete picture.

The question about the cause of alcoholism continues to plague us. Alcoholics Anonymous has been a very successful organization that recognizes alcoholism as an incurable or chronic—but very treatable—disease. Brian Mitchell, a program director with the Centre for Addiction and Mental Health, acknowledges that even today there are differing views on the causes of alcohol abuse and addiction (Mitchell, 2001). Some experts in the field have attributed drug and alcohol addiction to genetic or other biological factors, while others emphasize personality, or psychological, social, or environmental factors (Mitchell, 2001). Substance abuse is also listed as one of society's more common mental health disorders. In spite of extensive research, there is insufficient scientific data to point to one primary cause for addiction. Addiction to alcohol and drugs appears to result from a combination of several of the previously outlined factors.

What is known conclusively is that alcoholism is a devastating and very common condition. There are as many theories about its origin as there are definitions for alcoholism. In a nutshell, alcoholism is a significant physical impairment that results from persistent consumption of alcohol. *Significant impairment* means basically that alcohol begins to interfere with one or more aspects of one's life. Mitchell suggests that it's helpful to visualize alcoholism in terms of a continuum in order to understand the non-static nature of alcohol related problems.

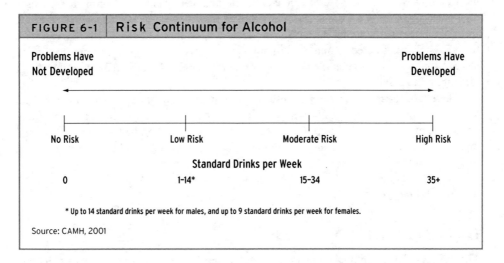

FIGURE 6-1 | **Risk Continuum for Alcohol**

According to the Centre for Addiction and Mental Health (2001), it may take several years for someone to become an alcoholic. Much is dependent on the amount and frequency of alcohol consumption. During this time, many psychological and medical problems can develop, and if unchecked, can even cause life-threatening problems. In 1995, an estimated 6,503 Canadians died as a result of alcohol consumption, and a further 80,946 were treated in hospital for alcohol-related causes (Canadian Centre on Substance Abuse, 1999). Motor vehicle accidents, cirrhosis of the liver, and alcohol-involved suicide led the way in cause of death (Canadian Centre on Substance Abuse, 1999). Furthermore, anywhere along the continuum, alcohol can takes its toll on friendships, jobs, and families.

> ### POINTS FOR PONDERING
> *Discretionary Powers*
>
> One of the great virtues of policing is that officers experience a great deal of variety and have a vast amount of discretion. Unfortunately, one of the great drawbacks of policing is that officers experience a great deal of variety and have a vast amount of discretion. The benefit is fairly obvious, but the flip side may not be. The drawback is that the right or wrong answer or approach is not always obvious. For example, when dealing with out-of-control, hysterical people, a veteran officer's approach is to be polite but firm, and to tell people to "grow up." A younger officer sees this approach work ten times out of ten. During one call, the younger officer takes the lead in dealing with an angry, ranting woman. With the words "grow up" still lingering in the air, the rookie ducks just in time to avoid a flying rolling pin and grabs the woman just before she throws a frying pan. What happened? First, the experienced officer has the look of someone with 20 years' experience and is six inches taller and 70 pounds heavier than the newcomer. As well, the younger officer has never dealt with this *particular* person before.
>
> What are some of the factors that make it difficult to deal with people "by the book"?

FACTORS CONTRIBUTING TO VIOLENT BEHAVIOUR

Before we deal specifically with people who have been drinking, it will be worthwhile to examine factors that contribute to violent behaviour in general. As we will see, alcohol does not cause violent behaviour. It is certainly related in many violent incidents, but its presence is more a window into the participant's lifestyle than a predictor of violent behaviour on its own. The intention of this section is not to stereotype people or promote a particular lifestyle, but rather to highlight the type of person or environment *most likely* to lead to violent behaviour. It is in any officer's interest to be able to anticipate trouble and therefore react appropriately.

Consider This...

Two males are scuffling outside of a bar at 2:00 a.m. One has a bloody nose, and they both look the worse for wear. As the officers approach to assist and try to break up the fight, both males begin to launch insults at the two officers.

To no one's surprise, the majority of violent offenders are male. Studies in Canada and the United States conducted in 1991 show that men make up 88 per cent and 89 per cent of violent offenders respectively (Corrections Canada, 1999). This is not to say that women are never violent. In the same 1991 study, it was found that women make up 12 per cent of the violent offenders, amounting to 13,000 charges (Corrections Canada, 1999), and the percentage of violent crime is on the increase for women. In 1970, 8.1 per cent of all Criminal Code charges against women were for crimes of violence. By 1991, that number had risen to 13.6 per cent (Corrections Canada, 1999).

It has been found in numerous studies that violent behaviour occurs most often in younger age groups (Hindelang, Gottfredson, and Garofalo, 1978; Moone, 1994; Junger-Tas, 1996). This does not mean that "the young people are out of control," but that there are reasons why young people are more prone to violence. Several factors may contribute to insecurity and therefore violent behaviour or inappropriate reactions. Included in these factors is the absence of a recognized **social structure** for the young, uncertainty about the future, and the diminishing **traditional links** within the family, the community, and society.

Without structure, people, and youth in particular, cannot find their role or limits. If a ten-year-old is given complete freedom, he will not know the limits normally placed on a ten-year-old. He may drink alcohol like a 20-year-old, but need to be fed and dressed like a toddler. He does not know what is expected of him, so he has no model to conform to. All too often, children today lack structure as a result of extreme poverty, the absence of a strong parental figure, strong media influence, or simply misguided indulgence by the parents. Ultimately the child behaves badly because the child does not know how to behave.

Uncertainty about the future is not a new condition. During the **cold war,** people built backyard bomb shelters and waited for nuclear annihilation. Until recently, the world appeared to be more stable, but there seems to be an ever-widening gap between the "haves" and the "have nots." As well, there is a greater than ever ability to access information and greater than ever choice. Further, many young people today shun the establishment and look for alternatives to traditional careers and lifestyles. The result is often confusion and despair, and therefore little hope.

Our society is changing at an incredible rate. While many of those changes have been positive, we have lost many support links. Families can pick up and move halfway around the world, cutting physical ties to extended family members. It is common for children to have two parental families, to have siblings from several relationships, or even to be the progeny of an unknown donor. The result can be difficulties in parental consistency or a lack of identity. Communities have become very transient, with neighbours often remaining strangers. Traditional religious affiliation, once a cornerstone of communities, has decreased sharply. Add to this the economics of longer work weeks and double-income families and we can see a loss in many elements that helped to secure one's position in society.

When people are under stress, their perceptions of instability, **marginalization,** and lack of support can lead to violent behaviour (Manciaux, 1993). The marginalized or isolated person believes that there is nothing to gain or lose, and that there is no person or institution that can help. Violence and misconduct is more prevalent in children and adolescents whose parents drink heavily (Plant, Orford, and Grant, 1989): a combination of modelling inappropriate behaviour and a lack of coping skills.

Aggression is most prominent where there are aggressive role models and where positive feedback is given for aggressive behaviour, as we discovered in chapter 5 (Fagan and Jones, 1984). Aggressive or violent behaviour becomes a way to find acceptance within the peer group. This reinforcement can be found not only in the street or criminal subculture. Recall your days in primary school and a fight in the schoolyard. The crowd gathered and circled the combatants, cheering them on. The child who was winning, the aggressor, got most of the support. After a teacher—not another child—stopped the fight, it was the winner who was talked about next day.

Following in the primary school theme, but with more serious stakes, is inappropriate responses to insults or jealousy. In a street subculture, violence can hinge on mere insults or perceived slights to one's honour (Horowitz, 1983). A common news feature is the account of a shooting or knifing over accidental bumps, unwanted eye contact, or the "dissing" of the attacker.

POINTS FOR PONDERING   *The Effect of the Media*

Is there in fact a greater amount of violence in society today, or does this perception stem from the huge volume of media input in our lives?

If the media do influence our perspective, do they also factor into violent behaviour as well?

Substance abuse itself can be a flag for violent behaviour. Heavy alcohol and drug use tends to be common in the lifestyle of those prone to criminal behaviour and violence. This does not mean that alcohol and drugs are always the cause of such activity; however, they are an integral part of the individual's coping mechanisms and social activity.

A study was conducted in Edmonton, Alberta, to find the role of alcohol in criminal violence. Although the respondents were youth spending a considerable time on the street, the results can easily be applied to the population that law enforcement personnel encounter (Baron and Hartnagel, 1998).

Overall, the study indicated that those who are on the street more and whose peers are involved in criminal activity are more likely to become involved in criminal violence. Further, people who are economically deprived and feel marginalized by society may harbour anger (Bernard, 1990) and are more likely to react with violence.

Victimization, too, was shown to be a factor in violent activity, because higher levels of victimization often correspond to higher levels of violence. Other factors cited in violent behaviour among street youths included loyalty to friends and peers, homelessness and poverty, and the concerns already discussed about personal status (Desroches, 1997; Baron and Hartnagel, 1998).

Consider This...

"I thought that she was my friend. We were all sitting around the fire, drinking and having fun, then she came up and called me a bitch and a slut. Then she just started punching me, first in the face and then in the stomach. Everyone just stood around, nobody did anything. I can't go back to school now, I can't face them."
—A fifteen-year-old girl's account of a Grade 9 field party.

ALCOHOL USE AND VIOLENCE

If we combine our knowledge of the effects of alcohol with our knowledge of factors that contribute to violent behaviour, it is easy to understand how alcohol plays a role in violence. Take someone prone to violence or out of touch with society and give him or her a drug that loosens inhibitions, significantly affects judgment, or reduces ability to accurately assess the environment. That person is a likely candidate to be a victim or aggressor in the right setting.

If someone finds confidence and sense of well-being in a bottle, and those feelings are torn away, violence may be the only avenue left to maintain self-respect or to vent frustration.

It is suggested that in Western society, people under the influence of alcohol are seldom held responsible for their actions. It appears that the rules of society do not carry the same weight when you are drunk. Intoxication reinforces feelings of masculinity, rebellion, and a general "party atmosphere" for young males who may see violence or thrill-seeking as a part of the night out (Alcohol and Public Health Research Unit, 2000). Alcohol further accentuates thrill-seeking by creating a feeling of being all-powerful, which reduces the perception of risk (Incardi and Russe, 1977; Baron and Hartnagel, 1998).

What about young people? As we know, peer pressure can be an enormous factor in the behaviour of youth. Along with the spirit of protest and experimentation, it leads many young people into early contact with drugs and alcohol. Alcohol is especially difficult to control for this segment of the population who are still developing their coping skills and aren't aware of their limitations. It appears that young teens, in particular, have difficulty in drinking moderately. Even those in their later teens show difficulty in maintaining moderate drinking levels. The result, more than in any other category, is often victimization.

Studies indicate a relationship between alcohol consumption and violent behaviour, and, in particular, violent behaviour and heavy or binge drinking (Room, Bondy, and Forris, 1995; Rossow, 1996). Statistics in the United States indicate that in 1996, 36 per cent of inmates in American institutions had been drinking at the time of the offence. Further, 40 per cent of offenders in crimes of violence had been under the influence of alcohol at the time of the incident (National Council on Alcoholism and Drug Addiction, 1998).

How does this affect police officers? While it is true that police officers cannot prevent people from drinking and becoming intoxicated, police officers can work within the community policing model to cut down on levels of intoxication and under-age drinking in licensed establishments. Even more important, police officers can assess situations and circumstances and can limit potential violent behaviour while dealing with individuals.

STRATEGIES FOR DEALING WITH INTOXICATED PEOPLE

The following strategies will help you to manage people who are intoxicated. Remember that people can act normally and then quickly escalate into much more dangerous behaviours, to themselves or to you.

- Do be firm, to demonstrate that you have the final control of the situation. This is perhaps the most important yet most difficult technique to master. An officer does not want to remove all of an intoxicated person's control and provoke a violent reaction, but if someone believes that he or she has control over the officer, violence might appear to be the ticket out.

- Do identify the subjects and use available resources to determine their criminal and incident history. Police officers have a wealth of information available to them. This information can help assess the likelihood of confrontation based upon previous police contacts.

- Do use acquired knowledge and skills to assess the particular person and situation you are dealing with.

- Avoid treating each person and situation the same way. People are too different for a "cookie cutter" approach.

- Do move the subject away from the crowd and try to initiate a conversation. A crowd of supporters may increase the person's sense of bravado or encourage a "perform-ance" for friends. Isolation is a good way to bring somebody back to reality. A simple conversation, as opposed to barking out orders, can achieve a positive initial rapport.

- Do use distraction techniques such as humour or small talk. People who are intoxi-cated may need a distraction to lower their activity level. Small talk is a good tool to slow people down, to forget whatever triggered the anger. Humour, when used appro-priately, can be very disarming.

- Do treat the person with respect, and show that police officers, too, are human. Treating a person with dignity will lower the level of defensiveness and put them more at ease. By being a person, and not just a uniform, an officer is more likely to be treated with respect, particularly if the intoxicated person has issues with authority figures.

- Do allow the person to "save face." Try to give options rather than ultimatums. A per-son who is backed into a corner seldom reacts well. This is well illustrated when you tell a four-year-old child to do something "or else." When someone is impaired and ego is on the line, the results are predictably disastrous.

- Do be patient. A police officer is paid by the hour to deal with clients, sober or otherwise.

- If arrest is not the preferred option, *do* find a sober peer and put the onus on him or her to speed the friend away, but *don't* depend on that person. If the choice of a peer is a poor one, the officer's workload just doubled.

- Don't belittle or humiliate the person, especially in a crowd scene. If the intoxicated person is drinking in order to supplement self-esteem, and if that self-esteem is further challenged, there is more likely to be violence in order to be assertive.

- Don't ever let your guard down. In policing, complacency kills. People are not pre-dictable, and intoxicated people are even less predictable. Intoxicated people's actions are less likely to correspond with what they say, so watching for nonverbal communi-cation is very important.

It is not always easy to show patience and restraint when dealing with intoxicated peo-ple. They are likely to treat police officers casually, if not rudely. Someone who can barely stand or speak coherently will paint a picture of himself or herself as a saint, and proclaim that he or she had "only two beers." (This is in contrast to the intoxicated person who is not in any danger of being arrested, who will proudly state that he or she has been drinking steadily since yesterday.) A police officer may also become frustrated by the unbelievable number of times that a person repeats herself, as if it were the officer who was the intoxi-cated one. When they demand unnecessary or unwarranted action, tell the officer how to do his or her job, or state, "If you weren't hiding behind that uniform, I'd take you to the cleaners," it's difficult to remember that their higher brain functions have been affected by a drug (alcohol) and that they *may* not act this way all the time.

The bottom line is that this is part of the job when you are a police officer. Superiors and the public expect professionalism, regardless of the situation. If the police officers' oath of office is not enough to remind them of their accountability, they can look to inter-nal discipline, civilian police watchdogs, the media, and civil and criminal courts. Any of these agencies will be only too happy to remind an officer that he or she has sworn to serve and protect all of society, regardless of their sobriety.

As stated earlier, it is not only suspects under the influence of alcohol that police officers deal with. Complainants, victims, and witnesses can also be experienced at less than their best. Officers must be extra patient with victims and witnesses who have been drinking and must try to obtain as much information as possible, even though intoxicated people are poor investigative resources. Follow-up interviews or even postponing the investigation may be necessary. It becomes more of a problem when the incident stems from the complainant's—or especially the victim's—state of intoxication. Not only are they unlikely to be much help to investigators at the time, but their intoxication may have been the chief cause of their victimization. The officer may have strong judgments about victims bringing their misery upon themselves. Again remember, police officers are professionals, and a fact of life is that they don't have the luxury of choosing their customers.

There is one more category of intoxicated person that tests the patience, and humanity, of officers more than all the others: the regular customer. These are the people who prompt officers to "**glove up**" the moment they are seen because it is well known how generous they are with their bodily fluids. Unless the officer is fortunate enough to talk an ambulance crew into transporting your party, the bottom line here is that the police are the bottom line. Police officers get paid to deal with things and people that nobody else wants to handle. One more time the officer will have to remind himself or herself that police are professionals and that no one's son or daughter aspires to be a "down and out drunk." These are the people at the far end of the alcoholic continuum, people who just couldn't handle that which life threw at them. It is sometimes difficult, especially because it is part of a police officer's coping mechanism to remain somewhat detached, but officers must try to treat the "down and outers" as real people. There otherwise is a danger of objectifying "drunks," and treating them as "things," rather than as people (Thibault, Lynch, and McBride, 2001).

SUMMARY

As demonstrated, alcohol abuse is a societal problem with few simple answers. Police officers are often given the task of dealing with the aftermath of alcohol use and abuse. There is no way to ensure a safe and successful resolution to conflicts with persons under the influence of alcohol; however, education, training, and professionalism will go a long way to improve the odds in the officers' favour. In this chapter we started with an overview of alcohol use, which has firm historical roots. It was observed that 9.2 per cent of Canadians are problem drinkers, and that alcohol costs our society $7.5 billion annually. People drink alcohol for many reasons: to de-stress, to gain or maintain control, to experience something new, and as a result of peer pressure.

We examined alcohol as a drug, taking note of its intoxicating effects. The chapter also covered reasons for addiction in general, and for addiction to alcohol specifically. Violent behaviour was addressed and was seen to be caused by many factors. Key among them is the prevalence of violence among young males, particularly where they feel marginalized and live in an environment where violence is modelled and rewarded.

We put together the areas of violence and alcohol and observed how the loosening effect of alcohol and its tendency to cause misjudgments of social cues can lead to violent encounters. It was also observed that heavy or binge drinkers are often prone to violence, regardless of the presence of alcohol.

Finally, guidelines were given to aid prospective police officers in dealing with intoxicated people, including awareness of officer safety and respect for the alcohol abuser.

CASE STUDY

Bill is a labourer who was recently laid off from his job. His skill set and education are limited, so prospects for new employment are not good. On Friday night Bill goes out drinking with his buddies, hoping to drown his sorrows. After three or four beers, the group settle at the local hotspot. They wait outside in a line-up for about ten minutes in the cold February air. Once inside the crowded tavern, Bill finds out the coat check is closed, so he is left to hold his jacket in the warm and smoky room. Because they are late arrivals, Bill and company are left in the undesirable spot near the washrooms. Bill is bumped or jostled several times by patrons going to and from the washrooms. One man spills some of his rye and Coke on Bill's jacket. The two exchange angry words, then the man goes on his way. Bill resumes drinking his third beer at the bar when he is grabbed from behind by a bouncer. Bill is told that he is cut off because he was causing trouble and that he has one minute to drink up and leave. As the bouncer is leaving, Bill steps in front him to plead his case and is grabbed by two more staff members. The three bouncers aggressively lead Bill to the front door and push him out to the sidewalk, where he falls. Bill tries to regain entry to the bar, shouting and swearing at the staff members who keep him out. Bill continues swearing and starts to kick the pop machine, which is just outside the front doors. You are walking the beat in the downtown area and happen upon Bill as he begins to kick the pop machine.

Questions

1. As first officer on scene, what is your initial approach with Bill?
2. Given the circumstances, how is Bill likely to react to your presence? What other factors could influence his reaction?
3. If you had not arrived on scene when you did, what is the likelihood that Bill's frustrations would have carried over to the first innocent passer-by?
4. How might Bill react to another intoxicated person, who is commenting on Bill's behaviour?
5. To what extent is the tavern responsible for Bill's behaviour?

KEY TERMS

Addiction: A state of dependence caused by the regular use of a drug or substance.

Aggression: A hostile or injurious behaviour or action, acted out without concern for others.

Community policing: The concept of the police service involving community groups in making policy and decisions, rather than the police and other government agencies acting unilaterally. In order to implement community oriented policing, it is generally acknowledged that frontline officers, too, must be empowered.

Cold war: The post–Second World War period of political tension between the proponents of Eastern bolshevism and Western democratic ideals. The nuclear arms race and the space race were two results of the international posturing.

Glove-up: Put on protective rubber gloves before contact with high-risk individuals.

Marginalization: Perceptions of being close to the lower limit of acceptability, function, or empowerment in society.

Neurotransmitter: A chemical substance that is released from nerve endings to transmit impulses to other nerves or to muscles or glands.

Objectifying: The projection of thing or object status upon a person, rather than that of a human being. These "things" can be hurt without feeling guilty, because they cannot feel.

Social structure: The framework of society including the family unit and its hierarchy, gender, friends, sexuality, recreation, ethnicity, and social institutions.

Traditional links: Typical supports in society that include the nuclear family, the extended family, and religious and social service groups, which offer aid and stability within a community.

WEB LINKS

www.camh.net
The home site for the Centre for Addiction and Mental Health contains a wide range of information and resources on addictions of all kinds.

www.nida.nih.gov/
An American based resource for information on different aspects of drug addiction.

www.ccsa.ca/stats.htm
A list of links to sites that include Canadian statistics on alcohol and drug abuse.

www.ou-edu/oupd/bac.htm
This site contains an on-screen calculator for the user to determine blood-alcohol content.

www.ias.org.uk/factsheets/crime.htm
This site shows the international scope of the relationship between alcohol and crime. Notable is a study sponsored by the British government.

REFERENCES

Alcohol and Public Health Research Unit (2000). The association between alcohol and violence. Auckland, NZ: University of Auckland.

Stephen W. Baron & Timothy F. Hartnagel (1998). Street youth and criminal violence, 1998. *Journal of Research in Crime and Delinquency, 35*(2), 166–89.

Thomas J. Bernard (1990). Angry aggression among the "truly disadvantaged. *Criminology, 28*, 73–95.

Canadian Centre on Substance Abuse (1999). Canadian profile. www.ccsa.ca/Profile/cp99alc.htm

The Centre for Addiction and Mental Health (1999). Drug use among Ontario students. Press release, Toronto.

Rae Corelli & Barbara MacAndrew (1994). Booze and the badge. *Maclean's, 107*(13), 52–56.

Correctional Service of Canada (1999). Understanding violence by women: A review of literature. www.csc-cc.gc.ca/text/prgrm/fsw/fsw23/fsw23e01.shtml

Fredrick J. Desroches (1997). *Behind the bars: Experiences in crime.* Toronto: Canadian Scholars Press.

Andrew J. Dubrin & Terri Geerinck (2001). Human relations for career and personal success. Toronto: Pearson Education Canada Inc.

Jeffrey A. Fagan & Sally Jo Jones (1984). Towards an integrated model of violent delinquency. In Robert Mathias, Paul De-Muro, and Richard S. Allinson (Eds.), *An anthology on violent juvenile offenders.* Newark: National Council on Crime and Delinquency.

M. J. Hindelang, M. R. Gottfredson, and J. Garofalo (1978). *Victims of personal crime: An empirical foundation for a theory of personal victimization.* Cambridge, MA: Ballinger Publishing Company.

Ruth Horowitz (1983). *Honor and the American dream.* New Brunswick, NJ: Rutgers University Press.

James A. Incardi & Brian R. Russe (1997). Professional thieves and drugs. *International Journal of Addictions, 12,* 1087–95.

Jean Kinney & Gwen Leaton (1987). *Understanding alcohol.* St. Louis: Mosely Press.

Michael Manciaux (1993). Violent youth. *World Health, 46*(1), 24.

Brian Mitchell (2001). Theories of addiction. Unpublished presentation paper, The Centre for Addiction and Mental Health.

J. Moone (1994). *Juvenile victimization: 1987–1992* (Fact sheet 17). Washington, DC: Office of Juvenile Justice and Delinquency Prevention, US Department of Justice.

J. Madeleine Nash (1997, May 5). Addicted. *Time,* 69–76.

National Council on Addiction and Drug Dependence Inc. (1998). *FYI: Alcohol and crime.* New York: National Council on Addiction and Drug Dependence.

M. A. Plant, J. Orford, and M. Grant (1989). Effects on children and adolescents of parents' excessive drinking: An international review. *Public Health Reports, 104,* 433–42.

R. Room, S. J. Bondy, and J. Ferris (1995). The risk of harm to oneself from drinking. *Addiction, 90,* 499–513.

I. Rossow (1996). Alcohol related violence: The impact of drinking pattern and drinking context. *Addiction, 91,* 1641–51.

J. Tas-Junger (1996). Youth and violence in Europe. *Studies on Crime and Crime Prevention, 5,* 31–58.

chapter seven

Dealing with People with Mental Health Disorders

Courtesy Peterborough Lakefield Community Police Service

LEARNING OUTCOMES

After studying this chapter, you should be able to

- Define mental illness.
- Describe types of mental health disorders.
- Explain some of the causes and treatment of mental health disorders.
- Interact with people with mental health disorders.
- Discuss the issues regarding mental health facilities.

On-the-Job Scenario

You respond to a call for service for a woman threatening suicide at a rooming house in your area. En route, you determine through an occurrences check that police have responded at this address seven times in the last two months. You also learn that the subject has been taken to hospital on five of those occasions. As it turns out, your backup officer has dealt with this woman before and thus establishes a rapport quickly. The apartment is in a mess and you see a number of pill bottles scattered about the kitchen. The woman states that she wants kill to herself by overdosing on pills. You transport her to the hospital and wait until she is seen by the emergency room doctor, then assessed by the psychiatrist. After ten minutes, the nurse tells you that the woman has been given a mild sedative and is free to go.

One of the greatest challenges for front-line police officers is dealing with people who are affected by a mental health disorder. Despite misconceptions to the contrary, people with mental health disorders are generally neither violent, nor dangerous. Their behaviour can, however, be very unpredictable and perplexing, particularly to those who do not understand mental illnesses. When those with mental health disorders are violent or aggressive, the police are often called upon to assist in transporting them for treatment. As well as dealing with people with disorders themselves, police officers also must deal with the role of society in regards to available treatment facilities and the incarceration of those with disorders.

In this chapter, we will examine a number of mental health disorders, concentrating on those more likely to be seen by police officers. First, we will define mental illness and mental disorders. Then we will examine several types of disorders. Strategies to assist you in managing people with these types of disorders will follow. We will end the chapter by discussing some of the issues around mental health and their impact upon policing.

MENTAL ILLNESS AND DISORDERS

Mental illness is a broad term that refers to all of the diagnosable mental health disorders. These disorders are characterized by abnormalities in thought, feeling, perception, or behaviour and may substantially impair judgment, distort reality, and lead to an inability to function on a daily basis. Mental illnesses vary greatly in type and severity. Some of the more widely known illnesses or disorders are listed in the *DSM-IV* and include substance abuse, psychotic disorders, personality disorders, mood disorders, anxiety disorders, and cognitive disorders (Baron, Earhard, and Ozier, 1998; Public Health Service, 2000). In this chapter we will cover schizophrenia and psychosis, mood disorders, personality disorders, anxiety disorders, and developmental disorders, which are not all of the disorders. However, people with such problems are more likely to come into contact with police, so they were included in this chapter. However, we urge you to learn more about emotional disorders as part of continued professional development.

The most prevalent mental illnesses in Canadian society are substance abuse, anxiety disorders, and mood disorders. **Substance abuse** is the abuse of alcohol, drugs, tobacco, or other addictive items, which were discussed in the previous chapter. **Schizophrenia and psychotic disorders** are disorders that we traditionally think of as "madness." **Mood disorders** include major or clinical depression and bipolar disorder (manic depression). **Personality disorders,** which affect behaviour with others, are classified as rigid and inflexible behaviour and result in social or occupational problems or distress for the individual. **Anxiety disorders** include panic attacks, phobias, and obsessive-compulsive behaviour. Occurring at birth or in early childhood, **pervasive developmental disorders** (including mental retardation) are characterized by inability to develop life skills and by impaired intellectual functioning. Close to 20 per cent of Canadians experience some form of mental illness annually (Baron, Earhard, and Ozier, 1998).

Mental health workers often stress that the vast majority of people who suffer from a mental illness are not violent; a recent MIMH Epidemiological Catchment Area Study

(1999) indicates that 90 per cent of people with current mental health disorders are not violent. However, mental health disorders could make a person more likely to require the assistance of the police or emergency services. The majority of such contacts are not likely to be confrontational. However, in instances of personality disorders, severe mood disorders, and periods of psychosis (definition below), conflict with police is a possibility. Therefore, as with other information in these chapters, it would be helpful to understand types of disorders you may come into contact with while on patrol. For each of the disorders, we define the disorder and its symptoms, discuss possible causes, and provide a very brief overview of treatment or intervention. Not all causes and treatments are discussed. The purpose here is to provide a few details to expand your understanding of the disorder and of what people go through who face the intimidating task of "getting better," managing their condition, or dealing with loved ones who experience these disorders.

TYPES OF DISORDERS

There is a wide variety of disorders. Obviously, we cannot cover them all, because entire books are written on each of them. Here we just want to give you enough information so that you can recognize some of the symptoms that people may display. Also, a note of caution: not all people who show these symptoms have the disorder. Similarly, people who may act fine can suddenly show a recognizable pattern of mental illness. The major source for information on the classification and symptoms of mental disorders can be found in the *Diagnostic and Statistical Manual of Mental Disorders IV (DSM-IV)*. However, most practitioners and counsellors who deal with emotionally disturbed individuals know many of the symptoms without consulting any manual. As a police officer, you will soon learn many of the disorders of individuals that you encounter regularly.

SCHIZOPHRENIA AND PSYCHOTIC DISORDERS

In this section we will examine schizophrenia and psychosis. Both disorders share symptoms that severely affect an individual's ability to function normally.

Schizophrenia

Before describing what schizophrenia is, it is worthwhile to get rid of a commonly held myth about schizophrenia. Schizophrenia is not **multiple personality disorder** or **dissociate identity disorder,** as it is now known (Wand, 2000; SSO, 1999; Hales and Hales, 1996). **Schizophrenia** is a series of psychological disorders that can grossly distort a person's perception of his or her surroundings or reality. It alters not only the perception of self, but also that of those around the affected party. As described by the National Institute of Mental Health, schizophrenia shatters "the inner unity of the mind" and erodes "the will and drive that constitute our essential character" (Hales and Hales, 1996). The term itself is derived from the Greek terms: *schizo*, which means "split," and *phrenia*, which means "mind" (SSO, 1999). The symptoms of schizophrenia are divided into two main categories. **Negative symptoms** reflect the absence of normal functioning—symptoms such as lack of emotional response, lack of initiative, social withdrawal, and absence of movement (catatonic behaviour). **Positive symptoms**, on the other hand, are those symptoms we usually associate with mental illness and include hallucinations, delusions, and fragmented speech.

Schizophrenia comes in many different forms, the main types being **paranoid, undiffer-entiated**, **catatonic**, **disorganized**, and **residual**. Of these main types, paranoid and undif-ferentiated schizophrenia are most likely to result in psychotic episodes that erupt suddenly. The United States National Alliance for the Mentally Ill describes schizophrenia as a "chronic brain disorder" that "impairs a person's ability to think clearly, manage his or her emotions, make decisions, and relate to others," often leading to symptoms that "leave them fearful and withdrawn" (NAMI, 1999). This description is clinically correct, but the words do not convey what the affected person goes through. To help, we will review an officer-training initiative in Montgomery County, Maryland. The police department was attempting to improve its officers' efforts in dealing with mentally ill people. One officer, while wearing a set of portable stereo headphones that filled his head with the sounds of people screaming, was required to enter a convenience store and buy a newspaper. He was next to ask for change in nickels and dimes and then ask the attendant her name. The officer not only found that this simple task was made difficult, but he also was made uncomfortable by the reactions of people around him. He said, "Here's a situation where you can't blend in. You're a public spectacle" (Ly, 1999). If we thought of more dramatic symptoms, such as severe hallucina-tions or delusions, and imagined what it would be like to experience them in our everyday lives, we begin to understand the challenges faced by persons with schizophrenic disorders.

Causes

The exact causes of schizophrenia are still not known. What is known is that its basis is strongly biological, making it largely a disorder of the nervous system (SSO, 2000). Within this scope are assumptions about brain dysfunction and biochemical imbalances. There are other possible contributing factors, including genetic factors and the home environment (Baron, Earhard and Ozier, 1998, 2000).

Although its severity varies, approximately 300,000 Canadians suffer from schizophre-nia (SSO, 1999), which is about 1 per cent of the population. This number changes dra-matically, however, with the occurrence of schizophrenia within the family. A person with a sibling or one parent with schizophrenia has approximately a 10 per cent chance of devel-oping schizophrenia, and if there is a sibling and a parent with schizophrenia, the chance jumps to almost 50 per cent (Baron et al., 1998; Public Health Service, 2000).

Treatment

Schizophrenic disorders are not believed to be curable, but the symptoms are highly treat-able. Medication can significantly reduce or eliminate the positive symptoms, but the neg-ative symptoms are much less likely to be helped by medication. Anti-psychotic medication often produces side effects for the user.

Psychosis

Psychosis is a term that refers to disturbances in thought and perception patterns. These disturbances make it difficult for people with psychosis to determine what is reality, or from the perspective of the people with the disorder, they experience a reality different from that experienced by those around them. Psychotic symptoms are broken down into two basic areas: positive symptoms and negative symptoms. These symptoms are shared by many schizophrenics as well.

TABLE 7-1	Symptoms of Psychosis	
Positive Symptoms	**Negative Symptoms**	
Hallucinations	Flat or blunted effect or emotional responses	
Delusions	Concrete thoughts	
Disorganized thoughts and behaviours	Anhedonia (inability to experience pleasure)	
Loose or illogical thoughts	Poor motivation, spontaneity, and initiative	
Agitation		
Source: Public Health Service, 2000.		

The negative symptoms have the greatest long-term impact on the person suffering with the illness (Public Health Service, 2000). However, it is the positive symptoms that are the most notable outward manifestation of the psychosis and the area that police officers must deal with in confrontational situations.

The two most frequent symptoms of psychosis are hallucinations and delusions. Hallucinations occur when the individual experiences things that have no basis in reality. This input can be experienced through any of the senses: hearing, sight, smell, taste, or touch (Public Health Service, 2000; Baron, Earhard and Ozier, 1998). Although hallucinations are not actually occurring, they are as vivid to the person with the disorder as a real event would be. Auditory **hallucinations** are the most common type. In these cases, people hear sounds or often voices that are not heard by those around them. These voices might tell them to do something that they would otherwise not do, such as assault a stranger or mutilate themselves. Visual hallucinations can cause great fear for individuals with the disorder. They may see knives coming towards them, or walls falling down around them. As the police officer may be confused by the lack of sensory input that causes the fear or agitation, the people with the disorder may be confused by the lack of the officer's response to the threat.

Delusions are more complex and potentially more dangerous positive symptoms of psychosis. Delusions are falsely held beliefs held by the person with the disorder. Delusions of grandeur may lead individuals to believe that they are a famous pop star, politician, or religious figure (Public Health Service, 2000; Baron et al., 1998). Although the subject of fixation, such as a Jesus or Mohammed, may not be at all dangerous, and in fact be very virtuous, such people may become so self-righteous in their new persona that they may act upon their judgments of others, then rationalize their extreme behaviour. Likewise, their self-grandeur may be so elevated that they will not take directions or commands from "common" people.

The presence of the police uniform may also lead affected people down another path, so that now they think they are a leader of the Mafia or Hell's Angels. This may lead to conflict, because the persona they have taken on is the complete opposite of the symbol of order and authority that the uniform represents. The delusion may take on a more temporary or convenient form as well, such as the gentleman who justified his claim to being President Stone by stating, "See, it says so on my jeans."

Another common, and potentially dangerous, delusion is that of persecution or control. These delusions can be observed in extreme paranoia. People who line their living room walls in tin foil in an attempt to block out satellite transmissions from the CIA, may see that eliminating a prominent politician is the only way to ensure their survival. Others live in constant fear of people in general. A police officer might find a person cowering under a car, fearful of the person across the street. An officer will, of course, attempt to calm these fears, but a uniformed police officer may be seen as a member of the highest level of a conspiracy against them. The most sincere efforts to render help, and mention of hospitalization in particular, may only intensify the belief in conspiracy.

It is worth noting again that these delusions seem very real to the person with the disorder. The fears brought on by these delusions are extremely difficult to dispel with logic and reason. People in this state can be difficult to manage, and the onset of violence is a possibility.

Psychotic thought and speech are typically unconventional and disordered, leading to further confusion and mistrust. The affected person may have difficulty linking concepts or coming to logical conclusions. The conversation that began as a discussion about the neighbours' discomfort with someone screaming in the night, may conclude with a lengthy talk about crooked floor tiles and how they relate to the prime minister. Even if people's thought is quite logical, they may have difficulty expressing themselves. Their sentences may be fragmented or the words out of order. Affected people may even make up their own words or jumble them into a nonsensical "word salad" (Baron et al., 1998, 2000). The result of these symptoms is that resolving the problem can be made difficult, if not impossible.

In total, the symptoms of psychosis are a representation of (disturbances of) the flow, processing, and interpretation of information in the central nervous system. This condition is treatable with the use of prescription medication, but limited knowledge about the functions of the brain means that there is still much to be learned about the causes of psychosis (Public Health Service, 2000).

Causes of Psychosis

Psychotic symptoms can be caused by a variety of mental disorders, most notably schizophrenia and severe bipolar disorders.

Psychotic Episodes Caused by Other Factors

- Medical ailments such as brain tumours, severe infections, diabetes, and epilepsy
- Reaction to alcohol, drugs, or toxins
- Injuries to the head
- A combination of reasons that are made worse by acute distress; for instance, death of a loved one, work or school pressure, or divorce

These factors may cause serious psychotic reactions, but if the underlying cause is treated, a full and speedy recovery is very possible (Hales and Hales, 1996).

Treatment

The treatment of psychosis mirrors the treatment of schizophrenia, with medication used to alleviate or relieve psychotic symptoms.

MOOD DISORDERS

Mood disorders are disorders that affect individuals' experience of emotion or affect. **Emotion,** as we saw from chapter 5, is a physiological state of arousal that we define subjectively, affected by a variety of factors, including the situation and our own internal states. **Affect** refers to a pattern of observable behaviours associated with subjective feelings. For example, if you are experiencing happiness (emotion), then you may smile (display affect). **Mood** refers to a continuous emotional response that can alter a person's perception of the world if it is sustained over time (APA, 1994). Different from emotions and affect, mood disorders encompass the person's life and interfere with ability to function normally. Mood disorders discussed here are associated with two specific moods: depression and elation. Mood disorders are defined, then, in terms of episodes and imbalances of emotional states when a person's behaviour is dominated by either clinical depression or mania.

Unipolar Mood Disorder (Major Depression)

Unipolar mood disorder is a disorder in which a person experiences episodes of depression. Depression is different from ordinary sadness or gloom. **Depression** is characterized by overwhelming feelings of gloom, despondency, and dejection. Some depressed people describe their condition as feeling as if they are drowning or suffocating (Oltmanns and Emery, 1995). Depressed people often note that their thinking slows down and they feel guilty and worthless. While not all depressed people think of harming themselves, some experience feelings of self-destruction and some do eventually commit suicide.

Bipolar Mood Disorder

Bipolar mood disorder is a disorder in which a person experiences episodes of mania (manic episode) and depression (depressive episode). **Mania** is the opposite of depression and includes exaggerated feelings of physical and emotional well-being. Manic patients often report that their thoughts are speeded up. Grandiosity and inflated self-esteem are also characteristics of the manic phase. They talk quickly and have a decreased need for sleep (Oltmanns and Emery, 1995).

While all of us have mood swings, the moods are exaggerated in this disorder. The person alternates between bouts of depression and mania (APA, 1994). These moods last much longer than our normal mood swings, and the behaviours are often more noticeable. Two most notable symptoms of depressive episodes are a prolonged depressed mood and diminished interest or pleasure in daily activities. Other indicators of depression include significant weight loss or weight gain, insomnia or hypersomnia (oversleeping), physical overactivity or inability to engage in activity, loss of energy, and inability to think clearly. The person may also experience suicidal thoughts.

During the manic phase or episode, the most noticeable symptom is the elevation of mood that can include extreme feelings of wellness or irritability. This symptom is long-term, often lasting for more than a week. Other symptoms include inflated self-esteem, decreased need for sleep, excessive talking, distractibility, and over-indulgence in pleasurable activities (such as eating, drinking, shopping that the person cannot afford). For a more complete list of symptoms of bipolar disorder and depression, consult the *Diagnostic and Statistical Manual of Mental Disorders* (1994) or texts on abnormal psychology.

Causes of Mood Disorders

Mood disorders are caused by the combined effects of biological and psychological factors. Biological factors play a significant role in depression; genetic studies have demonstrated that mood disorders tend to run in families (Egeland et al., 1987). Other findings suggest that these disorders may also involve abnormalities in brain chemistry (Delgado et al., 1990). However, not all family members succumb to depression, and some people with chemical imbalances are also not depressed.

Psychological mechanisms are also important in the development of depression, including **learned helplessness.** People who suffer from learned helplessness believe they have no control over their lives. While these beliefs may have arisen from past situations they could not control, people generalize this helplessness to situations they could control if they attempted to. As you can probably guess, feelings of learned helplessness can lead to depression (Seligman et al., 1988). Depressed persons also engage in faulty or distorted thinking and tend to bring unhappy experiences to mind and dwell on them. They tend to notice, store, and remember information consistent with their negative moods (Mason and Graf, 1993). As well, depressed persons typically possess negative self-schemas or negative conceptions and perceptions of their own traits, abilities, and behaviour (Beck, 1976).

Treatment of Mood Disorders

With the focus on biology, some effective treatments include the use of drugs to increase the supply of low levels of brain chemicals found in depressed individuals. Other drugs can be used to lower some brain chemicals in those displaying symptoms of mania. The most commonly used antidepressant is Prozac (fluoxetine). Depressed persons who take this drug often report they feel better than they have in their entire lives (Baron et al., 2001). One major drawback of the reliance on medication is that people may stop taking the medications when they feel better. Unfortunately, this usually leads to the symptoms' return. Also, some people experience uncomfortable side effects, which may also lead them to discontinue their use.

Therapies that rely on changing the negative thinking of depressed persons have been effective. Cognitive therapists help the depressed person to move away from faulty thinking processes and learn to view the world in a more positive light.

PERSONALITY DISORDERS

Personality disorders are a group of disorders based not upon affliction so much as upon self-perceptions. These disorders revolve around the self, how the person sees himself or herself, how he or she relates to others, and on coping abilities. To be classified as a personality disorder, the behaviour is rigid and inflexible and creates significant social problems for the person. Unlike someone you would label as a neat freak, a person with an obsessive-compulsive disorder would be so neat and have to be so neat that it would actually interfere with his or her ability to function normally. The *DSM-IV* table outlines the three major classifications of personality disorders.

TABLE 7-2	The *DSM-IV* Table of Personality Disorders
Odd and Eccentric Personality Disorders	
Paranoid personality disorder	Pervasive distrust and suspiciousness of others
Schizoid personality disorder	Pervasive pattern of detachment from social relationships and restricted range of emotions
Schizotypal personality disorder	Intense discomfort in interpersonal relationships, cognitive or perceptual distortions, and eccentric behaviour
Dramatic, Emotional, and Erratic Personality Disorders	
Antisocial personality disorder	Deceitfulness, impulsivity, irritability, reckless disregard for safety and welfare of others, lack of remorse
Borderline personality disorder	Pervasive pattern of instability in interpersonal relationships, self-image, moods
Histrionic personality disorder	Pervasive pattern of excessive emotionality and attention seeking
Narcissistic personality disorder	Pervasive pattern of grandiosity in fantasy or behaviour, plus lack of sympathy
Anxious and Fearful Personality Disorders	
Avoidant personality disorder	Pervasive pattern of social inhibition, feelings of inadequacy, hypersensitivity to negative evaluation
Obsessive-compulsive personality disorder	Preoccupation with orderliness, perfectionism, and mental and interpersonal control
Dependent personality disorder	Pervasive and excessive need to be taken care of

Table reprinted with permission from American Psychiatric Association (2000) *Diagnostic and Statistical Manual of Mental Disorders* (4th ed., text revision). Washington, DC: Author.

As you can see, there are personality traits within the table that on the surface appear to be fairly common. You may have a friend who is that neat freak, whom you dub compulsive, or another who is high maintenance and you could label dependent. It can be a fine line between cautious and paranoid, between vain and narcissistic. The key word within the table is *pervasive*. Pervasive connotes a behaviour that is all encompassing. The other key term, common in each scenario, is *disorder*. People with a disorder have life significantly affected by this behaviour pattern.

While many of these disorders have a major impact on the affected person, they do not factor into police-related conflict. You may feel empathy for people whose obsessive-compulsive behaviour drives them to wash their hands repeatedly, but they may not come into contact with law enforcement personnel. However, one personality disorder, the antisocial personality, is most likely to have police contact. Therefore, this disorder will be discussed in more detail than the causes and treatment of the other personality disorders.

Antisocial Personality Disorder

The personality disorder describes a pattern of behaviour that is "socially irresponsible, disregards or violates the rights of others, exploits and possibly harms others, and provokes no remorse in the perpetrator" (Hale, 1995). This disorder, more than any other, has a direct link with crime and criminals. People with an antisocial personality disorder often show no remorse towards their victims and may not need a reason to cause harm. They are impulsive and will risk negative consequences for personal gain. With little morality, many of these people will break laws willingly. They have disregard for others' rights and show no remorse when they violate those rights. The term *sociopath* has been used in the past to describe people affected by anti-social disorder. While other disorders such as depression are upsetting for the person who is experiencing the symptoms, with this disorder (and some other personality disorders), these people do not see themselves as disturbed. They find their ideas and behaviours acceptable. A puzzling feature of the anti-social personality is that people with this disorder do not seem to learn from experience. Delinquency in youth (many antisocial personalities were diagnosed with conduct disorders as youth) is followed with crime as an adult.

According to the *DSM-IV,* the symptoms include failure to conform to social norms, deceitfulness (lying, use of aliases, conning others for profit), impulsivity or failure to plan ahead, irritability and aggressiveness, reckless disregard for safety of self or others, consistent irresponsibility (such as not holding a job), and a lack of remorse. They also rarely form emotional attachments and are often emotionally unreactive (although they can pretend to feel many emotions). When someone with this disorder is intelligent, good-looking, and charming, the results can be devastating. Many confidence artists and serial killers have been diagnosed with anti-social personality disorder.

It is interesting that this population has a high rate of alcoholism and substance abuse, which may also lead them to increased contacts with law enforcement (Baron et al., 2001).

Causes of Antisocial Personality Disorder

Psychologists have studied the possible causes of this disorder more extensively than for any of the other personality disorders (Oltmanns and Emery, 1995). Many factors appear to play a role in the development of this disorder that starts in childhood. The impulsivity and aggression may be linked to an inability to delay gratification—a skill learned early in childhood and a major component of emotional intelligence (Sher and Trull, 1994). Biological factors may also have an influence. Some research suggests that persons with this disorder show disturbances in brain function, including abnormalities in the neuro-transmitter serotonin (Lahey et al., 1993). Another interesting finding is that persons with this disorder also show reduced reactions to negative stimuli, particularly punished responses. In other words, these individuals continue to behave negatively even in the presence of punishers (e.g., Newman et al., 1985). Current research continues to try to understand why people with this disorder have difficulty inhibiting responses that have negative consequences. Whatever the causes of such a disorder, one point is clear: People with this disorder often pose a threat to themselves and others (Baron et al., 2001).

Treatment

Treatment is rare with antisocial personalities, because they seldom see anything wrong with their behaviour. Because they see nothing wrong with it, they seldom seek professional mental health services unless forced to do so by the legal system. When they do seek treatment, it is rarely effective (Quality Assurance Project, 1991). This treatment failure may be the result of an inability to form trusting relationships, the foundation of most treatment programs (Baron et al., 2001). Research literature on treatment is sparse. Most programs that have been evaluated focus on juvenile delinquents, imprisoned adults, or others referred by the criminal justice system. Success in these types of programs focuses on the frequency of repeated offences rather than behaviour changes linked to personality changes (Baron et al., 2001). At this point outcomes are rather pessimistic with this population, and further research is required.

ANXIETY DISORDERS

We have all experienced **anxiety**: increased arousal accompanied by generalized feelings of fear and apprehension. You may have had the experience of lying awake with your heart pounding on the night before an important job interview. This is normal anxiety. But when these feelings persist for long periods of time, they can produce harmful effects and become an **anxiety disorder**. Anxiety disorders are psychological disorders that centre on the occurrence of anxiety. These disorders include generalized anxiety disorder, panic attack disorder, phobias, and obsessive-compulsive disorders.

Generalized anxiety disorder can be described as "free-floating" anxiety: the person has a general sense of unease, discomfort, and distress that cannot be attributed to any one thing or event. With panic attack disorder, the person experiences intense anxiety for relatively brief periods. These attacks may include dizziness, palpitations, heart pounding, sensations of short breath, trembling, feeling of choking, chest pains, tingling sensations, and other physiological effects of heightened arousal. For the person experiencing the attack, the effect is often overwhelming, because the attacks can "come out of the blue," or they can be tied to specific situations. Phobias are intense, irrational fears of objects or events. Such fears can be so strong that they interfere with daily living and activities; for example, having such a fear of spiders that a person will not walk outside in the summer. The last type of anxiety disorder, obsessive-compulsive disorder, is characterized by the inability to stop thinking the same thoughts (obsessions) or performing the same ritualistic behaviours (compulsions). The individual starts thinking the thoughts that lead to intensifying anxiety to engage in a specific repetitive behaviour (i.e., handwashing). Engaging in the same compulsive behaviour reduces anxiety, but only temporarily. After a short period of time, the cycle repeats itself (thoughts, behaviour, and so on).

Police are rarely called to assist in managing these types of individuals, but there may be instances when you are called to do so. For example, a person's obsessive compulsion may include bizarre behaviours such as taking off his or her clothes in a public place.

Consider This...

A police officer is called to a restaurant where a woman refuses to leave the bathroom. The establishment is about to close, and all efforts to persuade her have not worked. Her husband tells the officer that she has a phobia about spiders and that she spotted one under their table. She ran into the bathroom, and is now afraid to come out because the spider is still somewhere in the restaurant.

Anxiety attacks in a public place may warrant the call of an ambulance, because these attacks can mimic the symptoms of a heart attack or other illness. In general, however, it can be safely said that police are rarely called to deal with people with these disorders.

Causes

Interestingly, there is a genetic component in panic attacks. Approximately half of people with panic disorder have relatives with this disorder (Barlow, 1988). Psychologically, it may be that individuals who experience panic attacks are excessively sensitive to their own bodily sensations and tend to exaggerate their importance, which causes anxiety and panic (Baron et al., 2001).

Phobias are closely linked with a learning process called classical conditioning, which is learning based on associations that bring out strong emotional reactions. For example, when you were young, you went to touch a spider. Just as you were about to touch it, your mother screamed. The loud scream frightened you, and you began to cry. This pairing of the spider and the scream (especially if it is repeated), eventually leads to a "conditioned response." In other words, whenever you see a spider now, you become terrified.

Psychological explanations of obsessive-compulsive disorder centre on the inability of people with this disorder to put disturbing thoughts or experiences out of their minds. Most people can distract themselves from experiencing unpleasant or intrusive thoughts, whereas people with this disorder cannot.

Treatment

Treatment for these disorders is often a combination of medication and some form of therapy. Anti-anxiety medications reduce many of the physical symptoms of anxiety; they can relax muscles, decrease heart palpitations, and reduce gastrointestinal distress. Antidepressants are also used for treatment in panic attacks.

Psychological treatment includes such methods as desensitization, which uses progressive relaxation techniques along with exposure to the fear object or event, in gradual sequences, from imagining the feared object to handling it. This type of treatment is very useful for phobias.

Cognitive therapy is used extensively in the treatment of anxiety disorders and is similar to that of the treatment in depression (Oltmanns and Emery, 1995). This type of therapy helps clients change their thought patterns in order to change their inappropriate responses. Therapists help clients identify the thoughts (cognitions) that are relevant to the problem; recognize the relationship between these cognitions (worrying about germs) and their maladaptive emotional responses (anxiety) and behaviours (such as excessive handwashing); examine evidence that supports or contradicts these beliefs; and teach more useful ways of interpreting events in their environment (Schuyler, 1991).

MENTAL RETARDATION AND PERVASIVE DEVELOPMENTAL DISORDERS

Mental retardation and pervasive developmental disorders are not mental health disorders, but we include this section because police officers may respond to calls for service that involve individuals who are affected by either.

You might be asking how you would ever become involved with this group of people, but you will be at one time or another. For example, mentally retarded or autistic people may get lost and fail to return home. As well, with different levels of retardation, these people feel the same emotions as you and I, including depression and anger. If you recall from chapter 5, people with lower levels of intelligence are more likely to use aggression as a response to anger or frustration. They may also be pressed into involvement in crime by people who make promises of friendship, or they may not know about laws.

Consider This...

Police were called to get a person off the roof of the post office. The attending officer was informed that the person had Down's syndrome and was very upset. The person had a job at the post office, and the post office personnel did not want to get involved.

Here we will briefly examine mental retardation and the pervasive developmental disorder, autism.

Mental Retardation

Mental retardation is characterized by a significantly reduced intelligence level that can range from profound to mild, and an inability or limited ability to learn adaptive life skills (Oltmanns and Emery, 1995). Although not politically correct, this term is still used by practitioners and is still labelled as such in the *DSM-IV*. (More appropriate terms are *mentally challenged* or *persons with special needs*.)

Mental retardation is classified into four types based on Intelligence Quotient (IQ) Scores: mild, moderate, severe, and profound. About 90 per cent of mentally retarded people are in the mild category (Baron et al., 2001). Those who are mildly retarded (IQ between 50 and 70) can live and function on their own with minimal assistance, holding down jobs and even raising a family. In fact, you will be unable to identify most mentally retarded people unless they have a recognized cause for their deficit such as Down's syndrome, a recognizable disorder caused by the presence of an extra chromosome.

Causes

Mental retardation can be caused by many factors, with about one-quarter of cases having a biological origin (Grossman, 1983). The most common biological cause of mental retardation is the chromosomal disorder, Down's syndrome. Various infectious diseases and infection contracted during pregnancy, birth, or in infancy or early childhood may cause it (Oltmanns and Emery, 1995). Toxins can also cause mental retardation and include drug and alcohol use by mothers during pregnancy. While not an exhaustive list of causes, this small sampling gives you a good understanding of the complexity of causes for mental retardation.

Treatment

There is no treatment for mental retardation. Efforts usually focus on helping the individuals acquire life skills and to realize their potential. No longer shunned or institutionalized, mentally retarded children go to school and participate in a wide variety of programs and activities with other children of all capabilities. Mentally retarded adults often hold down jobs that they can perform within their limited abilities.

A focus in recent years has been prevention of mental retardation. Programs that educate mothers and fathers on the effects of alcohol and drugs, proper nutrition, and lead poisoning are examples of such prevention.

Autism

Pervasive developmental disorders are unusual problems that begin early in life and involve severe impairments in a number of areas of functioning. Most people with pervasive developmental disorders are also mentally retarded (Oltmanns and Emery, 1995). Individuals with pervasive developmental disorders show profound disturbances in relationships, engage in repetitive, stereotyped activities, and typically have severe communication problems (Oltmanns and Emery, 1995). There are many pervasive developmental disorders that we will not cover, but we will focus on **autistic disorder (autism)** because it is the most carefully researched disorder in this category, although there is some debate on what autism really is. It is also referred to as autism spectrum disorder (Tsai, 2000). Our purpose here is not to get into this debate but to give you some useful information that will help you deal with persons who have autism.

Persons with autism are most readily identified by their communication difficulties and repetitive behaviours (especially when under stress): they may be nonverbal or only repeat what has been said, may not respond to commands, may appear argumentative or belligerent (such as saying, "No," or ask "Why?" in response to all questions), and may appear to be not listening and withdrawn. You can imagine, then, how difficult it is to ask such a person questions or obtain required information. They may speak in a monotone and may use inappropriate volume. Also, they may not stay on topic and launch into their favourite topics (such as cars, baseball) and talk while you are talking. Behaviourally, they may gauge personal space poorly and stand too close or too far away. They may have repetitive motions such as rocking or swaying, which may become more intense when they become upset. Some people with autism have objects that they must hold or play with, perhaps twirling string or hair, self-touching, clapping, or indulging in other hand play. Eye contact, too, can be a problem. Some people with autism seem to stare (or glare) at you, while others will not make eye contact at all. They may not recognize danger or dangerous situations and may not be able to differentiate between minor and serious problems. The last characteristic to be aware of is that many individuals with autism do not handle change well and prefer that things be orderly. Even a change in routine can bring on a tantrum or upset.

Causes

Autism is rare, with only four or five out of every 10,000 children being diagnosed with the disease. It appears to have multiple causes, including biological abnormalities and genetics (Oltmanns and Emery, 1995).

Treatment

There is no cure for autism, and there is still controversy around the treatment options for autistic children. Early intervention (preschool years) with a focus on the development of language skills has a more positive prognosis for children with autism than those who do not develop language skills. The teen years also appear to be a critical developmental time. Autistic teens who develop higher thinking and social skills improve notably, while those who don't, decline. It is also during the teen years that almost half of autistic children develop seizure disorders, which also supports the biological idea of causation (Wing, 1988).

The focus of treatment is much like that for those with mental retardation. Teaching life skills and communication are the two areas of focus done, using a variety of methods, the most popular being behaviour modification (using rewards and punishments to obtain desired responses).

STRATEGIES FOR DEALING WITH PEOPLE WITH MENTAL HEALTH DISORDERS

In this section, we will explore techniques that help you manage interventions with some of these populations. Some strategies rely on your ability to calm the person with techniques to reduce agitation and confusion. Three approaches will be reviewed, those for persons exhibiting psychotic behaviour, followed by ones for mentally retarded and autistic persons.

Consider This...

A call is received by a distraught mother because her 21-year-old schizophrenic son has locked himself in the basement. He has been there for over 15 hours and has not taken his medication. Two officers arrive at 8:00 p.m. and talk the man into coming out of the basement. At first he is pleasant, although extremely dirty and rambling in his speech. Suddenly, he tries to attack one of the officers, screaming that he refuses to leave this planet.

Strategies for Dealing with Psychotic Behaviour

People who are displaying psychotic behaviours may be schizophrenic, in the manic phase of bipolar disorder, or under the influence of some sort of drug. Their mood can change very quickly, and you need to maintain your alertness at all times.

Here are some effective methods to assist with managing this population:

- **Don't become complacent.** Remember that the person is affected by a disorder. Outcomes that seem logical to you may not apply in these circumstances. You may be lulled into thinking that you have a genuine rapport with the subject, but then a seemingly innocuous gesture or action may trigger an aggressive response. As a police officer, you are trained to assist victims, and you may rightly see the affected party as a victim. You must, however, recall that the situation can become violent at any time, and that your complacency could harm yourself, the public, or even the affected party.

- **Don't try to convince the person that the hallucinations are not real.** Recall that the hallucinations are very real to the person experiencing the disorder. By trying to talk the person out of the disorder, you are putting your credibility at risk and increasing the tension between yourself and the subject.

- **Don't state that you share the person's delusion or see his or her hallucination.** You are playing with fire if you attempt to "play along" with the delusion. This approach has many possible negative ramifications, which include reinforcing the delusion or making it worse. It is also quite likely that the affected person will see through your attempt, and your empathy will be seen as condescension, or worse still, deception. The result is a loss of credibility.

- **Don't touch the subject, if at all possible.** This brings up concerns about *safe search* and *prisoner control*. However, touching a person during a psychotic, and especially a paranoid, episode often escalates the situation tremendously. If you cannot search surreptitiously, then announce and explain your intentions clearly and plainly. There is an additional concern when placing the subject in the back of the cruiser. A person suffering from paranoid disorders is likely to feel extremely threatened and vulnerable while handcuffed and behind a "cage," and may even feel in danger of being taken away to be killed. If possible, consider transporting by ambulance, but recall that the subject is your responsibility, not that of the ambulance crew.

- **Don't underestimate the power of your uniform in the situation.** Remember that the uniform is a powerful symbol. You may represent safety and order, but it is more likely that you represent power and control to the affected person. You might be seen as the instrument of the powers that are conspiring against them. Emphasize your humanity by showing that you care about the person's welfare. Engage in small talk, but stay with subjects that are neither controversial nor too personal. Try to project beyond the uniform.

- **Don't use humour.** Humour is often a great tension reliever, but people with mental disorders that lean towards paranoia may believe that you are making light of their condition or laughing at them. Unless you are familiar with the affected person and know that humour has a calming effect, save your new comedy schtick for the crew at the station.

- **Do use a calm voice and use plain language.** Recall the overwhelming sensory input that psychotic people can experience. By being calm and avoiding police or medical jargon, you can help settle the person down.

- **Do listen intently to the psychosis as described by the subject.** With auditory hallucinations, people may hear voices that direct them to take actions. These actions can be harmful or violent. By paying close attention to the content of these "messages" you may be able to anticipate acts of aggression. With visual hallucinations, the person may see innocent objects as being threatening. You may be able to remove these items and put the subject more at ease.

- **Do use the information resources available to you.** As you would with the intoxicated person in chapter 6, use **CPIC** and occurrence information to learn as much as you can about the subject. In the case of a mentally ill person, try to obtain as much information as you can prior to contact or out of earshot of the subject. If time allows, you may consider contacting your local hospital or mental health facility in order to ascertain his or her mental health profile.

- **Do be honest and open in your behaviour.** Be forthright in your actions. Do not tell the person that you are taking him or her to the hospital when your intention is to go to the station. Your credibility in this and future encounters could be compromised. Unless it could put yourself or others at risk, announce any overt actions that you intend to make. Your goal is to create an atmosphere of stability, not one of surprise and uncertainty.

Strategies for Dealing with a Person with Mental Retardation

The strategies here rely on your ability to understand mental retardation and the wide range of intelligence in this population. Chances are the person you will deal with will be mildly retarded and have some skills. While not a complete list, here are some techniques that are useful when communicating with this population:

- **Use simple language and short sentences.** If the person is lost or disoriented, he or she will be very upset, possibly crying. Reassure the person that you are here to help. Remember that although an adult, this person may have the cognitive capabilities of a child ranging in the Grade 2 to Grade 6 level of understanding. However, talking plainly and simply does not mean condescending or being child-like.

- **You may need to use physical guidance.** When managing a more profoundly retarded person, you may need to use physical guidance and signs. Someone with a very low level of intelligence may not understand requests such as "Get in the back of the car and I'll take you home." Gentle guidance may be in order, but if you encounter any resistance, try another approach.

- **Pay attention to nonverbal hand signs.** Some nonverbal mentally retarded people use rudimentary sign language, so if a person starts making gestures that you are unfamiliar with, it may be sign language rather than just random displays of hand play. Some wear aprons with symbols on them or have boards that they use to tell people what they want.

- **Check for identification.** Many mentally retarded individuals have identification with name, address, and contact information. Often it is not in a wallet, but on a bracelet or necklace, or sewn inside clothing. Check for this helpful information when dealing with someone you do not know or is unable to give a full name. Contact the person on the identification right away, because this person may have more information and could assist you immediately.

- **Remember that a mentally retarded person can also be a crime suspect.** Just because this person has a disability, it does not mean the he or she cannot be violent or dangerous.

Strategies for Dealing with a Person with Autism

Like mental retardation, autism varies in severity, and techniques will vary in their effectiveness, depending upon the person's skill and communication level. All of the previous approaches that help people with mental retardation also apply to individuals with autism. However, here are some additional techniques to assist you. These techniques are used by one of the authors and some of them are taken from a law enforcement handout (Debbaudt, 1999).

- **Allow for delays in speech and behaviour**. Many people with autism display delays to requests or in responding. Allow the person time to respond. Remain patient.

- **Display calm body language**. Do not move quickly. Use lower gestures and keep hands down. If you start talking excitedly or using forceful gestures, the person will "turn off," and worse, may become agitated. When they become agitated, many autistic people engage in self-abusive behaviours like head-banging or self-biting, or they try to run and hide.

- **Avoid touching and increase personal space**. Many autistic persons do not respond well to being touched, especially around the shoulders or face. Also, avoid standing too near or behind the person. Again, you do not want to increase agitation.

- **Do not try to stop repetitive behaviours**. The stereotypical or repetitive behaviours help relax the person. Do not stop the behaviour unless it is self-injurious or dangerous to others. If these behaviours increase in speed, this may indicate that the person is becoming more upset.

- **Check for injury.** Some autistic persons do not feel pain unless it is severe. If there has been an incident where injury may have occurred, do not rely on outward signs that the person is not in pain.

- **Be sensitive to the person's fears.** The person may have fears or be overly sensitive to a variety of everyday things such as lights, loud noises, and even smells. Try to remove these items if possible.

- **Err on the side of caution.** If you are not sure that the person is autistic and the person is being taken into custody, segregate the person from the general population. There is a high level of risk for abuse.

ARREST POWERS IN MENTAL HEALTH INCIDENTS

Of course, police officers have the power to arrest people who commit criminal offences. Police officers also have the power to arrest people in matters relating directly to mental health. The arrest powers in these cases are to be found in **provincial statutes,** such as the Mental Health Act in Ontario. The arrest powers will therefore vary somewhat from province to province, but in general a police officer has the authority to arrest a person where there is **reasonable grounds** to believe that a person acting in a disorderly manner may do something to cause serious harm to him- or herself or others, or is unable to care for him- or herself. The officer must also determine that it would be unsafe to delay, while attempting to use other sections of the legislation, such as the signing of a **form of committal** by a physician.

The most obvious use of these arrest powers is the apprehension of a subject who is threatening suicide or one who is wandering in and out of traffic, unaware of the potential for harm. While the need for action is obvious in these scenarios, it also has a great potential for conflict. People who have no regard for their own life, or have no concept of danger, could pose a significant threat to attending police officers. Strategies for dealing with suicidal people will be discussed in more depth in the next chapter.

A less clear-cut use of these arrest powers occurs when family members are concerned about someone who is acting irrationally but has not put anyone in danger. Another common concern is for an elderly person or one with a mental disorder who presents a risk to him- or herself by the improper use of electrical appliances that could cause a fire, or who shows a lack of ability to feed and care for him- or herself. In these instances, the attending police officer must gather as much information as possible in order to make a responsible decision.

In some cases, the subject's actions may not meet the threshold of need for arrest. This can be a very uncomfortable situation for the officer, because the family may be at their wits' end in dealing with the subject. The police may be their only hope in resolving the matter. This same family could become angry with the police, lashing out at what they see as their inability or refusal to take action. The appropriate response in matters such as this is to provide as much information as possible to the family, including specific referral contacts if appropriate. Officers must bear in mind the possible consequences if they make a mental health arrest without proper grounds. There are criminal concerns with regards to the use of force where grounds for arrest did not exist. There are civil concerns to be aware of; the same family that wanted the officer to act, regardless of the legislation, may want their pound of flesh if their family member is injured as a result of the arrest. The officer's best friend in these scenarios is good judgment, a sound knowledge of statutes and their authorities, and a solid base of conflict resolution skills.

| **POINTS FOR PONDERING** | *Mental Illness in the Prison Population* |

It has been estimated that people affected with anti-social personality disorder comprise up to three-quarters of the prison population (Hales and Hales, 1996). If substance abuse is factored into the equation, the percentage in Canada lies somewhere between 50 per cent and 90 per cent (Hodgins and Cote, 1990; Motiuk and Porporino, 1991; Wormith and Borzecki, 1985). A further 10 to 30 per cent of Canadian inmates are thought to be affected by serious mental health disorders such as depression, bipolar disorder, schizophrenia, or organic disorder (Correctional Service of Canada, 2000). These numbers are truly staggering, especially when it is taken into account that persons affected by mental health disorders are by definition victims themselves.

What are the reasons for these statistics? Part of the problem is sheer numbers. Figures in the United States indicate that people with mental health disorders comprise 13 per cent of offenders entering the judicial system every year, compared to their makeup of the general population, which is less than 2 per cent (The Center on Crime, Communities and Culture, 1996).

Not all offenders with disorders are incarcerated; some accused parties are re-routed through the mental health system for treatment or assessment. There are, however, problems with the mental health system in dealing with offenders. The health care system across the country is increasingly under pressure to decrease costs. The inevitable cost-cutting, not surprisingly, leads to decreased facilities available to treat and accommodate persons with disorders. If a mental health facility cannot accommodate a person arrested for an offence, the only alternative left to police is often to charge them. Then the offender is in the hands of the judicial system, not the health care system. Officers have the option of requesting that the courts require that the accused receive a forensic *psychiatric assessment*; however, this type of assessment only determines the accused person's mental state in relation to the specific charge. The accused person may well be found to be not responsible for his or her actions, but further treatment may not be ordered. The result is that this person may be released into the community without having had the disorder addressed.

The shortage of treatment facilities affects people with disorders even before police contact. If somebody with a disorder is unable to find proper treatment, the symptoms are likely to worsen. This, in turn, increases the chances of encountering conflict as a result of the disorder, leading quite possibly to arrest.

Treatment and assessment may be only a short-term solution, with the subject possibly returning to the street to reoffend.

SUMMARY

This chapter explored some of the mental health disorders that you may come into contact with during your career in policing. Mental health disorders are characterized by abnormalities in thought, feeling, perception, or behaviour, and may substantially affect judgment, distort reality, and lead to an inability to function normally. Four types of mental disorders were reviewed: schizophrenia and psychotic disorders, mood disorders, personality disorders, and mental retardation and pervasive developmental disorders.

Several individual disorders were discussed including symptoms, possible causes, and treatment. Schizophrenia, bipolar and unipolar disorder, and antisocial personality disorder were discussed in some detail, because individuals with these disorders are more likely to have police contact than with many other types of disorders. Mental retardation and autism were included because people with these disorders may come into contact with police for a variety of reasons including becoming lost or crime involvement.

Next, some of the issues concerning arrest powers were explored, for in some cases it may be unclear whether or not an arrest is warranted. Last, mental illness in the prison population was featured, because high numbers of people with mental illness reside in Canadian prisons.

CASE STUDY

You and your partner respond to a radio call at a group home for autistic adults where one of the residents has assaulted a staff member. When you enter the backyard of the facility, you observe a staff member speaking very firmly with a resident known to you as Norma. The staff member is trying to move Norma inside, but every time he tries to lead her by the arm, Norma slaps his hand and waves her fist at him. She is rocking back and forth on her feet and appears very agitated. Your partner, Bill, with six months' experience, and no experience with Norma, thinks that it is time to lay down the law. He approaches Norma from the side, shouts, "Hey, stop it," at her and holds the resident by the shoulders. Norma spins around and grabs his hands. Bill begins to panic when he realizes that he cannot free himself from Norma's grasp. Just as you worry that Bill might do something drastic, the staff member distracts Norma, and Bill breaks free, shaking his hands in pain.

Questions

1. What was wrong with Bill's approach to Norma?
2. Using what you know from this chapter, what would have been a better way to approach Norma?

KEY TERMS

Affect: The pattern of observable behaviours associated with specific subjective emotions.

Antisocial personality disorder: A personality disorder involving a lack of conscience, impulsivity, poor sense of responsibility, irritability, and aggressiveness.

Anxiety: Increased physiological and psychological arousal accompanied by fear or apprehension.

Anxiety Disorder: A disorder that involves intense anxiety out of proportion with the object or event.

Autism (autistic disorder): A pervasive developmental disorder characterized by severe problems in social interaction, communication, and stereotyped behaviours, interests, and activities.

Bipolar mood disorder: A type of mood disorder in which a person experiences periods of mania and depression.

Central nervous system: The brain and spinal cord areas, which are responsible for the integration of the nervous activities of the body.

CPIC: The Canadian Police Information Centre, a national, centralized database for the storage and retrieval of criminal records, criminal charges, wanted person information, and prohibition orders.

Depression: A psychological disorder characterized by intense sadness, lack of energy, and feelings of hopelessness and despair.

Delusions: Falsely held beliefs that are not based in reality.

Emotion: A state of arousal that is defined by subjective feelings such as anger, happiness, and sadness. Emotions are accompanied by varying degrees of physiological arousal.

Forensic psychiatric assessment: A court-ordered psychiatric evaluation that determines if the accused had sufficient mental faculties to be accountable for his or her actions at the time of the offence.

Form of committal: A document signed by a family physician, psychiatrist, or justice of the peace that gives authority for the involuntary admittance of a patient for a psychiatric assessment.

Hallucinations: Experiences of things that have no basis in reality, including seeing things that are not there.

Learned helplessness: Feelings of helplessness that develop after exposure to situations in which outcomes could not be controlled that led to later behaviour of helplessness when outcomes could be controlled.

Mania: A disturbance in mood characterized by elation, inflated self-esteem, hyperactivity, an exaggerated feeling of well-being, and accelerated speech and thinking.

Mental retardation: Considerably lower levels of intellectual functioning, usually with varying degrees of difficulty in meeting the demands of daily life.

Mood disorders: Psychological disorders characterized by extreme and prolonged mood shifts.

Multiple personality or dissociate disorder: A mental health condition that leads a person to believe that there is more than one person operating within himself or herself. There is much debate about whether this condition actually exists.

Negative symptoms: Absence of something normally present.

Panic attack disorder: An anxiety disorder characterized by relatively brief, but repeated, episodes of unbearably intense anxiety.

Personality disorders: Extreme and inflexible personality traits that restrict individuals' abilities to enter into and maintain social relations with others.

Pervasive developmental disorders: Disorders that involve lifelong impairment in cognitive and mental functioning.

Phobias: Unrealistic fears of objects or events, which have no basis in reality.

Positive symptoms: Presence of something normally absent.

Provincial statute: A law or regulation that is applicable only in the province of origin. This compares to the criminal code, which is national.

Reasonable grounds: Facts that would lead a reasonable person to draw a conclusion. This goes beyond mere suspicion. This used to be termed reasonable and probable grounds, or RPG.

Residual disorders: Disorders that occur after major psychotic episodes.

Schizophrenia: A group of psychotic disorders characterized by positive and negative symptoms and a deterioration in role functioning. There are four major types of schizophrenia:

Catatonic: Dealing with patterns of motor skills and activity, including rigid poses or repetitive speech.

Disorganized: A delusional state that lacks cohesiveness or order. The delusions do not follow a pattern or theme.

Paranoid: Delusions that are conspiratorial, with the affected persons believing that others are "after them" or intent on doing them harm.

Undifferentiated: A combination of symptoms including delusions, hallucinations, and incoherent thoughts.

Unipolar mood disorder: The depressive phase in bipolar disorder; also used to describe a major depressive episode.

WEB LINKS

www.apa.org
This is the site for the American Psychological Association. There is a "public" area that is searchable, containing information on a variety of mental health topics ranging from health care to mental disorders.

www.cpa.ca
This is the "sister" site of the APA, the Canadian Psychological Association.

www.clas.ufl.edu/users/gthursby/psi/directs.htm
Part of the World Wide Web Virtual Library, this is a directory to a wide range of psychology sites.

REFERENCES

American Psychiatric Association (1994). *Diagnostic and statistical manual of mental disorders* (4th edition). Washington, DC: Author.

Robert Baron, Bruce Earhard, Marcia Ozier (1998, 2001). *Psychology*. Scarborough, ON: Prentice-Hall Canada.

D. H. Barlow (1988). *Anxiety and its disorders: The nature and treatment of anxiety and panic.* New York: Guilford Press.

A. Beck (1976). *Cognitive therapy and the emotional disorders.* New York: International Universities Press.

The Center on Crime, Communities and Culture (1996). *Mental illness in jail: Diverting the nonviolent, low-level offender* (Research Brief, Occasional Paper Series, No. 1). New York: Open Society Institute.

Correctional Service of Canada (2000). Treating violent offenders: A Review of Current Practices. Diagnosis and Co-Morbidity. www.csc-cc.gc.ca/text/rsrch/reports/r38/r38e04.shtml

Dennis Debbaudt (1999). Avoiding unfortunate situations. www.geocities.com/HotSprings/Spa/7762/police_autism.html

P. L. Delgado, D. S. Charney, L. H. Price, et al. (1990). Serotonin function and mechanism of antidepressant action: Reversal of antidepressant-induced remission by rapid depletion of plasma atrytpophan. *Archives of General Psychiatry*, 47, 411–18.

J. A. Egeland, D. S. Gerhard, D. L. Pauls, et al. (1987). Bipolar disorders linked to DNA markers on chromosome 11. *Nature, 325*, 783–87.

H. J. Grossman (1983). *Classification in mental retardation.* Washington: American Association on Mental Deficiency.

Dianne Hales & Robert E. Hales (1996). *Caring for the mind: The comprehensive guide to mental health* (pp. 409–558). New York: Bantam Books.

B. B. Lahey, E. L. Hart, S. Pliszka, et al. (1993). Neurophysiological correlates of conduct disorder: A rationale and a review of research. Special Issue: The Neuropsychological basis of disorders affecting children and adolescents. *Journal of Personality and Social Psychology, 47*, 909–17.

Phuong Ly. Vanguard police training fosters empathy for mentally ill (2000, December 29). *San Francisco Chronicle.*

M. E. Mason & P. Graf (1993). Introduction: Looking back into the future. In P. Graf and E. J. Mason (Eds.), *Implicit memory: New directions in cognition, development, and neuropsychology* (pp. 1–11). Hillsdale, NJ: Erlbaum.

National Alliance for the Mentally Ill. The Nation's Voice on Mental Illness (1999). Information on Illnesses and Treatment. www.nami.org/illness/index.html

J. P. Newman, C. S. Widom, and S. Nathan (1985). Passive avoidance in syndromes of disinhibition: Psychopathy and extraversion. *Journal of Personality and Social Psychology, 48*, 1316–27.

National Institute of Mental Health (2001). When someone has schizophrenia. www.nimh.nih.gov/publicat/schizsoms.cfm

Thomas F. Oltmanns & Robert E. Emery (1995). *Abnormal psychology.* Engelwood Cliffs, NJ: Prentice-Hall Inc.

Public Health Service (2000). *Mental Health: A Report of the Surgeon General.* Pueblo, CO: Government of the United States.

Schizophrenia Society of Ontario (1999). What is schizophrenia? www.schizophrenia.on.ca/schiz.html

D. Schuyler (1991). *A practical guide cognitive therapy.* New York: Norton.

K. J. Sher & T. J. Trull (1994). Personality and disinhibitory psychopathology: Alcoholism and anti-social personality disorder. *Journal of Abnormal Psychology*, 103, 92–102.

Luke Tsai (2000). Children with autism spectrum disorder: Medicine today and in the new millennium. *Focus on Autism and Other Developmental Disabilities, 15(3)*, 138–46.

Quality Assurance Project (1991). Treatment outlines for anti-social personality disorders. *Australian and New Zealand Journal of Psychiatry, 25,* 541–47.

United States Surgeon General Report (2000). Mental Health: A Report of the Surgeon General.

L. Wing (1988). Autism: Possible clues to the underlying pathology—1. In L. Wing (Ed.), *Aspects of autism: Biological research* (pp. 11–18). London: Gaskell.

chapter eight

Negotiations and Mediation

Courtesy Peterborough Lakefield Community Police Service

LEARNING OUTCOMES

After studying this chapter, you should be able to

- Explain the basics of negotiation and bargaining.

- Understand third-party intervention.

- Assess the feasibility of negotiation situations.

- Explain the role of the first-response officer.

- Have more understanding of suicide and negotiation strategies to reduce the chances of suicide.

- Explain the role of mediation in some policing situations.

On-the-Job Scenario

While on patrol, you receive a call for a woman on the top of an overpass, threatening to jump into traffic. Arriving on scene, you find pandemonium. There is a trio of passers-by shouting well-intentioned but conflicting instructions at the distraught woman. Through the gathering crowd of onlookers comes a TV camera crew trying to set up for the perfect shot. You are only six months out of Police College and have never dealt with anything like this before. During the two minutes, which seem like two hours, that you are alone waiting for backup, all eyes are on you to resolve the situation.

The above scenario is not an everyday occurrence, yet it is not uncommon either. When the public sees a uniformed officer arrive at the scene, they do not look for grey hair to assess the officer's experience or capability. They expect to see the matter resolved quickly and professionally, whatever the situation.

Negotiation. The word conjures up visions of command posts, heavily armed tactical officers, and loud-hailers. A crisis, such as a hostage taking or a standoff with an armed person, is an occasion for a cohesive, tactical response. There are, however, many more everyday negotiations that police officers are party to. There are the suicide threats: people jumping from a bridge, slashing wrists, or taking pills. The stakes are no smaller, but there's often no time for a trained negotiator. Then there are the even more mundane negotiations: the neighbour disputes, custody disputes, and noise complaints. The urgency is diminished, certainly for the attending officer, but feelings, perceptions, and relationships may hinge on the skill of the mediating officer. Third-party interventions are a challenge, but they can provide dividends for the officer and complainant alike.

This chapter examines more closely the use of negotiation in policing, and includes an overview of negotiation, police applications of negotiation, third-party intervention, dealing with difficult co-workers, aspects of crisis negotiation, techniques for first responding officers, dealing with suicides, and mediation.

NEGOTIATION AND BARGAINING

The reader may, or may not, be surprised that police negotiation techniques had their beginnings not within police circles, but in the business sector. Police officers generally see themselves as being completely different from business people, and find the corporate culture to be counter to that of policing. If you want proof of this, just try to find one officer who has never said, "If a business ran like this department, they'd be broke." Law enforcement officers view their work as very different from the dollars and cents bottom line of the business world, and in a public service career this is only fitting. However, with a fiscal bottom line, and no government funding to bail them out, the corporate world has had to learn to negotiate successfully for its very survival.

Negotiation is the act of two or more people conferring in order to reach a mutually agreeable solution. This is a very basic definition, but one that conveys its essence. Whether it is a case of an employee seeking a raise from her employer, a customer and a salesperson haggling over the price of a car, or a police negotiator trying to resolve a hostage standoff with a bank robber, in each instance, the parties involved have their own objectives, but cannot obtain that objective alone. A dialogue is necessary for the participants to meet their needs. In business or everyday life, there are basic principles and techniques to a negotiation (Dubrin and Geerinck, 2001).

Police officers may operate with policing styles very different from their partners'. Rather than being at odds with the person seated beside you for ten hours or more, you could use negotiation skills to arrive at a style of policing that combines the two divergent styles. Here are several techniques that will assist you in negotiation with others.

Create a Positive Climate

Negotiations are not unilateral, so each side must believe that it is possible to achieve its objective. Opening a session on an upbeat note, where each participant is comfortable and feels secure, can set the tone for the entire negotiation. Open, nonverbal communications will go a long way to creating this positive climate. A smile and occasional affirmative nod demonstrates much more interest than a stern look and crossed arms. Demands will, of course, be made in the course of a negotiation, but they can be phrased as requests, sought cooperatively. The employee may have it in the back of her mind that she will quit if she does not get her raise, but cannot open the talks this way and expect to achieve her goals. By approaching the talks in a mutual problem-solving, rather than adversarial way, you can help to create a climate in which both sides respect one another.

If an officer polices with a more aggressive approach than her more senior partner, she can start the shift by opening, "I really like working with you. We do the job a little differently, but we complement each other well." This creates a cooperative atmosphere, yet suggests that compromise may be required.

Allow Room for Compromise, But Be Reasonable

A basic negotiation strategy is to open talks with a demand that still leaves room for compromise. The other participant can then allow for concessions that both sides can live with. The salesperson might target $10,000 for the car on the lot, while the customer may want to pay $7,000. It is very unlikely that either party will achieve the first price, but both can come away with their objectives. Should the customer start with a "lowball" figure of $5,000, or the salesperson start with an unrealistic $15,000, the other may become offended and end negotiations or bargaining there. As a result, this strategy must be tempered with a good deal of common sense. The satisfaction of those involved will depend upon their skills as negotiators, their eagerness to settle, and the integrity of the other party.

The more aggressive officer should not expect her partner to convert completely to her policing approach. She could achieve a compromise by choosing certain calls to express her wishes: "I think that in this case we should arrest this guy sooner rather than later and be done with it."

Focus on Interests, Not Positions

Keep the overall goal of the negotiation in mind, rather than focusing on individual points of the negotiation. If the woman negotiating for the higher salary is offered $500 less in yearly wages than she had desired, but is offered an additional $2,000 a year in benefits, she would be shortsighted to dismiss the offer without time for reflection. If her goal were to raise her standard of living, she would be $1,500 ahead of her goals.

In the case of the two officers, an all-or-nothing approach may not be advisable. By requesting a change of partner, the officer could sour a working relationship, or end up with a partner with a greater divergence in style.

Try a Final, Take It or Leave It Offer

In many cases, a believable final offer will end a deadlock. If the customer states that he will offer $8,900 for the car, "but not a penny more," he is indicating that he is no longer willing to negotiate. This may be $100 less than the salesperson's bottom line, but that sum may not be worth watching a prospective customer walk out the door and have to start from scratch. This should not be presented in the form of an ultimatum, but rather in terms of "this is as high as I can afford." This offer must, however, be believable. If you offer $90, but have $100 in hand, chances are that the other side will hold out for the $100.

At times, an officer might have a line that he or she cannot cross in a working relationship. Instead of waiting for trouble to happen and dealing with it then, she can state, "If we cannot agree on this, I'll have to request a new partner," and that is not a desirable situation. By clearly stating a bottom line, both officers are more likely to work towards a compromise.

Allow for Face-saving

This is more than a negotiating and almost deserves a separate heading. When negotiating, people can be hard-nosed, and after winning, rub the win into the other side's face. Buzz Hargrove of the CAW is known for this approach: once he showed up with a baby spoon and Pablum, after having his demands met by a major auto maker. He was quoted as saying that the company would take his demands "like babies to their first solid foods: they spit it out at first but learn to like it" (Canadian Press, 1996). While sensational, such tactics will not endear you to the other side and may hinder future negotiations. People prefer to avoid looking weak, foolish, or ineffectual during or after negotiations.

The more aggressive officer might have an opportunity for an "I told you so," where the two attend an address three times, yet eventually arrest the subject. A remark like, "Some people just don't see a break when it's given to them," puts the failure of the partner's "more accommodating" approach on the shoulders of the subject. As a result, the partner does not become defensive and is more likely to compromise in the future.

If you wondered if the police negotiation scenario could fit into these models, it certainly can. If you think hard enough, you could superimpose that situation into any of the techniques we've reviewed. This final technique is one of the most important of negotiation strategies. This technique means that you can win without completely destroying the other participant. It can easily be seen in business terms: developing a long-term client rather than a one-time customer. The idea of retaining the other's self-respect is equally important in police negotiations. Police officers would rather not have repeat customers, but the opposite is true, more often than not. If a negotiator "cons" a suspect into giving himself up, or embarrasses him in the process, future negotiations with that person will be much more difficult. Face-saving allows the party to retain his or her pride and dignity. Take the bank robber who botches the holdup and ends up with a room full of hostages. One of the first things he says, in the heat of the moment, is the familiar, "You'll never get me alive, coppers!" After several hours, the suspect realizes that he has no way out, but is too proud to merely surrender. The negotiator could ensure that the entire tactical team makes the arrest, rather than two regular uniformed officers. The robber could surrender, and with his self-respect intact, tell his buddies, "It took ten of them to take me down."

POLICE APPLICATIONS

While applicable to policing, the five negotiation techniques just mentioned are everyday approaches to resolving problems. There are other, more police-specific, negotiation guidelines.

Containment

Unless your boss is Attila the Hun, you will not have to establish an inner and outer perimeter in order to negotiate a raise. In a police setting, however, the area of negotiation must be made secure. The term to describe this process is *containment.* When a crime or incident scene is contained, it is made secure against people coming or going from the site. This restriction helps keep communications between the authorities and subject person free of intervention and interference. Securing the area helps to ensure the safety of civilians and police personnel and makes it easier to gather intelligence and deploy tactical personnel. The inner perimeter is the area immediately surrounding the suspect, but does not usually include the building, vehicle, etc., in which the suspect is located. When firearms are involved, a tactical team will ultimately have control of this area. The outer perimeter, as the name suggests, is a secondary zone. Control of this area ensures that personnel in the inner perimeter are unhindered, and allows for easier expansion of the incident site.

Teamwork

Policing relies on a coordinated team approach in order to be effective. On a given evening, a community of 100,000 people may be patrolled by as few as 25 officers. These odds are not at all good if each officer is working independently. During a negotiation, this team effort is equally important. The negotiators must be working with the uniformed patrol officers and tactical team members at all times. A breakdown at any stage could have tragic results. There must also be a team approach to the negotiation itself. If the incident is protracted, a single negotiator can become as fatigued as the suspect. This can lead to poor judgment or a hastened approach to the negotiation. Further, a secondary negotiator can offer advice and give perspective to the primary negotiator, while yet another member of the team can take notes and compile intelligence information (Wind, 1995).

Intelligence and Investigation

It must be remembered that any crisis negotiation is ultimately a criminal investigation. As with most suicide attempts, there may not be any criminal charges involved, but investigators must determine whether a criminal act brought about or will result from the incident. Intelligence gathering throughout the incident will aid in the negotiation by offering insight into the subject's motivation and personality (McMains and Mullins, 1996) and aids the tactical team in strategies and deployment.

Time

The Emergency Task Force, the tactical unit of the Toronto Police Service, employs a "three T's" approach to tactical operations: time, talk, and tactics. Tactics may, or may not, be employed in a negotiation scenario, but time and talk certainly are. The extension of time serves many purposes in a crisis negotiation, including the development of a rapport between the suspect and negotiator, the calming of the suspect, an increased ability to obtain intelligence and conduct a risk assessment, the wearing down of the suspect, and an increased likelihood of the formation of Stockholm syndrome (McMains and Mullins, 1996). Although talk is, of course, an integral part of the negotiation, negotiators allow for quiet time as well. These periods are referred to as "dynamic inactivity." While this may seem like a contradictory term, things are happening at the scene, just not being communicated to the negotiator. This dynamic inactivity time is often very helpful in the peaceful resolution of the incident (Wind, 1995).

THIRD-PARTY INTERVENTION

There may be situations where the two sides in a conflict cannot negotiate or use other strategies to resolve a conflict. The two sides may be hostile to each other, their differences may be perceived as impossible to overcome, both sides may be too exhausted to continue (emotionally and/or physically), or cultural preferences require third-party intervention (remember chapter 2?). Whatever the reason, *third-party intervention* of some sort may be the strategy of choice. Third-party intervention includes a wide range of activities that span a wide variety of conflict situations, from parents attempting to settle conflicts between siblings, to formal mediation attempts in labour negotiations, to attempts to mediate the release of hostages across international borders (Folger et al., 2001). **Mediation**, one type of third-party intervention, is one of the most common strategies. It is usually a formal process of conflict resolution in which an objective third party comes in to assist two sides in negotiations (Swanson et al., 2001).

Much of police work involves more informal mediation attempts. Think of the many types of situations in which a police officer helps settle conflict between two people, including answering domestic calls, dealing with two drunk individuals about to (or continue) to brawl outside a bar, responding to warring neighbours, or handling gang clashes. Any officer who becomes involved in assisting two parties to resolve an issue is engaging in mediation.

There has been considerable research on third-party intervention, in such areas as the style of intervention, the various phases or stages of intervention, and characteristics and behaviour of the mediator. Entire books and chapters in books have been dedicated to third-party intervention. Our goal here is for you to understand the steps in the process so that you may use it informally as a police officer.

Phases of Third-Party Intervention

There are many different models for third-party intervention, some with as many as seven different phases or as few as two. The four phases below are based on the work of two groups of researchers and seem to be the most relevant for the type of informal mediation that is seen in regular police work (Folger et. al, 2001; Sheppard, 1984). For each of the four phases identified by Sheppard (1984), additional research material has been added to more fully describe the phase. Remember that distinct phases are artificial and that there may be overlap between them. For each phase, an informal example of its use in policing will be presented.

Definition Phase

By the time a third party is called in, the two may have lost sight of important facts or events that were significant in the conflict. Part of the role of the third party is to review the sequence of events, which encourages parties to more carefully define their own problems (Folger et al., 2001). The essential component of this phase is to determine exactly what the dispute is about.

Two officers are dispatched to a residence where a fist fight has broken out between two males. Upon arrival, the officers separate the two and have one sit on a couch and the other on a chair. One officer takes the role of the third party. When each is asked what the fight is about, one states that the other owes him $200. The officer also notes that one who is owed money appears very drunk, while the second appears to be less intoxicated. The second claims to have repaid the $200 by paying the last two bar bills, which totalled more than the amount owing.

Discussion

This is a lengthy part of the process, where parties present alternatives after determining needs or requirements for solution. This stage includes identifying needs, clarifying issues, and discovering possible alternative solutions. Rather than fighting over solutions, the third party encourages the disputants to focus on needs, or what each party requires to feel that there has been resolution.

The intervenor is very active during this phase and must have people clarify their needs, discourage them from regarding each other as the cause of the problem, and prevent them from suggesting solutions before all needs have been clarified. Clarifying needs can be very direct and straightforward. The third party can turn to each person and ask, "What needs of yours must any solution fulfill?" or, "You have suggested that X should be done. Why do you want to see this solution adopted? What needs of yours would it meet?" (Folger et al., 2001, p. 303). In a formal setting, these need statements can be written on a blackboard or paper so that all can see them. By listing the needs in the more impersonal way, people begin to see the conflict as a problem to be solved by all involved in the dispute.

Once needs have been defined, the sides then determine alternatives for settlement that would meet the listed needs. When there are multiple issues to be clarified and then addressed, the intervenor may have to assist the parties in deciding which issues will be dealt with first.

After needs are defined, common goals may emerge that both sides want to achieve. If parents are fighting over methods of discipline, they can still agree on a common goal: to raise their child to become a competent and caring adult. Disputing departments in an organization also have a common goal: to assist the company in making money, and even more basic, to maintain their jobs.

Much as during the process of problem solving, alternatives that meet the parties' needs are proposed. Again the alternatives, like the needs, can be listed for disputants to view for evaluation.

Here the officer clarifies what each party wants (needs) and establishes a common goal. It becomes apparent that the drunker of the two wants his $200 and does not count paying bar bills as payback. The other states that he paid the bills to make up for the money owing and refuses to give him any more money. Through talking with each of the men, the police officer learns that they have been friends for over ten years. He also finds that both would like to remain friends. In fact, the more drunk person starts reminiscing about past fun times.

Alternative Selection

In this phase, "the parties and/or the intervenor determines the validity of information, weighs arguments, and selects an alternative" (Folger et al., 2001, p. 300). This phase involves inducing integration (coming up with a mutually satisfying solution) and finally reconciliation.

Three methods can be used to induce integration (Folger et al., 2001). One method is *suggesting common goals*. In many conflicts, people share common goals but fight over the means to achieve the goal. For example, both parents have the same goal for their child but differ in discipline methods. When common goals continue to be pointed out, conflict may not escalate further and parties can remain calm. A second method is *defining the integrative process* where the third party attempts to integrate the two sides around a shared issue. This method assumes that if given the process, the two parties can come up with a mutually acceptable solution. There are many step-by-step processes that can be used by the third party to help people come up with their own solution. One model is the earlier problem-solving model. Third, the third party can *induce cooperation*. Using this approach, the third party enlists one side as an ally in moves designed to get both sides to cooperate. This method works well when there is no trust or willingness to cooperate or endorse a proposed solution. When it is demonstrated that one side is willing to make concessions, both sides may be brought together and continue the negotiations. For example, if the husband and wife do not trust each other, the mediator or third party may talk to the husband to arrive at something that he is willing to do to re-open the door for communication. After the husband's concessions are presented to the wife, it might be possible for the two can get back together again to continue problem solving.

In our example, the officer states, "You both claim that you want to remain friends, yet are fighting over $200. If one of you had not paid the tabs, the other would have. Am I right?" After some discussion, with the goal of continued friendship in mind, they reach an agreement: the man owing $200 will pay $100 to his friend who has paid the bar tabs, because the cost of his share of the drinks was about half the tab.

Reconciliation

The final stage is reconciliation: both parties accept and carry out the agreement or apply the solutions they have agreed upon. This includes the enforcement of the decision and possible discussion of any problems with the solution. The parties may want to agree to an evaluation. For example, if the parents agree on a new style of parenting that both are willing to apply, they may want to review any problems with this method in one month's time. A third party may or may not be present for this evaluation.

The officer may end by stating that both men need to "sleep it off" and contact each other the next day to decide upon a time and place for payment of the $100. The officer also makes certain that the person can afford the payment. An alternative arrangement would have to be found if the person could not pay the total.

While this four-phase model is formal, it can be loosely followed for more informal conflicts where third-party intervention or mediation is required, such as in our example here. Mediation as a short-term strategy will be discussed in more detail later in this chapter.

DEALING WITH A DIFFICULT CO-WORKER

While many of us have great co-workers or co-authors, not everyone is as lucky. Most of us, at one time or another, will have to work with difficult people. In policing, this could be any number of other professionals whom you encounter, from other officers, court personnel, lawyers, mental health professionals, to other members of the community on whom you rely to perform their duties. People are classified as difficult if they are uncooperative, touchy, defensive, hostile, or unfriendly. Particularly in policing, having a difficult partner such as one who is overly aggressive with members of the public, as well as with you, may have serious implications. You may find yourself on the wrong side of civil or criminal charges. Here we offer several strategies to assist you in dealing with these difficult people (Dubrin and Geerinck, 2001). By using these strategies, you may avoid conflict. However, when these people overstep your rights or make confrontation necessary, rely on the strategies earlier in the chapter.

Take Problems Professionally, Not Personally

Difficult people may not be out to get you personally. It is what you represent or the requests that you make that have spurred the difficult behaviour.

Use Tact and Diplomacy

Sometimes people are unaware that their behaviour is annoying or irritating. For example, a social worker whom you frequently encounter continually refers to police officers as "coppers." You find this label insulting. You can tactfully change this behaviour by being diplomatic and using constructive feedback. Remember to start with something positive. For example, "Sonia, I really appreciate how fast you got the court order to remove the child from that home. And I like working with you. But when you continually refer to me as a 'copper,' it rubs me the wrong way. How about just saying 'cop' or 'officer'?"

Use Humour

Humour can be a valuable tool for pointing out difficult behaviour, as long as you don't use sarcasm. The humour should point out the unacceptable behaviour while not belittling the person in any way. For example, a co-worker who is grumpy in the last hours of night shift may be dealt with this way: "Hey, I hate to interrupt you when you are doing that bear imitation, but do you think you could stop grumbling long enough to stop for coffee?" In this way, you have pointed out that the behaviour is bothersome without humiliating your partner.

Listen and Respond

As stated previously, active listening improves communication. Allow the difficult person time to express his or her concerns. Then express your concerns and goals in the relationship. For example, "You're saying that management is just out to get us, so why try? However, I need to do good work and keep this job. I really rely on your input and I need that input to be accurate."

Reduce Differences Nonverbally

It is hard to get along with someone who seems to be very different from us. If you want to get someone to cooperate with you, reduce these differences on the nonverbal level. By matching these behaviours at this level, you unconsciously reduce the differences with that person (Kirschner and Brinkman, 1994). As discussed in chapter 3, this is a nonverbal technique (mirroring) used to establish common ground.

By using a combination of these strategies, you may be able to get along better with a difficult co-worker. If the problems escalate, choose from other conflict strategies in this or other chapters in this text.

THE FEASIBILITY OF NEGOTIATION

Not every conflict can be negotiated. There are times when people cannot be engaged in dialogue because they have no interest in talking. Their mind was made up before the second or third party arrived. A classic example of this is the person interrupted during a suicide attempt. This is not the proverbial "cry for help" of a threat of suicide, but the act in progress. The decision was already made, and help was not requested. Another such example is premeditated murder where the act or escape was again interrupted.

The American Federal Bureau of Investigation (the FBI) conducts criminal investigations in a multi-jurisdictional or national scope. As a result, it is often on the leading edge of research and the dissemination of information in the US. The bureau has compiled a list of eight conditions that should be present in order for a situation to be considered negotiable. This list does not mean that negotiations shouldn't begin if not all the criteria are present, but it does give the negotiator a realistic and tangible gauge to determine the likelihood that negotiations will succeed. You will note that this list is centred on hostage situations; however, we will be able to translate many of these points into other negotiation scenarios.

Is Negotiation Feasible?

- The hostage taker must want to live.
- The authorities must be capable of making good their threats to use extreme force.
- The hostage taker must make demands.
- The hostage taker must see the negotiator as someone who can do him harm, but is willing and able to help him.
- There must be time to negotiate.
- There must be an effective reliable line of communication between the negotiator and the hostage taker.
- The situation must be contained.
- Where there are multiple hostage takers, the negotiator must be able to deal with the person who is making the decisions.

Some of the FBI criteria are very straightforward, needing little explanation, while others should be examined more thoroughly in order to fully understand the negotiator–hostage taker relationship.

Points one and two are very closely related in that they deal with the bottom line. If the hostage taker establishes that he is ambivalent about his own life, then there are two major problems. The first is that there is little to bargain with or for, because it is difficult to offer incentives to someone who does not care about the most basic need: the need to survive (McMains and Mullins, 1996). The next problem is that if the hostage taker does not care about his own life, he is less likely to be sympathetic towards his hostages.

Former American president Theodore Roosevelt is often associated with the expression, Walk softly and carry a big stick, which became part of American foreign policy, but is also applicable to policing. Without the prospect of incarceration or hefty fines, it would be very difficult to enforce the law. On a more personal level, the uniformed officer has an array of use-of-force options, which not only weigh down the duty belt, but also demonstrate that varying degrees of force will be used if necessary. The vast majority of Canadian police officers will go through their careers without ever using the highest use-of-force option—the firearm—and only occasionally use the lower use-of-force options such as the baton or pepper spray. The very fact that the public acknowledges that police officers sometimes use extreme force has the effect of keeping these incidents to a minimum. In hostage situations, the hostage taker has already demonstrated his willingness to use force through acts or threats. By taking a hostage, he is liable to believe that he has a measure of control in the situation. If he believes that he can kill hostages without retribution, he likely will kill hostages. If the hostage taker believes that the police do not have the ability or the resolve to use extreme force, then the hostage taker has no incentive to listen to the negotiator. The negotiator must be able to establish a working rapport with the hostage taker, but while he talks, the hostage taker must be mindful of the presence of the police tactical unit, the negotiator's "big stick."

If no demands are made, it is very difficult to negotiate because there is little on the side of the hostage taker to negotiate for. As the FBI describes it, if "substantive demands" are not made, anyone held unwillingly is a potential victim, as opposed to being considered a hostage. If the hostage taker is suicidal, then his life can be, in essence, a demand.

The fourth criterion appears to be paradoxical. If the hostage taker sees the negotiator as someone who can do him harm, how can she also be seen as willing and able to help him? This relates back to the "big stick" approach to negotiation. The negotiator represents authority, and therefore has the capacity to do the hostage taker great harm. However, the negotiator is not the instrument of force herself. Put crudely, the negotiator is the master holding the snarling tactical team on leash. She can release the powers of extreme force on the hostage taker, or she can hold them at bay. These contrasting roles of the negotiator—the friend and the foe—can be a tool of great effect (McMains and Mullins, 1996).

There must be sufficient time for the negotiator to build rapport with the hostage taker. The negotiator requires time to find out what motivates the hostage taker, and what he is afraid of. Emotions must be calmed so that the hostage taker does not act impulsively. There must also be time to deploy the tactical unit and gather intelligence, both for the tactical team members and for the negotiation team. Finally, there must be adequate time for demands to be met. Unrealistic demands such as $10 million in cash and a Learjet waiting for him in five minutes are as bad as no demands at all.

In tactical operations, good communications are crucial. There are many factors involved in good communications. Without them, there can be no effective dialogue between negotiator and hostage taker, and the essence of negotiation is meaningful discussion among the participants (McMains and Mullins, 1996).

Whether the mode of communication is a telephone, portable radio, or face-to-face talking, the flow of conversation must be clear and uninterrupted. We have all had a telephone call cut short for technical reasons, and have became frustrated as a result. Recall other telephone conversations that were plagued by static, distortion, or, heaven forbid, an uninvited third party. Then imagine these scenarios with very high stakes and one party (the hostage taker) who is scared, angry, and distrustful.

Face-to-face negotiations do not include the possibility of technical breakdowns, unless a loud-hailer is used, but this form of communication has many inherent problems. There is the physical danger of being too close to an armed person, putting the negotiator at risk and complicating tactical operations. There is the obvious lack of privacy in the conversation, which does not help to build trust, and makes it difficult for the negotiator to communicate with tactical team members. There is also comfort to consider. Particularly if negotiations are long and drawn out, the negotiator should be in an environment that is at least as comfortable as the hostage taker's, and preferably more so. One must remember that high-stress situations are physically very fatiguing. Ideally, negotiators are rotated and kept fresh (McMains and Mullins, 1996), while the hostage taker has no such luxury. If part of the negotiation strategy is to wear down the hostage taker, then the negotiator must be in a position where she is not subject to the same attrition factors.

Recall the law of nonverbal communications: 93 per cent of what we communicate to others is through nonverbal channels (Dubrin and Geerinck, 2001). If you are left with only the remaining 7 per cent of the message, you must ensure that the 7 per cent is understood. Language barriers, particularly in a culturally diverse society such as Canada, are a very important consideration. If the hostage taker and negotiator cannot talk fluently in the same language, then the prospects of miscommunication are high. Within language there is also dialect. Canadian school children may be taught Québecois, Parisian, or Acadian French, depending on where they live or the background of the teacher. Minor variances in these forms of the language could be crucial in high-stress communications. It is important to be open to such differences when establishing communication. There are variances in jargon, slang words, and **semantics**. Recall from the chapter dealing with the mentally ill that they may have difficulty comprehending you and may even have developed their own vocabulary. Some negotiators will compile a log of idiosyncratic words that the hostage taker uses so that they will not stumble over those words a second time (McMains and Mullins, 1996).

Many of the previous criteria relate to the fact that the situation must be contained. This applies to both the site of the incident as well as to the lines of communications. In order for the authorities to be able to use extreme force, intelligence must be gathered and the tactical team must be able to adequately deploy. Both tasks would be next to impossible to accomplish if the scene were in any way mobile. The efforts of the negotiator to be seen as someone who has power over the hostage taker's fate is far less convincing if the police do not demonstrate control of the scene. Containment curtails negotiation time because a deadline implies inability to resolve the situation with force. Communications are of course severely compromised by a lack of containment.

We examined the challenges of establishing good communications; the prospect of re-initiating these procedures from site to site would be daunting and perilous. There are also dangers involved in giving the hostage taker access to outside communications. This is a difficult problem to address, now that cell phones are commonplace, but if the hostage taker can communicate outside the channels of the negotiator, then his reliance on the negotiator as the only person who can extricate him from the situation is greatly undermined. Furthermore, the hostage taker can gather intelligence on the police operations if he has allies in the area. Even if the hostage taker is working alone, there is also the threat that he, along with the television audience, can "watch it live on CNN." If the media are not closely monitored by the police, there is a real chance that the hostage taker can see the tactical team members deploy, with the result that their safety would be greatly compromised. Finally, when practising containment, plans must be made for action to be taken if the negotiation efforts fail and the hostage taker attempts to flee. Not only could the hostage taker make good his escape, but civilian lives could also be put at risk.

The last criterion of the negotiable conditions is that, when dealing with multiple hostage takers, the negotiator must be able to deal with the person who is making the decisions for the group. It would be difficult for the negotiator to develop a rapport with the hostage taker if he varied his contact person or his power base. The group could become unstable if a spokesman agreed to conditions that the leader turned down. Not only could this instability work against the hostage takers; it could also increase tensions and make the situation explosive. The negotiation team puts great effort into analyzing the personality of the hostage taker and tailoring their negotiation and tactical plans around him (McMains and Mullins, 1996). If, in fact, he is not the person who is calling the shots for the group, then the intelligence gathered could be erroneous and therefore dangerous.

The Stockholm Syndrome

The term *Stockholm syndrome* refers to a psychological phenomenon that sometimes develops in hostage taking incidents. In such cases, the hostages develop a close bond with the hostage taker that can extend beyond the termination of the crisis. This syndrome was named after a 1973 bank robbery attempt in Stockholm, Sweden, turned into a five-day hostage situation. Even though the incident was resolved peacefully, the hostages emerged from the bank with sympathy for the two hostage takers and hostility towards the police. One of the hostages, a bank employee, even became engaged to one of the hostage takers.

There are three elements of the Stockholm syndrome:

1. The hostages develop positive feelings toward the hostage takers.

2. The hostages develop negative feelings toward the police.

3. Following the situation, the hostages retain a degree of compassion and empathy for the hostage takers (McMains and Mullins, 1996).

The Stockholm syndrome can be both a positive and a negative development within a hostage situation. The greatest asset is that the hostages' positive feelings toward the hostage taker are somewhat returned. This means that the hostage taker may begin to put a human face on the hostage, therefore reducing tension and the potential for violence on the part of the hostage taker (McMains and Mullins, 1996). On the other hand, if the hostages' bond with the hostage taker is too strong, the hostages may become an obstacle to police operations. Hostages have been known to try to help the hostage taker escape. They have also disrupted the police after being released, and have purposefully given the police misinformation when questioned following their release.

Regardless of the negative effects of the Stockholm syndrome, negotiators will attempt to foster the Stockholm syndrome in order to increase the hostages' chances of survival. The negotiator will attempt to determine the names of the hostages from the hostage taker if those names are not already known. This information may even become a bargaining tool. Once she knows them, the negotiator will use the names of the hostages during talks. If she doesn't know them, then the hostages are referred to in a personalized manner so as not to de-humanize them. The term *hostage* is replaced by *people, employees,* and *your family* (McMains and Mullins, 1996). Efforts are also made to make health inquiries about the hostages, making the hostage taker aware of medication needs and possible allowances for age, whether very young or very old. The negotiator can also minimize the "us and them" mentality of the hostage taker by generalizing needs so that the whole group is considered, rather than just focusing on the needs of the hostages and then the needs of the hostage taker (McMains and Mullins, 1996).

POINTS FOR PONDERING   *When Negotiation Fails*

Hindsight is, of course, 20-20, and criticizing how others act in a difficult situation is not kind. However, to quote another old maxim, Those who ignore history are doomed to repeat it. By breaking down and analyzing failures in negotiations, we can learn how to do a better job next time. One classic, high-profile failure in negotiations was the FBI-ATF standoff with the Branch Davidian in Waco, Texas. Notwithstanding the tragic opening and closing pages of this incident, the negotiations themselves were flawed and often unproductive. The PBS program *Frontline* documented several such difficulties. Members of the tactical team and the negotiators did not communicate well and were therefore unaware of each other's actions. This lack in coordination led to an almost antagonistic relationship between the two units. If the stakes had not been so high, other breakdowns would have been comical. In an effort to harass and therefore break down the resolve of the people within the Davidian compound, authorities began playing loud music in the direction of the compound at all hours of the day. However, the Davidians had a sound system that was better than the authorities', and they returned the favour of overpowering music towards the tactical positions. The result was in an even poorer line of communications between the negotiators and tactical officers.

The negotiation team in Waco had difficulty in establishing goodwill among its own personnel; it is little wonder that they had no better luck establishing goodwill with the people with whom they were trying to negotiate.

FIRST RESPONSE BY UNIFORMED PATROL OFFICERS

The reality of a police call for service does not always correspond to the situation as it was originally described. Take, for example, the break-and-enter in progress that turns out to be a neighbour who forgot his keys and squeezed through a kitchen window, or the truck that was reported to be furiously driving around a parking lot, in a cloud of smoke, that turned out to be a street sweeper. With this in mind, a uniformed patrol officer must assess a situation before summoning the negotiators and the tactical team. Police resources are not unlimited, and citizens do not appreciate having the streets blocked off, even for police operations. As a result, it is up to the first responding officers to discover what, in fact, is happening and to determine an appropriate level of response.

With calls for service involving weapons, hostages, or possible negotiations, the first-response officers must initially treat the call as legitimate and act accordingly. The officers' mindset must switch over to a tactical approach even before their arrival on scene. Prior to arrival, officers should obey the following guidelines (ETF, 2001):

- **Determine the best route of approach to the scene.** Gather as much information as possible from police communicators to determine exactly where the suspect is located. If possible, officers should approach from a direction that keeps them out of possible lines of fire. Keep use of vehicle sirens to a minimum near the scene so that police arrival is unannounced.

- **Drive safely to the scene.** No call is worth injuring innocent people. If the officer is involved in an accident, chances are that he or she will never get to the scene. A quick but calm approach to driving to the scene will see the officer arrive less tense and in a better frame of mind to make difficult decisions.

- **Scan the area for danger cues en route.** Hastily parked vehicles or people who look out of place could be signs of accomplices, just as the absence of persons in a busy area could signal the danger zone.

- **Position the police cruiser safely.** On television, police often arrive with sirens blaring, right in front of the location. But no part of the car, with the exception of the engine block, offers much protection from gunfire. The cruiser should be parked far enough away to avoid detection, in a position where it can be used to block off traffic if necessary.

- **Wait for backup officers.** The situation has not yet been confirmed, but it must be treated as real until determined otherwise. The term **tombstone courage** was coined for good reason.

Once the first officers arrive on scene, they must speak to witnesses and make observations in order to determine if there is indeed a crisis. Basic investigation and some background checks are required in order to determine the potential threat. At this stage, the attending officers are not concerned with a complete intelligence gathering operation, but in establishing that there is need to summon additional units and treat the call as legitimate.

Once the first responding officers have verified the information and called for additional units, the team concept to crisis management is applied. Information on safe approach routes and set-up locations is passed on to units that are on their way to the scene. This can be coordinated by one of the first officers on scene, who establishes a temporary **command post**. Once additional officers arrive, they are deployed to isolate and contain the suspect. Containment has been previously mentioned, but it differs somewhat in the initial stages of a crisis. At this point, many factors are still unknown, so the situation is uncertain. Safety must be foremost in the minds of the officers on the scene. A "reactionary gap" should be created to give the officers time to analyze and respond to an emergency or to the presence of a hostile party (ETF, 2001). This extra distance between the officer and the subject is similar to the half car-length "stop swerve space" that one leaves between a stopped car and the vehicle in front. Another consideration is the formulation of an arrest plan, should the subject wish to surrender, or an escape route if an armed or suicidal subject closes quickly on the officer (ETF, 2001). Communications are particularly important during the initial containment period, to avoid crossfire (ETF, 2001) and to identify citizens and prevent them from entering the perimeter.

The "Three T's" of time, talk, and tactics are the best tools for the first responding officers. Unlike specially trained negotiators and tactical team members, uniformed patrol officers approach most situations with the intent of dealing with it as quickly as possible. Such an approach is understandable, because the officers bounce from call to call, resolving each matter in turn. It is important to reinforce that time is the officers' ally and that the longer the incident lasts, the greater the likelihood of a peaceful resolution, and the lesser the likelihood of violence (ETF, 2001). The initial-response officers should not necessarily attempt to establish communications with the subject. They should try to distance themselves from the subject and keep a tactical withdrawal in mind (ETF, 2001). A tactical withdrawal is a safe, deliberate disengagement from a dangerous situation. An example is a situation in which a lone person, armed with a knife, barricades himself in a room. If no one else is in danger, and the matter cannot be resolved quickly, it is quite acceptable to back off and contain that person in the room until a negotiator arrives. This is, however, not always an easy decision for a police officer to come to. By nature, police officers want to act in a situation and not simply be bystanders. It is very important, however, to impress upon officers that a tactical withdrawal is sometimes the safest and preferred option for all involved. It can de-escalate a situation and buy that crucial, additional time. If communications between the first-response officer and the subject become a reality, the officer should keep the overall plan in mind. By keeping the subject talking, and not making any promises, the officer can gather information about the subject and establish a rapport that will aid the negotiator.

SUICIDE

Suicidal intentions come from various sources including mental disorders, chronic pain or terminal illness, unresolved emotional and psychological problems, and response to hopelessness, or, particularly with young people, frustration (Hales and Hales, 1996).

Statistics in the United States indicate that suicide accounts for 1 per cent of deaths annually. It is more prevalent among the elderly, divorced or separated, unemployed, and impoverished, and men are three times more likely to commit suicide than women (Hales and Hales, 1996). But suicide happens within every age range and socio-economic status.

Ninety per cent of suicide attempts fail. Attempts are largely unplanned, an impulsive reaction to one's environment. More often than not, the attempt is designed to fail. This is the "call for help" that will hopefully lead to professional help and a change in attitude about one's life. Sadly, though, 10 per cent of those who attempt suicide will be successful in a subsequent attempt (Hales and Hales, 1996).

Of particular concern to police officers is the method of suicide attempt. Women are more likely to be unsuccessful in their suicide attempts, which most often involve overdoses of drugs or medication. While the ramifications of attending these types of attempts are certainly disturbing for police officers, they, by their nature, seldom lead to confrontation. Men are more likely to attempt suicide by using firearms or other weapons, and are subsequently more often successful in their attempt. Further, men who attempt suicide often suffer from depression or abuse chemicals. We have previously examined the effects of mental disorders and alcohol abuse on reasoning abilities and in the concluding chapter will discuss the added effects of stress. All these factors contribute to a situation that has high potential for being dangerous for attending officers.

For the first responding uniformed officer there may be little or no time to assess the risk factor of a suicidal individual. If there is a protracted negotiation, then assessment becomes a much more readily available tool. Regardless of the situation, a risk assessment will help to determine the level of danger befalling the suicidal individual, and consequently the level of danger for the attending officer.

Risk Factors

- **History of previous suicide attempts.** As with the other police contacts mentioned, CPIC and occurrence checks will indicate previous suicide attempts as well as a history of violence or weapon use. As well, intelligence gathered from family, friends, or neighbours can contribute to a current picture of the person's state.

- **History of mental disorders.** People with mental disorders and/or a history of substance abuse comprise up to 95 per cent of those attempting suicide (Hales and Hales, 1996). Once again, much information can be gathered en route to a call.

- **Indications of hopelessness.** Statements such as, "What's the point of living?" and, "It doesn't matter" point towards someone who has given up on life.

- **A recent loss of a loved one.** Such a loss can be as a result of death or a failed relationship, and can leave someone without a sense of purpose or meaning.

- **Isolation.** A person who lives alone, by circumstance or choice, is at higher risk. Those without friends or social support are more likely to act upon suicidal thoughts.

- **Chronic pain or terminal illness.** A history in either area can indicate a wish for a final escape from an unbearable situation.

- **Planning or leaving a suicide note.** A written plan of action, or a number of calculated actions leading up to the attempt indicate a greater willingness to succeed. Putting one's affairs in order, giving away money or possessions, or leaving a suicide note is often a point of no return.

As in any other crisis negotiation, the key to dealing with a suicidal person is in solid communications. Developing rapport or a relationship with the individual is of prime importance. Among the best ways to communicate with people in crisis is to listen to them. By listening, we have the opportunity to understand what such people are dealing with and how they feel about it. They may fit a case study to perfection, but if you treat that them like an exercise, chances are that you will lose them. Everybody wants to be thought of as unique and to be treated accordingly. In the case of a person with suicidal thoughts, this is even more important. To demonstrate that you do value what the individual is saying, practise active listening: reflect back to the speaker the content and feelings or his or her message (Devito, 1996). This empathetic feedback employs personal terms such as, "I understand that your wife's death must be difficult for you," or, "Losing your job must be a real strain on you, Peggy." This technique is described as portraying the "nurturing parent"

(McMains and Mullins, 1996). Suicidal people tend to be, understandably, self-focused. By showing your understanding of the person's feelings and putting that understanding into words, you begin to share the person's hardship and hopelessness, and therefore help him or her feel less isolated.

Intervention Strategies

- **Do be safe.** Police officers by nature want to act and want to help, but by putting themselves at risk, they jeopardize other emergency personnel.

- **Do be honest and direct in communications.** Do not lead people to believe that their actions will have no ramifications even if they walk away from the attempt. Similarly, do not lead them to believe that five minutes in the emergency room will solve all of their problems. Recall that many people who attempt suicide will make more than one attempt.

- **Do use other resource people such as medical professionals or police negotiators.** It is not appropriate to use non-police personnel in high-danger or hostage situations, so use family members as a last resort. The history of family relationships can be difficult to trace, so they can lead to uncertain results.

- **Do use open-ended questions to promote conversation.** If such people are acting on impulse, drawing them out of their immediate situation may give the perspective required to successfully intervene. If you ask, "Do you feel sad?" the answer will likely be, "Yes." But if you say, "I understand that you feel sad. Can you describe the sadness to me?" you do not give a simple yes or no alternative to the response.

- **Do try to instill a sense of hope in the suicidal person.** To instill such hope, two beliefs must be challenged: that the person's pain will not subside, and that his or her loss or pain overshadows everything else in life (McMains and Mullins, 1996). The officer is not curing the subject's problems, but rather helping the person to see that there is a way out of the present state.

- **Don't sugar coat the act of suicide when talking to a person at risk.** Use phrases such as "kill yourself" and "die" instead of "take your life" and "pass away." Suicide is ugly to witness and devastating to survivors. Let the individual know this, and do not give an easy out. Do not confuse such directness with being blunt and unsympathetic.

- **Don't interrupt the person.** When taking a verbal statement from a witness, it is estimated that most police officers interrupt the respondent within ten seconds. When a person is contemplating suicide, such an interruption could be enough to cut short your attempts at dialogue. Be patient, remember that your input, while valuable, is only a minor part of the suicidal person's recovery.

- **Don't use reverse psychology.** Police officers are not psychologists. Stay within your abilities. Dirty Harry Callaghan can successfully use the "you don't have the guts to do it" approach, but in the real world this could lead you to the wrong side of a judge's gavel.

- **Don't punish yourself if you cannot talk an individual out of a suicide attempt.** If people are determined to take their own life, they will. If you can show people that you care for them, you have given them some solace in their final moments.

Consider This...

"I talked to him for two hours. I felt as if I was getting to know him. We even joked around. We had a rapport; we were on a first-name basis. I really thought that I could talk him out of it. Then he jumped. He didn't say a word. No warning, he just jumped. I don't know what else I could have done, but I should have done more."

Suicide by Cop

Police officers must approach each encounter with a suicidal person with extreme caution. It is, or should be, foremost in the officer's mind that a person who does not presently value his or her own life may have similar sentiments about the lives of responding emergency personnel. In most cases this does not apply, but as when dealing with people with mental health disorders, the risk is there.

Sometimes, suicidal individuals do reach the stage where they intend to harm others in their attempt, or to have the police take their lives for them. In these situations, they will provoke a confrontation with the responding officers in the hopes that the officers will kill them. The possibility of these "victim-precipitated suicides" is another reminder for officers to conduct the best possible risk assessment.

It goes without saying that scenarios such as these are a high risk for the responding officers. What are equally treacherous are the post-incident stresses that they can cause. Taking a life runs completely counter to a police officer's values. In cases where victims brandished a replica or inoperable firearm, an officer who had to use extreme force can carry a heavy burden of guilt. Further, even in cases that appear to be clear cut, in Canada a police or independent review body will fully investigate the matter, and a coroner's inquest will likely be ordered. Such an investigation, even in the best of scenarios, is an unnerving and stressful experience. Chapter 10 examines police stressors like this one in more detail.

POINTS FOR PONDERING   *Teamwork in a Medical Emergency*

The man was clearly out of control. Handcuffed and pinned to the bed by four police officers, he continued to rant, strain, and curse loudly. The paramedics on the scene were less excited by the ordeal than the officers were. This was partially because they did not have to restrain the man themselves, but also because the man was a diabetic, and they had just found that he had a low blood sugar level. Their calm words, echoed somewhat less calmly by the officers, were to relax: "Things will be better in a minute or two." Soon after the paramedics started an intravenous drip, the man began to settled down, his struggles became less pronounced, and his threats less frequent. Then suddenly, as if by magic, the man was calm, wondering what all these people were doing in his bedroom.

This hypoglycemic or insulin-shock reaction created a potentially violent situation. Without the presence of trained medical personnel who were able to quickly diagnose and treat the condition, the possibility of injury or a protracted, fruitless negotiation was likely. Scenarios such as this one illustrate the need for cooperation and trust among emergency services personnel. Because the officers were open to the advice of the para-medics and trusted their judgment, they were able to treat this threatening, out-of-control man as a person in need of assistance, not as a criminal. As a result of the professionalism of all parties involved, this and situations like it can end peacefully and without injury.

MEDIATION

Mediation is similar to, but not the same as, negotiation. In mediation, an independent third party helps the involved parties resolve the dispute on their own. In negotiation, the third party acts on behalf of the hostage or victim, or where the suspect is alone, on behalf of society. The negotiator works with the subject party, but has a definite interest in the outcome.

According to Bush and Folger, the mediator allows "the parties to clarify their choices, resources, and decisions by recognizing each other's perspectives" (Folger, Poole, and Stutman, 2001). This is not always an easy task; often by the time police are called to disputes, the involved parties will not even talk to one another. The attending officer may have expertise in the matter if it involves a provincial or municipal statute, for example. But the dispute may hinge on where a neighbour placed a newly installed fence. Regardless of the issue, the role of the attending officer is to enable the disputants to solve the problem themselves.

Police officers are not always eager to mediate. Mediation takes time and often a great deal of patience on the officer's part, not to mention that officers, in general, like to be in control of a situation. In mediation, the involved parties have the ultimate say in resolution. So why mediate? In the case of the disputed fence line, the officer could merely attend and dictate a decision: "You tear down the fence and put it up on your own property," or, "Stop whining. The fence is only six inches over your property line. You can live with that." The problem would be resolved, but only temporarily. Many neighbour disputes have a history that precedes police involvement. If the dispute gets to the point of officers attending, there is likely to be an escalation of conflict. On the other hand, if the police are involved in the first dispute, and one party does not get satisfaction, there may again be an escalation of conflict, followed by an "I'll take care of it myself" approach, because the police did not intervene on their behalf. The bottom line is that officers will attend and re-attend the address, possibly until one party is charged. As with many things in life, a little more time invested initially can save a lot more time in the long run. To illustrate how beneficial mediation can be at reducing calls for service, the Pittsburgh Police Department has not only instituted a mediation training program for front-line officers, but mediation is man-dated for certain types of dispute calls (Cooper, 2000).

Not all disputes lend themselves to effective mediation. The best mediation scenario is an isolated incident, involving participants who are unlikely to have future contact (Cooper, 2000). In these instances, there is usually less pride and animosity involved, and the participants can expect the outcome to be successful. Long-term disputes will not likely be solved by a single mediation session. A good effort by the attending officer may lay the foundation for future results, but many times the best outcome is an "agree to dis-agree" position, backed up by advice on criminal and civil repercussions. An incident such as the fence-line dispute may be mediated, but if the officer has a hunch that the involved people will fall back into dispute, advice on civil liabilities and processes like small claims courts and local tribunals should be added. The police should not mediate matters that involve large sums of money. A question of ownership over a valuable family heirloom is not within the realm of police intervention. In such cases, the attending officer should play the role of short-term peacekeeper, if necessary, and provide advice and information on civil law and professional mediators. Disputes over child custody matters are another situation that has no place for police mediation. Advice can be given, but these cases are in the jurisdiction of family courts. Incidents involving previous criminal charges such as assault and mischief to property should have restraining orders and court-imposed conditions as their chief method of de-escalation. In some cases, a lesser degree of mediation may help to maintain a truce of sorts. In the end, the attending officer must analyze the participants and make a judgment about whether mediation is a viable option.

The Mediation Process

Regardless of the setting or type of dispute, some basic mediation guidelines can be used (Cooper, 2000). Recall that the goal is to allow the participants to resolve the situation themselves.

- **Determine a suitable location.** Before starting any mediation proceedings, select a place for the talks. This is not always as easy as it sounds. Any disputants who are at home, on their "own turf," are at a distinct advantage. Neutral ground outside is an option, but it is subject to unfavourable weather, and if there is a possibility that neighbours will eavesdrop, the parties may not be comfortable enough to be forthright. A third-party location, such as a neighbour's house, a community centre, or the police station is a good option. The police cruiser will do if necessary, but the close quarters may make the participants feel rushed.

- **Vocalize the goal.** If mediation begins with a reminder of the intended outcome, participants are more likely to focus on the result than on personal differences.

- **Establish ground rules.** A framework is necessary to allow the parties to start from a more or less level playing field. Neither side should feel at a disadvantage from the start. Structure will help keep the parties on topic and can ensure that a one-hour call does not take the better part of the shift. Finally, by setting the limitations of the police in non-criminal matters, the participants will understand that the solution must come from them.

- **Listen fully to both sides of the story.** Every dispute has two or more sides to it, with the truth emerging from some middle ground. Once both sides are heard out, the truth or underlying issue becomes more apparent, and a perception of equity is demonstrated to the parties.

- **Reiterate what was said.** By recapping each person's story, the officer shows that each has been heard, and puts the issues into context. One person may have felt threatened by the other, but by re-examining the use of the word, the officer may determine that the "threat" was to call the police. This technique may also allow for a change in perspective. An earth-shattering problem may, as heard coming from someone else, be seen as much less significant.

- **Brainstorm solutions.** Many times in a dispute, each participant has only one solution firmly in mind. By helping with brainstorming and by offering suggestions, the mediating officer can help both parties see beyond their own vision of a solution. As well, when there are now many options on the table, the participants can make a choice and own the resolution.

- **Communicate the solution in straightforward terms.** There is little point in arriving at an agreement that is vague or interpreted differently by each side. If the discussions have all been made separately, this is the time to bring the two sides together to ensure clarity and to determine if conformity to the resolution is likely.

- **Explain the repercussions of violating agreements.** The involved parties must be made aware that if arrangements are not honoured, there will be consequences. These consequences can range from criminal or civil action, to frequent police attendance, to having life made miserable by a disagreeable neighbour.

- **Follow up.** It is not always necessary, or realistic, to follow up on a mediated dispute. At other times, follow-up will add greatly enhance compliance. There are times when an effort as simple as a phone call will keep the parties on track. The officer can make the follow-up personal by offering a business card in case of future problems. Another option is to use a third party to monitor the situation. An independent community group can check on the status of the situation or act as a neutral ground for further talks.

SUMMARY

This chapter will not to transform you into a trained crisis negotiator, but has passed on some basics of negotiation and mediation that can be used in everyday policing. We covered some general negotiation techniques, which include creating a positive atmosphere in which all the involved parties feel at ease and believe that the outcome is mutually beneficial. Third-party interventions were discussed, including the phases of intervention. The very practical concerns of dealing with a difficult co-worker were examined, accompanied by possible strategies for solution. We also examined negotiation principles that were specific to police, such as containment, teamwork, information gathering, and using time to advantage. Eight conditions of a feasible crisis negotiation were discussed, along with the ramifications if those conditions were not present. The Stockholm syndrome, its origin and implications in hostage-taking, was examined. The role of the first responding officer was discussed in the context of being one member of a team effort to resolve a crisis.

The issue of suicide was explored, including risk factors of suicidal individuals and an outline of the topic of "suicide by cop." Some suicide intervention strategies were presented, with officer safety and respect for the affected person being stressed. The advantages of attempting mediation with disputing parties were discussed. Some basics of mediation were reviewed, including guidelines that can help in solving the problem.

CASE STUDY

You and your partner arrive at a bank is response to a customer who has become irate and the bank would like removed. The man, who has recently lost his job, had come to discuss the mortgage payments on his house. The man was notified that, regrettably, he would not receive an extension on his payments, and that foreclosure on the house was imminent. As you enter the bank, the man pulls a handgun from his jacket and points it at the head of the mortgage manager. You are told, "Back off, or this guy is dead." The man, with the manager in tow, withdraws to a closed office, from where he refuses to respond to your questions.

Questions

1. As the first responding officer, what are the chances of beginning a fruitful negotiation?
2. Would you feel empathy for the hostage taker?
3. What background information would you, as a negotiator, like to receive?
4. What are your sources of intelligence on the hostage taker?
5. Is this a negotiable incident?

KEY TERMS

Command post: An on-site location used as a base for communications and coordination of a major event. This is often a large vehicle designed to house a negotiation or operations team and communication and information-gathering equipment.

Mediation: A formal method of resolving conflict that includes an objective third party.

Negotiation: The process of conferring to reach a mutually acceptable solution.

Semantics: The differences in perception of written or spoken words.

Tombstone courage: Courage that goes beyond common sense and puts the life of the individual, as well as the lives of colleagues, at risk.

 ## WEB LINKS

www.stressdoc.com/difficult.htm
This site provides helpful tips for dealing with a difficult co-worker.

www.mapnp.org/library/intrpsnl/negotate.htm
"Negotiating with Others" has good links to all kinds of articles on negotiation.

www.bbraham.com/html/negotiation/html
This site has a list of negotiating tips.

http://suicide.mentalhelp.net
A site about suicide, including symptoms of a suicidal person, where to get help, and online resources.

REFERENCES

Canadian Press (1996, November 6). Big three talks end with Ford deal. *Canadian News Digest.* www.canoe.ca/NewsArchiveNov96/candigest_nov6.html

Christopher Cooper (2000). *FBI Law Enforcement Bulletin, 69*(2), 7.

Joseph A. DeVito (1996). *Messages: Building interpersonal communications skills* (3rd ed). New York: Harper Collins.

Andrew Dubrin & Terri Geerinck (2001). *Human relations for career and personal success* (2nd Canadian ed.). Toronto: Prentice Hall.

Emergency Task Force (2001). *A training guide for first responders.* Toronto: Toronto Police Service.

Joseph P. Folger, Marshall Scott Poole, and Randall K. Stutman (2001). *Working through conflict: Strategies for relationships, groups, and organizations* (4th ed.). Toronto: Addison Wesley Longman Inc.

Dianne Hales & Robert E. Hales (1996). *Caring for the mind: The comprehensive guide to mental health* (pp. 559–73). New York: Bantam Books.

Rick Kirschner & Rick Brinkman (1994). *Dealing with difficult people: How to bring out the best in people at their worst.* New York: McGraw-Hill.

Michael J. McMains & Wayman C. Mullins (1996). *Crisis negotiations: Managing critical incidents and hostage situations in law enforcement and corrections.* Cincinnati: Anderson Publishing Co.

B. H. Sheppard (1984). Third party conflict intervention: A procedural framework. In B. Staw and L. L. Cummings (Eds.), *Research in organizational behavior* (Vol. 6). Greenwich, CT: JAI Press.

Charles R. Swanson, Leonard Territo, and Robert W. Taylor (2001). *Police administration: Structures, processes, and behavior.* Upper Saddle River, NJ: Prentice Hall.

Waco: The inside story (1995). In *Frontline.* Boston: WGBH.

Bruce A. Wind (1995). A guide to crisis negotiations. *FBI Law Enforcement Bulletin, 64*(10), 7.

chapter nine

Dealing with Domestic Abuse and Family Abuse

Courtesy Brookside Studio

LEARNING OUTCOMES

After studying this chapter, you should be able to

- Understand the nature of domestic disputes.
- Learn strategies to de-escalate domestic disputes.
- Understand domestic violence, its dynamics, and the risk factors.
- Understand the effect of family violence on children.
- Understand child and elder abuse.

On-the-Job Scenario

You and your partner attend a townhouse unit for a report of a domestic dispute. The complainant, a neighbour in the next unit, told the communications call taker that she could hear shouting and smashing sounds. The complainant adds that this is a frequent occurrence. Both you and your partner have less than 5 years' police experience and are under 30 years old. The door is answered by a man in his mid-50s; he is obviously agitated and is gruff, bordering on rude. You invite yourselves into the residence and see broken plates on the kitchen floor. There are no signs or complaints of an offence, but you believe that some mediation or problem solving is required. The woman remains silent, and the man states dryly, "What could a couple of kids like you tell us about being married?" After ten fruitless minutes, you leave the residence frustrated and convinced that you will be back.

Part of a police officer's job is to deal with domestic and family abuse. Responding to this type of call can be very frustrating and will rely heavily on your ability to resolve conflicts, use mediation and negotiation, and be alert for signs of serious family dysfunction where lives may be at stake. In this chapter, we will look closely at abuse, including domestic disputes and domestic violence, effects of domestic abuse on children, child abuse, and elder abuse.

DOMESTIC DISPUTES

Domestic disputes are trouble for any police officer. Perhaps that is worded a bit too strongly, but domestic disputes are one of the most challenging and frustrating calls for service that police attend regularly. The challenge comes from the complex and unique nature of domestic disputes. The frustration often results because a victim, or potential victim, does not recognize the danger of the situation. It's really not surprising that this is such an undesirable type of call to attend when you look at its components.

We have already examined at great length how to deal with alcohol users and abusers. Alcohol is a component in many domestic disputes and in even greater percentages where violence is involved. A police officer's negotiation—or more to the point, mediation—skills are brought into play, but these are situations that fall at the lower end of the continuum in terms of a successful outcome. Children are often the true victims in domestic disputes, and their involvement can be enough to melt the heart of the stoniest police officer. And in repeat calls for service, domestic disputes are a frequent cause. It's not unheard of to reattend an address two or three times in a single shift. The final challenge in dealing with domestic situations lies in the investigation itself. With provincial standards and police service policies becoming more and more prevalent, preparing a report for every domestic call is now standard practice, and where charges are laid, the attendance at a scene and accompanying paperwork can occupy much of a shift. In the vast majority of incidents, police officers have discretionary powers in their decision to arrest. The officer *may* arrest if certain criteria are met. Today, in many jurisdictions, police service policies dictate that officers *shall* arrest if the same criteria are met in cases of domestic violence. But regardless of the many challenges, police must treat domestic disputes seriously, and their investigations must be thorough and complete in order to protect the safety of all involved.

Attending a Domestic Dispute

Police officers are dispatched to deal with domestic disputes for several reasons. If a neighbour calls, it usually means that family fights are a regular occurrence at that address and that the caller is tired of the accompanying noise, or that things have gotten out of hand and that somebody is being injured. If one of the involved parties calls in the dispute, it indicates that he or she (and it is usually she) is no longer able to cope with an ongoing situation, that she was assaulted by her partner, or is in fear for her safety. A family member may call on behalf of one of the involved parties, in which case the attendance of the police could be a surprise to both spouses. En route to a domestic dispute call for service, it is helpful to find out the identity of the caller, as well as any history of such calls at that address.

Regardless of the origin of the call, the officers' purpose at a domestic dispute is to resolve conflict and ensure safety. As we already discussed in the negotiation chapter, it can be a tall order to solve somebody else's problem. The high emotions and personal baggage involved make domestic situations that much more difficult to handle. Such disputes can be between parent and child, siblings, or in some other family relationship. In this chapter, we will focus on intimate relationships, which are typically husband–wife, common-law, or boyfriend–girlfriend situations. Some attention will also be paid to former partners who continue to intimidate or harass their "ex."

Officers will mediate in a domestic dispute in an attempt to reduce future calls for service and to prevent violence from occurring. Although there are no guaranteed results from a determined mediation effort, it is almost guaranteed that if officers do not do a good job, they or their co-workers will be back.

Another aspect of domestic disputes to keep in mind is their volatility, and as a result, the need to consider officer safety. There is the cliché of battling spouses suddenly turning on officers when one of them is about to be arrested. Whether or not this scenario is realistic, it is true that for many years in North America, domestic dispute responses were the primary call for service that led to police officer deaths.

De-escalation Strategies

The following strategies are used to calm a tense domestic dispute, which is quite different from spousal assault. In assaults, de-escalation is accomplished with the arrest and removal of the offender. (Note that among the de-escalation strategies are many references to officer safety.) While arrest and removal is not a method of resolving the conflict itself, the attending officers cannot operate effectively in an unsafe environment.

- **Explain your attendance.** The officers should convey that they are responding to a complaint, but are primarily concerned for the welfare of the residents. It is important to maintain the confidentiality of the complainant, although the parties involved may guess the caller's identity. The officers should let the residents understand that they want to help and not unnecessarily intrude, but that they will not leave without being certain that everyone is okay.

- **Remain calm.** In a heated verbal exchange, it is important for the attending officers to act professionally. Professionalism includes being calm, objective, and respectful. This action, in turn, can help to lower the anxiety and activity level of the participants. An officer may, on occasion, need to use more assertive verbal control with one party in order to settle people down or gain control of the situation. A shout or loud warning can be effective in restoring order. Note that this technique is a tool to use, not an attitude.

- **Pick a safe location.** Many domestic disputes occur in or near the kitchen. The kitchen, with its readily available supply of knives and cast-iron frying pans, is not a safe place to be with an angry person. A bedroom, with its personal memories, is not a desirable place to mediate, either. A better location is a living room or family room where there is a place to seat the participants.

- **Separate the participants.** A warring couple do not magically become calm, regretful, and accommodating just because the police arrive. Partners will move around an officer just to throw one final verbal barb at the other. By putting distance between the participants, officers have a better chance to deal with the issues, rather then the personal animosities. When the participants are separated, there is less likelihood that a partner will be intimidated into not speaking. Something as innocent as eye contact can prevent a spouse from being forthright with police. When creating space, it is important to maintain visual contact with your partner. Not only are the officers monitoring possible physical flare-ups, but also there is less opportunity for one partner to feel jealous about the other being alone with an officer of the opposite sex. This can also cut down on fear of conspiracy in the spouse with the more guilty conscience.

- **Maintain control.** During any mediation, it is important to allow participants to solve their own problems. To help, the officers must listen, be empathetic, and allow the involved parties to have some measure of control. This is the ideal time to use active listening skills and to develop a supportive climate for communication. In a domestic situation, however, there is much more potential for violence than in the average dispute, so officers must be firm in reducing belligerent or hysterical behaviour. In heated situations, some diplomacy must be sacrificed for respect of authority.

- **Distract.** Distraction can be an effective technique to calm an irate person. "That's some kind of hot weather we've been having," can be a useful line. Better still is using common ground or obvious signs of interest. Seeing a well-used baseball glove, an officer might comment on how the Blue Jays or Expos are doing or the latest trade. Such a remark can help to promote dialogue, which can act to calm the subject. Again, by using this type of strategy, you are also developing a supportive climate and reducing the defensiveness of the other person. The disadvantage of this approach is the danger of straying too far off topic, and therefore increasing the length of the call or de-emphasizing the solution.

- **Show empathy.** Showing empathy will demonstrate that the officers are concerned about the involved parties. Without getting too personal, officers can show that they relate to the problems that the participants face. An officer who is a parent may offer, "I remember when my kids were small, and we were always sleep deprived. It made it tough to deal with our problems." Not only does this put a human face on the officer, but also it emphasizes that conflicts are shared and that they do end. Take care to avoid patronizing.

- **Remove one of the participants.** In many domestic disputes, particularly when there is alcohol involved or ultimatums have been made, calmer heads do not prevail. These are good times to initiate a cooling-off period. By removing one of the combatants from the residence, preferably the more angry person, both parties have the chance to reduce their anger or stress and gain some perspective. Done properly, this can be an occasion to build some consensus: "Okay, I'll leave, and you can watch the kids." If the situation warrants, and if one party will not leave voluntarily, the officers can act on **preventing a breach of the peace section of the Criminal Code,** and forcefully remove the party more likely to escalate matters.

- **Check backgrounds or previous history.** Canadian Police Information Centre (CPIC) checks en route can reveal criminal history and specifically a history of family violence. Occurrence checks can reveal incidents of previous domestic disputes and their resolutions. Occurrence checks can also detail if a resident has a firearms licence. Officers must be very vigilant to the presence of weapons in a residence, even if legally possessed. Statistics Canada reports that police were previously aware of domestic violence between the suspect and victim in 56 per cent of spousal homicides, and that between 1977 and 1996, one-third of all homicide victims were killed by family members (Statistics Canada, 1998).

DOMESTIC VIOLENCE

According to a Statistics Canada survey from 1999, 7 per cent of people involved in a marriage or common-law relationship suffered violence at the hands of their partner during the previous five years. This means that over 1.2 million victims reported at least one incident of domestic violence (Statistics Canada, 2000). These are staggering numbers, particularly when it is taken into account how many others are touched by this violence. The children of the victim, family members, and friends are all touched by domestic violence.

Domestic violence can be described as the use of physical force, threats, or intimidation in the context of a sexually intimate relationship. The relationship does not have to be active, because many offences are committed by former spouses or intimate acquaintances. Offences within this area include homicide, sexual assault, assault, uttering threats, intimidation, mischief to property, and criminal harassment. Emotional or verbal abuse is part of the cycle of domestic violence, but this abuse is not governed by enforceable statutes.

The Dynamics of Domestic Violence

Although each incident of domestic violence is unique, there are common threads throughout. Lesley Harries-Jones is the victim services co-ordinator with the Peterborough Lakefield Community Police Service and as such deals with countless domestic abuse victims. She believes that every instance of domestic violence is preceded by verbal or emotional abuse (Harries-Jones, 2001). This is not to imply that every incident of verbal abuse is followed by violence, but rather it shows that domestic violence is a result of an escalation of conflict. This is one of many reasons that police officers must be thorough in conducting any domestic dispute investigation.

It is virtually guaranteed that any violent domestic dispute call that police attend is not the first incident of violence within the household (Harries-Jones, 2001). Chances are that there has been prior violence, but that the violence has now escalated to the point that a victim, witness, or neighbour has decided that a line has been crossed and that the police need to attend.

For the abuser, domestic violence is often a calculated act. The spouse who had a tough day at work and comes home to take it out on the family, will often do so deliberately, if not consciously. Take, for example, the man who is reprimanded by his boss at work. He does not take his frustrations out on the cause of his anger—his boss. Nor does he damage his place of work or assault his co-workers. The person goes to the beer store and treats the clerk with civility. He walks home with his 12-pack tucked under his arm, without picking fights with passers-by. The moment he enters the house, his partner is aware that trouble is brewing. The man sits down in his favourite chair and begins to drink silently. He begins to vent his anger as he consumes his beer. With each passing bottle, the blame is greater and the nastiness increases. The man continues to use his wife as a scapegoat for all of his problems, and pushes the buttons that he is sure will elicit a response from her. Finally, the wife tires of being blamed and argues back. Now when the man's dominance is threatened by his partner's defence, his tone and gestures escalate to the point where he loses control and lashes out physically. We are not suggesting that this is a blueprint for domestic assault, or that men are the only perpetrators of domestic violence. Rather, this example is used to demonstrate that domestic violence is not an accident; it is a response.

As the preceding paragraphs indicate, there is a progression found in many assaults (Harries-Jones, 2001). Here is a common sequence of events:

* Emotional abuse demonstrated by verbal abuse and insults
* Disregard for the spouse's property or the destruction of common property
* Loss of control followed by assault or threats

There is another consistency that often occurs in domestic violence: the abuser's pattern of behaviour, which can be a ritual. The offender comes home and begins to drink. After finishing the sixth drink, the offender begins to push his spouse, then slap her. The offender may lash out at his spouse, repeating the same phrases just before the violence. The assault can also follow a pattern. For instance, the abuser may hit his spouse twice in the stomach each time there is violence. Not only can these patterns recur consistently in a relationship, but they may also even transcend one relationship to another (Harries-Jones, 2001). The pattern may be a **modus operandi** that is unique to the abuser. It is interesting to note that another area where offenders appear to "follow a script" during an incident is in sexual assaults.

Risk Factors

Statistics Canada has compiled a list of risk factors that can show who is most likely to be a victim of domestic violence. It must be emphasized that domestic violence cuts across the entire fabric of our society and that no category of person is immune to its effects.

Gender While men and women reported violence on a more or less equal basis, women are more likely to have weapons used against them, are more likely to be injured, and are more often in fear for their safety (Statistics Canada, 2000).

Age Younger men and women (under 34 years of age) report a much higher incidence of domestic violence (Statistics Canada, 1998).

Form of union Those involved in a common-law relationship report four times the number of spousal assaults than do those people in a marriage (Statistics Canada, 1998).

Income Although domestic assault occurs throughout all income ranges, it is more often reported in households with incomes lower than $30,000 (Statistics Canada, 1998). Those in higher income groups may have greater access to legal and therapeutic advice and therefore may be less likely to report violence to police. But money does not protect people from domestic violence.

Alcohol Any police officer can attest to the fact the alcohol plays a prominent role in domestic disputes. Not only is it often found that one or both of the involved parties in a dispute have been drinking, but many times at least one party is intoxicated. Lowered inhibitions and confused thinking caused by alcohol can cause discussions to become arguments, and arguments to become unrestrained and vocal.

In domestic assaults, the role of alcohol is much more complex than it is in relation to violence in general. Surprisingly, the frequency of drinking does not play a large role in domestic violence. It is only when drinking becomes heavy (five or more drinks on five or more occasions in one month) that the incidence of violence increases noticeably (Statistics Canada, 1998). It is found that intoxicated males injure their spouses more than non-drinkers (56 per cent compared to 33 per cent) and that serious acts of violence increase when alcohol is involved, from 40 per cent to 65 per cent (Johnson, 2001).

As we discovered in the chapter on alcohol abusers, alcohol itself does not create violent behaviour. It has been found that the *type* of person who drinks excessively often does so for psychological reasons and that this *type* of person may tend to be physically abusive with his wife, whether or not he was drinking at the time (Barnett and Fagan, 1993; Fagan, Barnett, and Patton, 1988).

The alcohol may, in fact, become a manipulative tool for the abusive spouse (Harries-Jones, 2001), as when the spouse returns home and begins to drink, not socially, but for a purpose. This partner becomes more abusive as the consumption of alcohol progresses, not because of lowered inhibitions, but because a pattern or ritual is followed. The abusive spouse knows that before the alcohol is gone, he or she will have confronted the partner and will be firmly in control of the situation. The impairment becomes an excuse: it lets the abuser blame the substance and avoid personal responsibility.

Family history Studies have concluded that men who witnessed abuse against their mothers are more likely to abuse their spouses (Jaffe, 1990; Allan, 1991; Rodgers, 1994). Further, children who witness domestic violence are also at higher risk of being abused in their own domestic relationships (Statistics Canada, 1998). If you recall from chapter 5, social learning theory supports the notion that witnessing violence can lead to later imitation of such responses, as the abused or the abuser.

Verbal abuse and control During domestic calls, police officers frequently hear remarks like "He abuses me every day." Then just as the officer is reaching for the handcuffs, there's clarification: "He abuses me verbally. Take him away, Officer." The handcuffs return to the holder, and the officer replies impatiently, "We can't arrest him for verbal abuse. There's not enough room in the jails." While the officer's reply is technically correct, about powers of arrest and jail space, it glosses over a serious risk factor. Conflict, as we have discussed, seldom begins at the upper end of the continuum; it begins with verbalization, taunting, and then progresses.

Some women report that they suffer more from the effects of emotional abuse than they would from physical abuse (Walker, 1984; MacLeod, 1987). **Emotional abuse** can be described as degrading comments, verbal tirades, overt jealous behaviour, and isolation. This long-term emotional abuse can lead to perceptions of powerlessness and hopelessness, and to lowered self-esteem. These factors can lead a person to be more susceptible to abuse by the spouse. Control by a spouse can also be financial. By limiting the spouse's access to money, and the means to use it independently, a controlling husband or wife can take on a parental role. By doling out money on his or her own terms, an abusive spouse can manoeuvre a partner into a subservient role, and therefore a vulnerable position.

Spousal control, particularly in men, is very much a result of their perception of their environment. If a man believes that men have a right to dominate women within the society, he is unlikely to accept challenges to his masculinity, and therefore there is a much higher incidence of violence upon female spouses (Daly and Wilson, 1988; Schwartz and DeKeseredy, 1997; Wilson, Johnson, and Daly, 1995). As seen with alcohol use, violence against a spouse is an exercise of power for the male who is not in control of other aspects of his life. The abuse becomes a means, even if it is illegitimate, to accentuate his male status (Johnson, 2001). It is suggested that a man's attitudes and beliefs about to his dominance over his spouse is a greater barometer of potential spousal abuse than consumption of alcohol, age, type of relationship, or class variables (Johnson, 2001).

The issue of spousal control and its affect on family violence raises the question of what we, as a society, can do to empower the marginalized and change stereotypical views, in this case about the status of women in our society.

Reporting of Domestic Violence by Women

Time and time again, police officers see women who have not reported long-term abuse by their spouse or who return to their spouse after suffering physical abuse. Officers may spend a great deal of time on a spousal assault investigation only to discover that the victim wishes to have all charges dropped. This is a very difficult situation to comprehend, and it leaves many officers shaking their heads and questioning the victim's sanity. The reality is that there are many obstacles faced by a victim of an abusive relationship.

Domestic relationships are very complex and highly valued. About half the songs you hear on the radio, or movies you watch, tell you, "It's all about love." We search far and wide for love, and when we find it, we want to keep that loving relationship. In doing his or her job, the officer focuses on the criminal or safety aspect of the abusive relationship, sometimes forgetting that the involved parties started off in a romantic and loving relationship. This can be difficult to imagine while dealing with the pain and anger. But in many cases, the victim will focus on only the spouse's "good" aspects, choosing to ignore or bury the abuse (Harries-Jones, 2001). The abused spouse may believe that her partner will change and become that person she fell in love with. The emotional attachment between the two builds over a long period of time. Even when there is abuse and gradual erosion of emotional ties, love does not leave the relationship overnight. For a woman to break free from an abusive spouse, she must understand that she is at risk, despite her love for him (Harries-Jones, 2001). This is one area where a first responding officer can be instrumental in breaking the cycle of violence. We spoke earlier in the chapter about demonstrating empathy during a domestic dispute. By showing the victim empathy and understanding, after the fact, the officer can help empower that victim. A simple statement such as, "I know that you love your husband and there's nothing wrong with that, but it is not safe for you to be with him," or, "You don't deserve to be treated like this," can help the victim differentiate between the emotional bonds of the relationship and the reality of an unsafe environment. If you have ever been unkindly "dumped" by a partner, yet would still run to the telephone, hoping that it was that same person calling to make up, you may be able to relate this concept to your own reality.

The status of the family unit is also a factor to consider in the termination of a spousal relationship. Despite the abuse that the victim endured, she may still insist that her husband is a good father, alarmed by the prospect of not having a father figure in her children's lives.

Fear is another major obstacle for the victim to overcome, and it can take many forms. Victims may be afraid that their partner will return and do them more harm after being charged. An officer can reassure victims, explaining how the investigation will proceed, describing the conditions of release that provide a measure of safety for them. The officer must let victims know that the police will continue to support them and can refer them to a number of support agencies (which will be described at length later in this section). Unfortunately, the reality is that an officer cannot guarantee safety to anyone, but all available resources can be used to provide the highest degree of safety possible.

Other fears are less tangible for the investigating officer, but are very real for the victims. One major concern is about economic hardship. Victims may depend on their spouse for the family income, in whole or in part. Despite the availability of shelters and assistance programs, victims may see their standard of living drop significantly as a result of charging their partner. If there are children in the household, then financial fears are increased by concern for providing for those children. Prolonged absence from the job market, lack of gainful job opportunities, or concerns about childcare are issues that victims must face.

Another fear is that of "going it alone." Suddenly victims no longer have someone else in the household with whom to share life's burdens; the abused spouse may be overwhelmed by the prospect of caring for children alone. This breaking of ties may include the extended family of the spouse. Spouses may worry that children could become alienated from grandparents as a result of the breakup of the relationship.

When the abusive spouse is controlling, fears are heightened. A spouse who isolates his partner removes her supports. Over time, he may have made it so uncomfortable for her to carry on relationships with friends and family that it was easier for her to let those relationships slip away than to continue with them. In more manipulative cases, the controlling partner may have caused his spouse to cut off her support ties herself (Harries-Jones, 2001). This can be accomplished by continually undermining those people. One can imagine how difficult it would be in such cases to try to re-establish those old relationships. In addition to the real fears, the victim's self-esteem may so low that she does not believe that she can cope without her spouse. A controlling spouse can create a dependency that is difficult to overcome.

Another obstacle to reporting domestic violence is the confusion over the meaning of *abuse*. We have addressed the concept of emotional and verbal abuse and touched upon the fact that it is not criminal. As mentioned, there are cases where women feel more lasting effects from verbal abuse than from physical abuse. The physical abuse may occur monthly, but the verbal abuse is a daily event. In such cases, the partner may not understand that police cannot lay charges. It is up to the officer to convey that no criminal offences have been committed, but that there is clearly cause for concern. On the other hand, victims will often downplay acts of physical violence (Harries-Jones, 2001). Criminal offences such as assault, uttering threats, mischief to property, and harassment may not even be associated with abuse. In such cases, the victim may become frustrated by the officer's focus on the physical abuse to the exclusion of the emotional abuse.

There have also been instances, in a still male dominated profession, where male officers were unsympathetic to the female victim. In such cases, the officers have been reluctant to intervene, and the victim, even if willing to pursue charges, was left to her own devices. Matters such of these are few, and are on the decrease, but even one publicized case can erode a police service's credibility in a community.

POINTS FOR PONDERING   *There's No Place Like Home*

Dorothy finally got it right in *The Wizard of Oz:* your imagination might lead you elsewhere, but home is the safest place to be. Or is it?

One factor that makes domestic disputes so dangerous for officers and involved parties alike, is the home setting (Harries-Jones, 2001). When a new child arrives into a home, that home must be "child proofed." This entails blocking off staircases, covering sharp corners of furniture, and removing sharp or heavy items that can be grabbed or knocked off the counter. During a physical confrontation, the objects that make a house a home can lead to serious injury. A simple push can send a spouse tumbling down a set of stairs or falling onto a hard tabletop. A spouse may retreat to a bathroom, where there is likely a door lock, but the hard and slick bathroom ceramics, and the confined area make it a particularly dangerous place to be.

Take a look around your home and consider if you would want to be there when push came to shove.

Police Reporting and Arrests

Spousal violence is not a new issue in Canada. Several tragic, high-profile cases of spousal violence, such as the **May-Iles case** in Ontario, have attracted more attention from the media and police services. In the hope of increasing awareness, understanding, and sensitivity in domestic abuse cases, many police services in the country have instituted a mandatory reporting procedure for domestic disputes. This means that any time the police receive a call for service in a domestic dispute, the attending officer will generate a report. This not only applies to domestic assaults or actual disputes, but also when everything appears to be fine. In the latter case, spouses may be so intimidated by their partners that they will convince the officers on scene that the call was without merit. A pattern of several such reports can reveal that, in fact, a problem exists.

In response to victims' concerns, many police services have instituted a policy by which officers shall arrest where there are **reasonable grounds** to think that an offence has been committed during spousal violence. The word *shall* is not common in policing, where discretion is the norm. In incidents of domestic violence, however, the officer does not have discretion, and does not require the victim's compliance. The arrest is made. The reasonable grounds apply only to the commission of the offence, and whether there is likelihood of a court conviction is of no consequence. This practice removes the responsibility from the victim for initiating complaints against a spouse. Attending officers make it very clear to victim and accused alike that they are obliged to lay charges in these matters.

In every case where one spouse is arrested, that spouse is removed from the household. As under the **arrest sections of the Criminal Code**, police can continue an arrest if it is believed that it is in the interests of the safety of the victim to do so and to prevent a continuation of the offence. Due to the increased concern for the safety of battered spouses, the accused spouse is usually held in custody pending a court appearance. At this court appearance, the accused may be released, but with bail or a surety, and with conditions imposed. These conditions frequently include provisions not to communicate directly or indirectly with the victim and not to attend the family residence, unless accompanied by police in order to pick up belongings. Should the accused be released from the police station, the non-communication conditions are imposed by virtue of an **undertaking given before an officer in charge**. The accused in a domestic violence matter who breaches one of the release conditions would be re-arrested, and would almost certainly be held until a court appearance.

Another new procedure adopted by many Canadian police services is the videotaping of a victim statement. A videotaped statement serves several purposes. It captures the devastating physical and emotional effects of a domestic assault much more vividly than can a simple written statement. These results are even more dramatic if the statement is taken at the scene, at the time of the incident. The viewer of such a videotape can see the trauma of the victim and the disarray of the family home. Many services have portable video cameras available for this purpose. It is believed that the practice of videotaping statements leads to an increased proportion of guilty pleas by the accused as well as a higher conviction rate in domestic assault cases. Another feature of the video statement is that the victim is asked to swear to the truthful content of the evidence right on tape. This makes it much more difficult for the victim to later recant a statement, because it offers independent evidence of the incident.

Another new facet of the domestic violence investigation is a history and risk-assessment follow-up. This risk assessment was recommended by a coroner's jury after a tragic spousal homicide case. The investigating officer in domestic violence will often thoroughly question the victim spouse. Questioning goes beyond the current incident and delves into past actions and behaviours of the accused. Included are questions about previous assaults, threats, and intimidation. Such information is very useful for the investigating officer when making a case to keep the accused in custody. Questions are also asked about past behaviour outside of the relationship, such as about the use of weapons, suicidal tendencies, and even cases of cruelty to animals. This information helps to build a profile of the offender, giving the police and the courts an assessment of how likely he or she is to reoffend and escalate the amount of violence.

Note that due to recent case law, police officers could find themselves personally liable where it is proved that an investigation has been conducted improperly. In the past, it was generally the police service itself that was litigated against when something went wrong. Now if it is found that an officer is negligent in following mandated guidelines and procedures, and someone is seriously injured or killed, the officer could find his or her assets taken away in a civil court decision.

POINTS FOR PONDERING
Is Mandatory Arrest a Desirable Practice?

On one hand, the concept of mandatory arrest signals to society that domestic assault is not a personal matter and will not be tolerated (Stark and Sherman, 1994). As discussed previously, it is very important to reinforce the fact that old notions of male domination will be challenged. Previous campaigns, such as the publicity against impaired driving, have produced tangible results. Yes, people do continue to drive while impaired, but society as a whole no longer perceives impaired driving as acceptable. Mandatory arrests take the responsibility away from the victim, and by making that first step, help to end the cycle of violence (Stark and Sherman 1994).

The deterrent effects of mandatory arrest laws are not conclusive, as demonstrated in several studies (Mignon and Holmes, 1995). There are concerns that knowledge of mandatory arrest policies can actually discourage spouses from calling the police, or that a vengeful spouse can use these policies to advantage (Petkau, 1998). There are some who believe that alternate measures to arrest and incarceration have not been fully explored (Stark and Sherman, 1994). Australia, for example, has instituted "cooling off centres" for men to attend before being re-introduced to their domestic situation.

Victim Support

As previously mentioned, officers on scene can have a tremendous impact on the victims' reaction to domestic violence. However, officers helping victims to recognize the abuse and realize that they are not to blame for the violence is only the first step.

Officers can spend only so much time with victims until another call must be answered. In many cases, follow-up is necessary in order to ensure that victims do not lose sight of the true dynamics of the relationship and so that victims who emerge from an abusive situation know where to go next.

Most police agencies offer a victim support service within the organization itself. These support personnel will offer counselling and advice, often at the scene. They will also monitor reports to determine if intervention is necessary in cases where referral was not made or where the victim did not pursue it. If the victim support personnel are not able to deliver service directly—for example, where psychological therapy is necessary or alternate accommodations must be found—they are able to see that the victim finds the appropriate agency. Another concern for the victim is the possibility of having to testify in court. A victim who has made a clean break may have to face the abuser again during a trial or sentencing. Victim support personnel can provide information and assurance to help the victim deal with the emotional and technical aspects of court appearances.

Even with the detention time and conditions that can be imposed on an abusive spouse, victims will sometimes prefer to make a fresh start, away from the family household altogether. At such times police will refer them to alternate accommodation. Although the concept of a shelter for abused spouses is not new, there is a now a greater partnership between shelters and local police. Because the users of such services are almost always women, shelters are geared to abused women and their children. Shelters for men are available in most large centres, but their focus is more general, not specifically geared to victims of family violence.

Signs of a Controlling Partner

A number of signs indicate that a partner is controlling: points that could be considered symptoms of an ill relationship. Note that these signs apply not only to a domestic relationship, but also to an adolescent or young adult dating relationship. Such behaviours point to the type of person who is a potential abuser or harasser.

The following information is presented by police community services officers to students at senior grade school and high school levels, in order to address abusive relationship situations proactively.

Jealousy Not only jealousy in intimate relationships, but also in relationships with close friends. It leads to demands to account for the partner's whereabouts at all times.

Isolation Attempting to separate the partner from family and close friends, creating dependence on the controller.

Verbal abuse Demeaning or degrading comments as well as loud, intimidating behaviour.

Destructiveness The tendency to destroy personal possessions, which demonstrates the power of the controller.

Ultimatums The use of phrases such as, "If you leave me, I'll kill myself." Such demands are intended to draw out sympathy, but demonstrate the true insecurity of the controller.

Frequent apologies Apologies for recurring bouts of abusive or harmful behaviour are often followed by the inevitable "I'll never do it again."

Threats or acts of violence Actions directed at the partner or at others, which are dismissed as mistakes and are rationalized by such disclaimers as, "I didn't mean it."

The Effect on Children

Statistics Canada estimates that half a million children have witnessed or heard a parent being assaulted between 1994 and 1999. Many more children have been present for raucous arguments that do not lead to assaults, but are nevertheless damaging.

In order to address the concerns about children in domestic disputes, police services are involving more outside support agencies to assess the status of the children. In Ontario, the **Child and Family Services Act** stipulates that when a police officer investigates a domestic dispute and there are children in the household, present at the time or not, the officer must notify the Children's Aid Society about the situation. Regardless of any criminal investigation, the Children's Aid Society will review the matter and determine whether intervention is required. Intervention can range from a consultation, or a prescribed parenting skills course, to removal of the children from the household. Legislation has also dealt with the issue of battered spouses returning with their children to an unsafe environment with the abusive spouse. In such cases, the mother can be found neglectful in providing a safe home for her children. This is another tool for the attending officer to use to underscore the dangers of an abusive relationship to an abused woman.

Children who are exposed to ongoing verbal and physical battles between their parents can become desensitized to the strife around them. A child who is unable to do anything about the conflict around him or her is likely to cope by blocking out that conflict. One author has spoken to adult witnesses in domestic disturbances who continue to use avoidance as a coping technique: "I heard plenty of this stuff as a kid: arguing, yelling, hitting. Tonight? I just shut the door, and turned up the volume of the TV. I've seen it all before."

Whether this response is typical or not, it is obvious that regular exposure to domestic violence has a lasting impression on children.

Anybody with children can see how great their capacity is to absorb information from the world around them. Regrettably, this does not apply only to areas of positive reinforcement. Research indicates that children do not even have to be present during domestic strife for it to take its toll on them (Jaffe, Wolfe, and Wilson, 1990). The children may be in their rooms or playing outside the house. The parents may even make a conscious effort not to argue in front of the children in the false belief that this will shield them from adverse effects. The children still do suffer; however, they often internalize their anxiety, not knowing what to do with it, and not feeling safe in disclosing it to others. It happens that the harmful effects of the conflict around them seldom manifest until much later, when it appears in the form of emotional, behavioural, and relationship difficulties.

CHILD ABUSE

Abuse within a family is not limited to violence between adults. Children are also abused by parents and older siblings. Although there are mandatory laws nationally that require people to report child abuse and neglect, it is estimated that as much as 90 per cent of child abuse is not reported to the authorities (MacMillan et al., 1996). This low reporting figure can be attributed to several factors including the child's lack of comprehension that he or she is being abused (Duffy and Momirov, 1997); the dependence on and fear of the caregivers; and inadequate training for health care professionals in identifying cases of abuse (Loo et al., 1999).

The major components of child abuse are neglect, physical abuse, sexual abuse, emotional abuse, and verbal abuse (Government of Alberta, 1999). Neglect is the only factor that is not, generally speaking, consistent with abuse in spousal relationships. Neglect is the failure to provide the necessities of life and a safe environment. Neglect is not always obvious, but it can affect a child's physical, emotional, social, and psychological well-being. Physical and sexual assault may become part of punishment or correction as well as being an angry response. Emotional and verbal abuse are quite similar to the manifestations observed in a spousal relationship, but the child has far less capacity to cope with this behaviour and is more likely to internalize his or her feelings.

Fathers are found to be much more likely to physically harm the children in the household. A 1999 study found that fathers were responsible for 98 per cent of sexual assaults and 71 per cent of non-sexual assaults (Statistics Canada, 1998). Girls are the victims of 80 per cent of the sexual assaults and 53 per cent of the non-sexual assaults (Statistics Canada, 1998). Girls are most vulnerable to sexual assaults when between 12 and 14 years of age, while boys are most vulnerable when between 3 and 6 years of age (Statistics Canada, 1998). Non-sexual assaults increase with age for both girls and boys.

Cases of child abuse are generally very difficult for the police to investigate. Not only are the incidents vastly under-reported, but very young victims can have difficulties in adequately communicating the incidents to police officers and child welfare workers. Children's evidence may be filled with inconstancies that weaken their credibility. Quite often the offence occurs while in isolation with the suspect, and if there is no physical evidence for corroboration, there may be difficulty in substantiating the allegation.

Another increasing trend is the use of children in child custody disputes. In today's society, many children live in more than one family setting as the result of marital breakups. If the separated parents become involved in a bitter custody dispute, one parent may allege child abuse by the other parent in order to appear to be the superior caregiver. Although it seems unthinkable that parents would use their children as pawns in battles over their care, it is a reality.

ELDER ABUSE

Elder abuse can take on dynamics similar to those in child abuse. The victim often depends upon the abuser for care and therefore may have much to lose in alleging abuse. Unlike children, the elderly do not have an advocate system that can place them in alternate housing if they are at risk in their home. Like young children, who may have difficulties communicating their abuse, the elderly may suffer from medical conditions, dementia, or other psychological conditions that prevent them from being able to adequately present their case. Neglect becomes a larger issue in elder abuse, because the elderly are often isolated and therefore have fewer contacts to assess their condition.

Abuse of the elderly can be caused by several factors including family situations and caregiver issues (APA, 2001). If an elderly relative is put into a pre-existing family setting, there are many possible stresses put upon that family: additional financial burdens, new lifestyle dynamics. and potential intrusion on private time. Previous abuse may resurface in an elderly couple, or the elderly spouse of an abuser may "turn the tables" on the other when they become less physically capable (APA, 2001). Similarly, an abused child may abuse the parent in the parent's old age.

There are many possible qualities in caregivers that can increase the potential of abuse. Caregivers may have not had adequate training, facilities, or capabilities to provide stress-free care. Caregivers may have their own addiction, or financial or health problems, and may therefore have difficulties in caring for themselves. Even a fully capable caregiver can succumb to frustration and anger in fulfilling this very challenging role (APA, 2001). This is not to suggest that violence is an appropriate response to stress, but as we have already discovered, violence is often a result of inadequate coping abilities.

Elder abuse is becoming a greater problem as our population ages. In 1999, 12 per cent of Canadians were over 65. This group will comprise 17 per cent of the population by 2016 and 23 per cent by 2041 (Statistics Canada, 2000). As resources to care for the elderly diminish, more people will take in their aging relatives, and therefore there will be a greater likelihood of abuse of the elderly.

SUMMARY

In this chapter we have examined facets of domestic disputes that make them stressful and challenging for the attending officer. Calls to attend domestic disputes originate from various sources and this source may be an indicator of what to expect. The purpose of police at a domestic dispute is to ensure the safety of everyone involved. We covered some de-escalation strategies at domestic disputes: explaining police attendance, remaining calm, picking a safe location, separating the participants, maintaining control, using distractions, demonstrating empathy, removing one participant if necessary, and checking the background of those involved and their domestic history.

We introduced the subject of domestic violence and discovered that 7 per cent of Canadians suffer violence at the hands of their spouse. The dynamics of domestic violence were discussed, with emphasis on the likelihood that the violence is not a one-time event and that the violence often progresses from emotional and verbal abuse, to the destruction of property, to assaults or threatening behaviour. Many factors put people at a statistically greater risk of being victimized. Each factor was explained in context. The presence of emotional or verbal abuse was found to be the highest risk factor for a spouse, even though it is not, itself, a criminal offence.

Police services have adopted policies and procedures to help ensure the safety of victims and to increase awareness and understanding in domestic violence. Among the policies are mandatory arrest guidelines and in-depth investigation procedures. Failure to follow pre-scribed procedures could result in the personal liability of the attending officer. Victim sup-port is an important component of domestic violence investigations. Follow-up and referrals for the victim can be vital for the victim to carry on with life after an incident. Offered was a list of warning signs that a partner may be controlling. This controlling behaviour puts a partner at high risk for domestic violence. We also examined how children, present or not, can also become real victims of their parents' violence against each other.

The topics of child and elder abuse were introduced. Child abuse—which can be neg-lect or abuse that is physical, sexual, emotional, or verbal—is vastly under-reported, with only 10 per cent of cases being brought to light. These cases are difficult to investigate and to prove. Elder abuse is becoming more prevalent. Family situations and caregiver stress are two leading underlying factors of elder abuse. The isolation of elderly victims can cause these cases to go undetected.

CASE STUDY

You and your partner receive a 911 radio call for a domestic dispute. You are familiar with the involved parties, being one of many officers who have attended for similar complaints. The usual scenario is that both parties are intoxicated and very verbally abusive towards one another. The husband appears to be the aggressor, but there has never been a complaint or evidence of violence. Neither party has heeded your advice to seek counselling for alcohol abuse or for obvious marital difficulties. The last two times you attended, the wife was more upset than the husband, and small furniture items appeared to have been broken.

On this occasion it takes longer than usual for the door to be answered. The wife finally answers the door, but she is subdued. You observe the husband sitting on the couch, a towel plastered to his forehead, stemming the flow of blood. At his feet are the shattered remains of a beer bottle. Your partner speaks to the man, and when asked what happened he replies, "Nothing, nothing at all."

You speak to the wife for several minutes, and then she blurts out, "I couldn't take his cursing anymore. He's been talking that way to me, threatening me. He had it coming."

Questions

1. Your police service has a mandatory arrest policy in domestic assault cases. What action will you take?

2. If an arrest is made, what conditions of release might you consider?

3. What, if any, mitigating circumstances are present?

4. If you arrest and charge the wife, is it fair to remove her from the family home, even though investigation reveals that the husband has been emotionally abusive towards her for years?

KEY TERMS

Arrest sections of the Criminal Code: These sections of the Criminal Code refer to arresting a person (continuing to detain after apprehension) only if certain conditions exist. Unless the offence is exempted in the Criminal Code, a person shall only be held in custody where the identity of the person must be established, where release would jeopardize evidence, to prevent the continuation or repetition of the offence or the commission of another offence, or to ensure the presence of the accused in court.

Child and Family Services Act: A provincial statute in Ontario that deals with the protection and welfare of young people (under 18 years of age) and families. Other provinces have comparable statutes, for example, the Child Welfare Act in Alberta.

Domestic violence: use of physical force, threats, or intimidation in the context of a sexually intimate relationship..

Emotional abuse: abuse that is not physical and includes verbal degradation, verbal tirades, isolation of the victim from friends and family, and jealousy.

May-Iles case: In March 1996, Arlene May was killed by a former boyfriend who subsequently committed suicide. The ex-boyfriend had been threatening and harassing May for a number of months. Arlene May was not only fearful, she in fact indicated that she was resigned to her fate of being killed by Iles. A coroner's inquest was held with recommendations made to help prevent further such tragedies from recurring.

Modus operandi: Latin phrase meaning "method of operating." Commonly referred to as "M.O."

Preventing a breach of the peace section of the Criminal Code: Section 31(1) of the Criminal Code gives police officers the authority to arrest a person who, on reasonable grounds, they believe is going to act in a way that will result in disturbance of the common peace. This section does not carry a charge with it, but rather is a procedure to hold a person until it is found that his or her return will cause no further problems.

Undertaking given before an officer in charge: An undertaking may be issued in conjunction with a release form for arrested persons. It can be issued by an officer in charge of a police station or by a justice. In this undertaking, a list of conditions can be placed on an accused in the interest of protecting the victim and witnesses and preventing repetitions of the offence. The accused must agree to abide by these conditions, and failure to do so would result in an additional charge of failure to comply with an undertaking. Typical conditions implemented in domestic violence cases are a prohibition to contact the victim directly or indirectly and/or to attend the victim's residence or place of work; to not possess or consume alcohol, drugs, or other intoxicating substances; to surrender firearms and firearms licences; to obey a curfew; to report to a police service or to notify the police service of changes of address or occupation.

WEB LINKS

www.hc-sc.gc.ca/hppb/familyviolence
This is the National Clearinghouse on Family Violence, a Canadian site from Health Canada.

http://home.cybergrrl.com/dv
Resources for women on domestic violence.

www.library.utoronto.ca/aging/onpea.htm
The Ontario Network for the Prevention of Elder Abuse.

www.womanabuseprevention.com/html/question_6.html
Read this article from the Web site of Education Wife Assault that answers the question, "How common is child abuse in Canada?"

REFERENCES

American Psychological Association, Public Interest Directorate (2001). *Elder abuse and neglect: In search of solutions.* Washington, DC: Author.

Beth Allan (1991). *Wife abuse: The impact on children.* Ottawa: The National Clearinghouse on Family Violence, Health Canada.

O. Barnett & F. Fagan (1993). Alcohol use in male spouse abusers and their female partners. *Journal of Family Violence, 8,* 1–25.

M. Daly & M. Wilson (1998). *Homicide.* New York: Aldine.

S. Duffy & J. Momirov (1997). *Family violence: A Canadian introduction.* Toronto: James Lorimer and Company.

F. Fagan, O. Barnett, and J. Patton (1998). Reasons for alcohol use in maritally violent men. *American Journal of Drug and Alcohol Abuse, 14,* 371–92.

Government of Alberta Departments of Health and Wellness, Learning, Justice and Attorney General and Children's Services (1999). *Responding to child abuse: A handbook.* Edmonton: The Crown in right of the Government of Alberta.

Lesley Harries-Jones, Victims Services, Peterborough Lakefield Community Police Service (2001). Interview by G. Stark.

Peter Jaffe, David Wolfe, and Susan Wilson (1990). *Children of battered women.* California: Sage Publications Inc.

Holly Johnson (2001). Contrasting views of the role of alcohol in cases of wife assault. *Journal of Interpersonal Violence, 16*(1), 54.

S. K. Loo, N. M. C. Bala, M. E. Clarke, et al. (1999). *Child abuse: Reporting and classification in health care settings.* Ottawa: Minister of Public Works and Government Services.

H. L. MacMillan, J. E. Fleming, M. Wong, et al. (1996). *Relationship between history of childhood maltreatment and psychiatric disorder in a community sample: Results from the Ontario Health supplement.* Conference Reporting, International Family Violence Research Conference, Durham, NH.

Sylvia I. Mignon & William M. Holmes (1995). Police response to mandatory arrest laws. *Crime and Delinquency, 4*(4), 430–43.

Theresa Petkau (1998). *Patrol constables' perceptions of wife assault sensitivity training: A qualitative evaluation.* www.vix.com/menmag/batpetka.htm

Karen Rodgers (1994). *Wife assault: The findings of a national survey* (Juristat. Catalogue 85-002-XPE Vol. 14 No. 9. Canadian Centre for Justice Statistics.) Ottawa: Minister of Industry.

M. Schwartz & W. DeKeseredy (1997). *Sexual assault on the college campus: The role of male peer support.* Thousand Oaks, CA: Sage.

Evan Stark & Lawrence Sherman (1994). Should police officers be required to arrest abusive husbands? *Health, 8*(5), 32.

Statistics Canada, Canadian Centre of Justice Statistics. (2000). Family violence in Canada: A statistical profile. Ottawa: Author.

———. (1998). Family violence in Canada: A statistical profile. Press release May 28, 1998. Ottawa.

M. Wilson, H. Johnson, and M. Daly (1995). Lethal and non-lethal violence against wives. *Canadian Journal of Criminology, 37,* 331–61.

chapter ten

Managing Stress

Courtesy Peterborough Lakefield Community Police Service

LEARNING OUTCOMES

After studying this chapter, you should be able to

- Define stress.
- Explain how stress affects a person both physically and psychologically.
- Understand you own reactions to stress.
- List the stressors in police work.
- Use a variety of techniques to manage stress to prevent the psychological and physical effects of stress.
- Understand post-traumatic stress disorder and its impact upon police officers.

On-the-Job Scenario

"I don't understand what's wrong with me. I can't sleep at night, and my stomach is upset all the time."

"Maybe the shooting you were involved in is bothering you."

"No. That was two months ago, and I slept great the same night it happened."

"Well, I've heard that stuff can start to bother you months after something has happened. I mean, it was the first time you had to use your gun, and you did kill him."

"Look, don't try the psychology crap on me. I'm fine. Let's get back to work and finish these reports!"

As the above scenario depicts, people suffer a variety of symptoms after stressful events, whether or not they realize that their symptoms arise from dealing with those events. Stress can affect us long after the stressor is over, and symptoms may take months to appear. Dealing with conflict and tense situations can profoundly affect health and well-being. However, everyday hassles can also have impact. Part of being an effective police officer is understanding stress and learning how to manage it. Many police authors firmly believe that if law enforcement officers know what aspects of their job are likely to create stress, they will be better prepared to handle that stress (Anderson et al., 1995). Policing has many stressors that you must be able to manage effectively if you want a long and rewarding career in the field. And we believe that examining and exploring stress-reduction and stress-management techniques before they are needed is good preparation for inevitable stress that will be experienced.

This final chapter concentrates on stress. Some occupations, including policing, are more prone to stress than others (Violanti and Paton, 1999). In other words, by choosing a career in policing, you are choosing a job with higher levels of stress than many other jobs. To effectively deal with all the types of conflict that we have discussed in the book, you need to keep yourself healthy. An important component of being healthy, aside from the physical aspects, is appropriately dealing with all the stressors of policing, which range from engaging in fatal shootings to dealing with the belligerent drunk who refuses to leave the bar at closing time. Even keeping up on paperwork and other mundane features of the job can create stress. First, we will define stress and examine how stress affects us. Then we will concentrate on the stress of policing. A critical part of this chapter is the exploration of a number of techniques that you can use to assist with stress reduction. Last, an often-ignored area of stress in policing, post-traumatic stress disorder, will be discussed within the context of policing.

STRESS AND STRESSORS

Stress can be defined as "a reaction to any event that requires an organism to adjust in some manner." This adjustment can be emotional, psychological, and/or physical. Stress is a response to life experiences that challenge or threaten us. **Stressors** are the events or situations that cause these reactions or cause stress. Stressors share three characteristics. First, they put us into a state of overload, making it more difficult for us to adapt. They also invoke incompatible tendencies. For example, you may be excited about graduating but also be afraid of walking across the stage to receive your diploma. Third, the stressor is uncontrollable, such as losing a job or having a loved one die. Not everyone has the same stressors, and people can react differently to the same stressor. For example, while many people find tests stressful, tests are not a stressor for everyone. Some people may actually find tests fun, in which case these people do not suffer from negative stress, but may experience **eustress** or positive stress that gears us up for positive action. Also, the same stressor may affect the same person differently at various times. For example, slow-moving traffic may be a stressor for you one day, but not bother you at all on a different day.

What Makes Events Stressful?

Some types of events or stressors are more likely to cause stress than others. Any event that makes you adjust, make changes, or expend your resources (physically and/or mentally) has a potential to be stressful. The event can be one that makes you happy such as sky-diving or getting married, or one that is perceived as negative, such as shooting an offender in the line of duty or losing a loved one to cancer. According to one text, four types of events are more likely to lead to experiencing stress (Taylor et al., 2000).

Numerous studies point out that *unpleasant or negative events* cause people more psychological distress and produce more physical symptoms than do more positive stressful events (for instance, Sarason et al., 1978).

Events that are *unpredictable or uncontrollable* are more stressful than ones that are controllable or predictable (Bandura et al., 1988). This is, of course, one of the reasons that the field of policing is stressful. Officers often become involved in events that they cannot control, such as one family member shooting another family member or a mother who abuses her infant. Instead, police officers are often called in to deal with the aftermath of ruined lives and needless tragedy. Even experienced police negotiators cannot predict the outcome of a situation, even with their skills and training. When events such as these cannot be controlled, the person experiencing the stress is unable to plan or develop ways to cope (Taylor et al., 2000). For example, if my television is too loud, I can turn it down, but if the neighbour's television is too loud, there may be little that I can do about it.

Events that people know little about and that are therefore *ambiguous,* are more stressful than those that are clear-cut and obvious. In many police situations, officers are unsure about what is going on, such as when watching a "suspicious character" in a mall. People also lie to police officers who then cannot be sure when suspects or witnesses are telling the truth. When stressors are clear, people can actively use their problem-solving skills to find solutions (Billings and Moos, 1984).

The last type of stressful events are those that are *irresolvable.* Irresolvable events are more stressful than ones that can be resolved. People usually attempt to solve their problems, and failure to do so can be frustrating. For police officers, continuous calls at one particular residence, the continuing view of the damage that drug and alcohol abuse can do to people, or even feelings of guilt after shooting an armed and dangerous suspect may lead to cynicism and the view that nothing can be done. Some research has indicated that it is irresolvable stress that leads to the most harmful psychological and physiological responses (Holman and Silver, 1998).

Physiological Responses to Stress

In chapter 2, we examined emotions and how they cause physiological changes in the body through the sympathetic nervous system. Stress, which creates emotional states, also causes physiological changes in the body. The latest research on stress points out that its effects are more profound than previously thought. Stress changes people, and when people experience and cope with it, stress alters people's bodies and brains (Carpi, 1996). If you have ever had a close encounter with a car, you know how your body reacted: your heart rate went up, hands clenched the steering wheel, blood pressure soared, your mouth became dry, and you may have even begun to sweat. These physical changes, along with the accompanying emotional states, prepare you for "flight or fight." Usually, our responses to this type of incident are brief, and our body returns to a normal state fairly quickly. However, if the stress is ongoing or chronic, there is a longer sequence of events caused by our efforts to return to "normal" (Baron, 2001).

Hans Selye (1974), a major researcher in the area of stress, developed the **general adaptation syndrome**, a sequence of three stages, to help explain the effects of stress and long-term stress. The first is the *alarm stage*, in which the body prepares itself for immediate action. The sympathetic nervous system is aroused and releases hormones to prepare the body to meet threat or danger. If the stress continues and is prolonged, the *resistance stage* begins. During this stage, arousal is lower but the body continues to use up its resources at a higher than normal rate in order to continue coping with the stressor. With continued exposure, the body enters the third stage, *exhaustion,* where its capacity to resist is depleted. If this stage continues, illness and even death may result. Figure 10-1 summarizes these three stages from the work of Selye (1974).

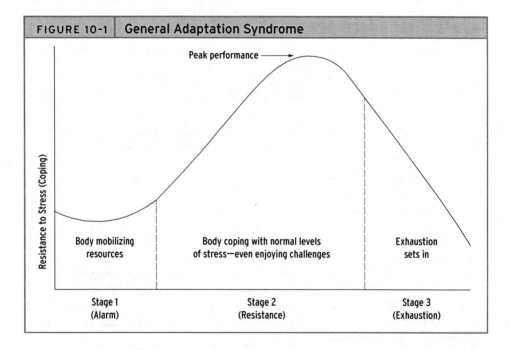

FIGURE 10-1 | General Adaptation Syndrome

The body's response to stress is complex and spread throughout the body. The sympathetic nervous system (which activates you), the parasympathetic nervous system (which calms you), the endocrine system (which releases hormones and chemicals), the pituitary gland, and the immune systems are involved in managing stress. The cerebral cortex of the brain assesses the stress and helps to regulate emotional responses so that control is maintained. With this continued activation of the body, the resources tend to "burn out" as the body continually tries to regain its balance or **homeostasis**—a physiological steady state in the body. For example, if you are hungry, your body is no longer in a steady state. Once you eat, homeostasis is restored. The same is true with stress. While trying to actively resist stress and maintain the body at a steady state, eventually the body runs "out of gas," leading to exhaustion and burnout.

However, as stated earlier, we cannot ignore the fact that people react differently to stressors, because they appraise them differently. Basically, how the individual perceives the stress will dictate how the person responds. This is an important point to remember, because restructuring and changing appraisals is a major stress-reduction strategy (similar to cognitive restructuring to reduce conflict). Continued negative appraisal of stress also leads not only to physical illness, but also to emotional and psychological problems.

Positive versus Negative Stress

While it may be hard to imagine that any stress can be positive, it is important to remember that stress is defined as any bodily reaction to a stressor, and that a stressor is a challenging event. Selye (1974) coined the term *eustress* to describe this positive stress. The basic principle underlying eustress is that many stressful situations bring out the best in us; for instance, making us more creative and resourceful. Also, there is little doubt that most of us need some stimulation and risk, although this need varies greatly among individuals. The field of policing is often chosen by individuals who crave more risk than those who enter low-risk fields such as accounting or computer technology. That is not to say that people who enter these fields do not crave excitement or adventure; they just choose not to pursue it on the job. There are accountants who skydive, race cars, and climb mountains! Selye believed that healthy individuals need a certain amount of stress, and that inactivity and boredom can lead to **distress**, or negative stress.

Police officers have a higher-than-average need for activity, and one group of authors (Anderson et al., 1995) has labelled these officers as *stress-seekers*. The fact that law enforcement can be a dangerous, exciting, and dirty job is exactly what makes it attractive. Stress becomes a problem only when it becomes distress and taxes or goes beyond the person's ability to cope or manage. It is worth noting that the 24-year-old who enters policing, and craves excitement, may no longer have the same degree of craving at 42.

SOURCES OF STRESS

Here we will examine many sources of stress, including stressors unique to policing. All of us share a number of sources of stress as well as sources of stress more unique to positions that involve enforcing laws. "No matter how hardy or tough people think they are when they join (a police service), the pain and suffering they are exposed to, the administrative hassles…and the hostility of some of the people they are trying to protect will eventually have negative…effects unless effective stress-coping strategies are learned and practiced (Anderson et al., 1995, p. 3). First, we will review common stressors and follow with police stressors.

Life Events, Stress, and Personal Health

Some of the earliest research on the physical effects of stress explored the relationship between stressful life events and the onset of illness. Rating scales such as the Social Readjustment Rating Scale (SRRS) listed potentially stressful events that required people to make changes in their lives, such as getting married, leaving home, or having a spouse die (Taylor et al., 2000). People responding to the scale would check off which events had occurred to them in the previous year. Each event had a point value associated with it; the higher the points, the more readjustment required of the person. Although most people will experience some of the stressors on the scale, those who experience many are more vulnerable and therefore more likely to become ill. (If you recall from our earlier discussion, prolonged stress depletes the immune system.) The stressors range from the death of a spouse (given a score of 100) to minor events such as a change in sleeping habits (a score of 15) and a minor violation of the law (score 11). According to Holmes and Rahe (1967), most people reach a critical level of stress at about 300 points, where there is an approximately 80 per cent chance of developing some kind of stress-related symptoms in the next year. Note that the life event scales also include positive stressors such as getting married, having a baby, and even Christmas and other celebrations. It is the amount of readjustment that creates the stress, and even positive events can cause a great deal of change in a person's life (ask any new mom or dad).

Research has consistently indicated that as stress increases, depression and other illnesses are more likely (Baron et al., 2001). The more events and the higher the total score, the more likely that the individual will suffer a health problem in the following year. One author has consistently noted the number of student illnesses that occur during examination weeks, and many students report becoming ill immediately after exams are over! The work of Holmes and Rahe (1967) and Holmes and Masuda (1974) has paved the way of updated versions of these scales, including ones about work-related stress, the stresses of being a student, and, as we shall see shortly, the stresses of police work.

Everyday Hassles

While major life events can be stressful, they do not occur every day. However, all of us experience **everyday hassles** or minor annoyances that can also be stressful. Standing in lineups, coping with overcrowded schedules, balancing family and work, dealing with inflation, and doing your taxes are all examples of hassles that are ongoing and experienced over and over again.

Social and Family Problems

Friends and family are the main sources of affection, love, and support in your life but can also be sources of stress. For example, if someone close to you is ill, you may worry about this person.

Physical and Mental Health Problems

While stress can make you ill, illness can create stress. In jobs such as policing, where physical health is important, health problems can be extremely stressful. When people are not well or have had surgery, they worry about recovery and implications if a full recovery is not possible.

Similarly, experiencing mental health problems can also be stressful. People are often unwilling to discuss these kinds or problems or seek help from a mental health professional.

Financial Problems

A major stressor for many people is financial problems. Credit card debts, high mortgages, and car payments add stress for many people. Just barely making ends meet can become very stressful if anything breaks down or needs replacing.

Personality Factors and Stress-Proneness

Some people are more stress-prone than others and thus feel the stressors that others do not or react with more stress than others, when faced with the same stressor. Here we will quickly examine Type A behaviour, external locus of control, and negative affectivity.

Type A Behaviour

People with **Type A behaviour** characteristics often get themselves into stressful situations because of these characteristics. People with Type A behaviour have the major behaviour problem of trying to do too much in too little time, which leads to a continual personal sense of urgency that can be very stressful. The second problem area for Type A's is their often free-floating hostility. With this sense of urgency combined with hostility, these people become irritated by small things, are impatient, and can be very demanding. On the positive side, they tend to be hard-working, but their aggressive tendencies can get in the way (Dubrin and Geerinck, 2001).

Certain features of the Type A behaviour pattern have been related to the development of coronary heart disease. According to this research, hostility, anger, cynicism, and suspiciousness lead to heart problems, whereas some of the other characteristics such as impatience, ambition, and being driven by work do not show this relationship (Dembrowski and Costa, 1987; Rosenman, 1975).

Belief in External Locus of Control

People who believe that they cannot control the events and things that happen to them have an **external locus of control**. In other words, what happens to them appears to be a matter of fate. People with an **internal locus of control** believe that they can control the things or events around them (Dubrin and Geerinck, 2001).

How are such beliefs related to stress? Let's illustrate with an example. Suppose you find yourself unemployed, an adverse and stressful event. People with an external locus of control believe that they can do very little to change the situation, so they do not actively seek employment and they continue to suffer the stressor of unemployment. Also, people with an external locus of control may worry about such events as unemployment even when employed. If, however, you believe that you can find another job, you are more likely to seek work if you are unemployed and less likely to worry about unemployment or other possible negative events or stressors.

Negative Affectivity

Have you ever met someone who also sees the negative side of everything and is often in a bad or upset mood? This person may have **negative affectivity**—a tendency to experience adverse emotional states and a predisposition to experience emotional stress. These emotional states include feelings of nervousness, tension, and worry. They also tend to experience other feelings such as anger, scorn, revulsion, guilt, and self-dissatisfaction more than others (Chen and Spector, 1991). These negative people search for problems rather than solutions and are often distressed even when working under conditions that others would find interesting and challenging.

Personal Differences and Stress Sensitivity

Some people appear to handle stress very well with laid-back attitudes, rarely overreacting to any stress in their lives. Others immediately go into crisis and have strong reactions to stress. While some research has pointed out such factors as the "resilient or hardy" personality, other research has explained that the differences in ability to cope with stress may have to do with the kinds of stress that we encountered in the past, particularly when very young. For example, losing a parent when very young is more difficult to deal with than losing a parent as an adult.

This newer research finds that our reactions to stress are similar to allergies. Just as with pollen or other allergens, our body can become sensitized, and then when in the presence of the allergen, react strongly. As with an allergy, we become sensitized or acutely sensitive to stress. Even the mildest event releases the entire cascade of the general adaptation syndrome and all of the related biological effects. Therefore, while we all start out with the same biological makeup, how we managed stress in the past has great influence on how we manage it in the present. As a result of early life events, some people become more sensitized to stress and react more acutely to stressors (Carpi, 1996). People who manage stress well early in life tend to cope with it better when they are older and suffer fewer damaging physiological and psychological effects.

This research has some direct relationship to policing. First, police organizations may want to investigate the type of life stress that recruits have already experienced prior to a policing career. Second, if sensitization occurs, officers who have been in the field for many years and have dealt with a variety of serious calls (such as a shooting), may be in need of stress management training before they show symptoms of stress. In other words, this research strongly emphasizes the need for stress management training for officers throughout their careers.

THE STRESSORS OF POLICE WORK

There are stressors unique to police work. While some may be shared by other public service employees, such as the stress of shift work and dealing with traumatized people and death, police work also includes uncommon stressors dictated by the facts that police officers carry weapons, must make split-second decisions, and may be called upon to use force at any time. It is the unpredictability of the work that may create much of the stress. For example, a paramedic may deal with death and gruesome accidents, but this is a regular part of the job. In a single shift, a police officer may have to tell loved ones about a death, view the body of a suicide victim five days after the fact, use force on someone with a weapon, and receive notice of a court appearance. Or, on the other hand, an entire shift may be one endless patrol with little to relieve the boredom. Another difference between police work and other emergency services is that there can be a built-in animosity towards a police officer. People seldom curse the firefighter who saved their house or the paramedic who bandaged their wounds, but the police officer who took away their father may be an object of scorn. In this section, we will first examine stressful law-enforcement events and then target some of the specific stressors of police work.

Life Stress Events in Law Enforcement

Similar to the Life Events Scale by Holmes and Rahe (1967), law-enforcement events scales have also been designed to assist law enforcement personnel in gauging stress from the stressors of law enforcement. Although most theories, as we saw earlier, see stressful events as cumulative or building on each other, in law enforcement one event such as the killing of a partner has the potential of driving an officer into a full-blown post-traumatic stress reaction (see later in the chapter for more information on post-traumatic stress reaction) (Anderson et al., 1995). James Sewell (1981), in his article on police stress, lists the top 25 stressors in law enforcement. It is interesting that none of those 25 items are positive stressors; all are negative events.

---

25 Most Stressful Law-Enforcement Critical Life Events

1. Violent death of a partner in the line of duty
2. Dismissal
3. Taking a life in the line of duty
4. Shooting someone in the line of duty
5. Suicide of an officer who is a close friend
6. Violent death of another officer in the line of duty
7. Murder committed by a police officer
8. Duty-related violent injury (shooting)
9. Violent job-related injury to another officer
10. Suspension
11. Passed over for promotion
12. Pursuit of an armed suspect
13. Answering a call to a scene involving violent, non-accidental death of a child
14. Assignment away from family for a long period of time
15. Personal involvement in a shooting incident
16. Reduction in pay
17. Observing an act of police corruption
18. Accepting a bribe
19. Participating in an act of police corruption
20. Hostage situation resulting from aborted criminal action
21. Response to a scene involving the accidental death of a child
22. Promotion of an inexperienced or incompetent officer over you
23. Internal affairs investigation against self
24. Barricaded suspect
25. Hostage situation resulting from a domestic disturbance

Source: James D. Sewell (1981, April). Police stress. *FBI Law Enforcement Bulletin*, p. 9. Reprint courtesy of the *FBI Law Enforcement Bulletin*.

Two things should be noted here. First, this list is not new, although many of these events would most likely still be in the list. For example, in recent decades police corruption has been more closely scrutinized, and participating or getting caught in some sort of corruption would likely be perceived as more stressful today. Second, this is an American listing. However, when examining the list, particularly the top ten items, Canadian officers would most likely agree that these events are extremely stressful and difficult for many to cope with.

In a recent speech by an officer, Dan Goldfarb said that the biggest police stressors are killing someone in the line of duty, having your partner killed in the line of duty, lack of support by departments/bosses, shift work, and the daily grind of dealing with the "stupidity of the public" (Goldfarb, 2001). If we were to re-examine everyday life event stress and then add a couple that are specific to the field of law enforcement, it can readily be seen how stressful law enforcement is and how important the development of coping strategies is for officers.

Shift Work

Although many people work in shifts, the physiological and psychological demands of shift work are often overlooked as a significant stressor. While most of the country operates under the usual routine of being awake during the day and sleeping at night, police officers (among other shift workers) continually make adjustments to various shifts. Many studies, such as one examining many shift systems, including the Ottawa shift system, illustrate the stress of shift work, which upsets natural rhythms (Simpson and Richbell, 2000). Our bodies work according to a certain rhythm called the **circadian rhythm**, a 24-hour cycle of activity ranging from sleep to activity. Temperature, heart rate, blood pressure, and other bodily processes follow this day/night cycle, usually reaching a peak in the afternoon or early evening and a trough during the night (Simpson and Richbell, 2000). Shift work upsets this natural cycle and can create such symptoms as irritability, loss of appetite, fatigue, feeling hot or cold at certain times, and sleep difficulties. Often, just as a person is getting adjusted to one shift, the shift changes and creates the same problems all over again.

While shift work can be physiologically stressful, it can also be psychologically stressful. Night shifts particularly can be difficult and interfere with life that operates on a daytime schedule. Night shift routines interfere with dating opportunities, child-care routines, and even simple things such as cutting the grass, watching a child in a school play, or going to a movie. Officers with spouses and children may find shift work especially stressful. One study found that 30 per cent of police divorces were related to the stress of the profession, mostly resulting from shift work (Baxter, 1978).

Supervision

With the ability to use force and to act with discretion, police officers have considerable power. Having these powers, which could lead to corruption, is a concern for police managers and supervisors. The resulting supervision has placed unneeded stress on many police officers without resolving the problems of the occasional abuse of power and corruption (Anderson et al., 1995). This can become a "Catch-22" for many officers. While they need these powers to act quickly and to make decisions, they may come under fire by superiors (not to mention public scrutiny) if they are perceived as misusing them in some way. For example, if an officer spots a person trying to open car doors in a parking lot, should he or she stop and search the person? Should the officer wait until the person enters a vehicle, takes something out of the vehicle, do nothing? What if the officer stops and searches the person, finds nothing, and that person files a complaint against the officer? In the event of a complaint, how will the supervisor deal with the officer? It is important that supervisors recognize the continued complexity of police work and support those officers on patrol who are, for the most part, operating with little direct supervision.

Several writings on police organizations have pointed out that current management methods, coupled with a rigid hierarchy of decision making, are poor organizational structures for proper supervision in such highly changing and volatile times (Anderson et al., 1995; De Paris, 1998). While these authors urge restructuring, the reality is that officers must deal with whatever structure and supervisor is in place.

Several supervision problems create stress for officers. Of course, many of them are found not only in policing, but supervision problems compound the stress from police stressors, especially if officers feel unsupported "back at the office." One has already been alluded to, which is the supervisors who do not support their officers and engage in unjustified criticism. The lack of counselling skills in supervisors who do not listen or offer support and show insufficient concern for their officers is all part of supervision with poor interpersonal communication skills. As well, supervisors who are contemptuous of patrol officers have been cited as stressful (Sparrow, 1990). Last, supervisors who do not consult with officers and who are autocratic in decision making can create stress for officers. This points to a very important method of stress reduction for police officers: supervision that is fair, supportive, and allows officers some latitude in their own conduct within a legal framework.

Dealing with Death and Severe Injuries

Most new police officers are mentally and emotionally unprepared to deal with the dead, dying, or seriously injured. Skills must be acquired to help deal with the stress that is caused by dealing with dead bodies, people who have been seriously or fatally injured, and people who have experienced a traumatic event such a car accident, or a victim of rape or assault (Anderson et al., 1995).

Consider This...

An officer of 30 years still recalls vividly his first death call involving a baby. The infant had died in her crib, a victim of crib death. As he describes the incident, he almost gets tears in his eyes, even after all of these years. He says that the first tragic incident is the one you never forget, even when later incidents become blurry in memory.

Many officers deal with these situations by withdrawing their feelings from the scene or by no longer seeing the victims as people (dehumanizing them). Some develop a sense of "black humour" that members of the public may find disgusting or immoral. The key is to find some way to handle these situations, otherwise the officer may become depressed or unable to continue in the job. As well, if you recall from our earlier discussion, unresolved stress continues to affect the person, even if the person is largely unaware of these effects.

According to one text on police stress, four situations are likely to traumatize even the most experienced and conditioned officer:

1. Making a death report to next of kin.
2. Receiving a call to an incident involving a death that has special personal meaning, such as that of a friend.
3. Dealing with the death of another officer.
4. Dealing with a major catastrophe, where there are many dead, such as an airplane crash (Anderson et al., 1995, p. 88).

Testifying in Court

Frustration with the judicial system is one of the most commonly acknowledged stressors for police officers (Territo and Vetter, 1981). Rulings by the court are often perceived as too lenient, compelling evidence may be excluded, charges are reduced, and officers themselves may be scrutinized for their behaviour during the arrest (White et al., 1985).

While not a popular activity for officers, testifying in court is part of the job, even though it may be infrequent, often occurring months after the arrest was made. The officer must locate the case file, search memory for details, try not to confuse this case with similar ones, and put up with a cross-examination that makes the officer feel as if he or she is the one standing trial. A trend that makes it more difficult for officers in court is the tendency for plea bargains to be made. These arrangements save money and court time, but the result is that officers rarely testify in court. Police officers are expected to be competent and professional witnesses, but with little experience, they are often poorly equipped to deal with major court cases. As with any other aspect of law enforcement, the officer needs to be trained, equipped, and mentally prepared to deal with court appearances (Anderson et al., 1995). Additional stress can be added to a court appearance if the case is personally important to the officer, such as the shooting of another officer or a particularly heinous crime such as sexual assault of a child.

Dealing with Organizational Change

One Canadian author added that stress can result from the profound and extensive organizational changes presently occurring in Canadian policing (McKenna, 1998). These changes include restructuring with more focus on community orientation, amalgamation of services, and legislative effects such as changes in discretionary powers and use of force.

Dealing with the Public

Dealing with members of the public can be very stressful. Here we will look at a few specific types of people that officers are routinely called in to manage or they meet during patrol.

Often, police officers must deal with people who are traumatized. They may have been in an accident, have witnessed or have been involved in a traumatic event, or have been a victim of crime. Police officers may note several characteristics as the traumatized try to come to grips with what has happened, including crying, incoherence, dazed expressions, and difficulty understanding. These people may be in crisis and so must be treated as if they are. (Refer to chapter 5 and managing crises.)

Police may also have to deal with people who are basically anti-police. These people are hostile, uncooperative, and while not committing any crimes or suspected of committing a crime, react defensively and may be rude. Patience is required, and that can be difficult, considering the kind of treatment police are given. Being patient with people such as these can be trying and stressful.

A third type of person can be lumped under the label of simply irritating. This person requests assistance for matters out of the normal routines of policing. Requests range from talking to a neighbour about wandering cats to fixing stuck windows. Most officers treat these calls with kindness and understanding, but over time such calls can become annoying.

Fourth, members of the public who have strong opinions about what police "ought" to be doing are a constant stressor. When giving out a speeding ticket, this kind of person tells the officer that he or she should be out there getting the "real" criminals rather than bothering honest citizens who pay the officer through his or her taxes. Sometimes belligerent, these individuals act as if they know the role of police officers better than officers themselves and are not reluctant to share this knowledge.

Last, people who are suspected of crimes, gang members, and other marginal persons are a source of stress. Often, the hostility between the police organization and these groups prohibits good communication, making it all the more difficult to deal with these people. These people can be hostile and very aggressive. The officer may have to use the tactics studied in chapter 5 to manage conflicts.

In general, the range of required behaviours when dealing with the public may be the cause of stress. On one hand, police officers are supposed to be gentle, approachable, impartial, and kind. On the other, they are supposed to be tough, aggressive, and able to get people to obey the law. Bouncing from one set of expectations to the other can be difficult while still maintaining vigilance to expect the unexpected.

Suicide by Cop

In the world of police work, suicide by cop actually refers to an incident in which a suicidal individual ends his or her life by using a police officer as a weapon for the suicide. Usually the person sets up the situation so that it appears as if he or she is going to shoot the officer (or someone else), and the officer is forced to respond by shooting the individual.

Consider This...

A patrol officer spots an erratic driver and pulls the car over. The driver, a 19-year-old male, gets out of the car and approaches the officer with what appears to be a rifle. Despite repeated requests for him to drop the weapon, he lifts the rifle towards the officer. The officer shoots and kills the male. Afterwards, the officer finds out that the rifle was a convincing look-alike toy.

This type of incident is very stressful because the officer may find himself or herself questioning his or her behaviour. In this type of event, the officer is also a victim. Critical here is the immediate support of the officer's service to help the officer understand that the actions were ethically correct and professionally justified (Vanzandt, 1993).

Critical Incident Stress

Every year, hundreds of police officers must deal with intense, traumatic events that have serious long-term effects for them, their families, and their service (Kureczka, 1996). These critical incidents create extreme stress that may be long-term. A **critical incident** is defined as a psychologically distressing experience that is outside the range of normal or usual human experience (Blau, 1994). These incidents are extreme stressors—the ones at the top of our earlier lists—such as killing someone in the line of duty or in personal life, the death of a child, or divorce.

What distinguishes a critical event from other stressors is that it threatens the ability to function, or maybe even to survive. It may be so intense as to produce post-traumatic stress disorder (see post-traumatic stress disorder below). According to Blau (1994), critical incidents have the following common characteristics:

1. The event is sudden and unexpected.

2. The event is perceived to be a threat to officer survival or well-being.

3. The event includes an element of loss.

4. The event causes a sudden shift in the officer's values, ideals, or confidence.

Of course, none of us respond identically to critical incidents, because of differences in our personality, values, and beliefs. For example, the responses of police officers who kill someone in the line of duty vary and include such responses as feeling guilty, feeling immobilized, and feeling they have compromised their religious beliefs. Other officers appear to have no reaction and feel little, if any, guilt (Lippert and Ferrara, 1981).

MANAGING STRESS

There are many strategies to choose from to manage stress. This section will explain several of them. Some deal with specific stressors and deal directly with attacking the source of the stress, such as testifying in court, while others are techniques that can be used for all types of stressors and are more indirect in their focus. The key is to find stress-reduction and stress-management techniques that you can use. What works for one person may not help you. You may need to try several techniques before you find the ones that help you.

Recognize Your Stress Symptoms

While it sounds simple, we are not always in tune with our own bodies and may not realize that what we are experiencing is stress. We rationalize, deny, or ignore the early warning symptoms until we become really ill—mentally or physically. Recognition may be the most important strategy in the list. Stress often manifests with physiological and/or psychological symptoms. Recognizing these symptoms early can reduce the chance of their getting worse and you can more quickly make use of the help you need.

Consider This...

After witnessing the shooting of his partner, an officer started to have bouts of nausea and vomiting. It was only after he started to notice blood that he went to the doctor and was diagnosed with an ulcer.

Below is a chart that lists the symptoms of stress. Many people are "in tune" with their bodies and know when something is not quite right. However, symptoms can be overlooked when we get too busy to slow down or we can deny that we are experiencing stress.

This is by no means a complete list, but you can use it as a checklist when you have experienced several stressors and are unsure about the stress symptoms you are experiencing. Also, these symptoms can vary in their intensity; the more intense the symptoms, the more severe the stress is likely to be.

TABLE 10-1	Stress Symptoms Checklist

Physical Symptoms

• Sleep difficulties (cannot get to sleep, stay asleep, wake too early, or want to sleep all the time)	• Physical tension in back, neck, jaw, or other body areas
• Sweating or chills	• High blood pressure
• Difficulty breathing	• Higher than normal heart rate that is prolonged and noticeable even at rest
• Unexplained rashes, including hives	• Overeating or under-eating
• Blurred vision	• Weight loss or weight gain
• Headache	• Lack of energy, fatigue
• Stomach upsets (including nausea, vomiting, and heartburn)	• Teeth grinding during the night or during the day
• Bowel problems (constipation or diarrhea)	• Sense of choking or tightness in throat
• Chest pain	• Swallowing excessively
• Back pain	• Dizziness or lightheadedness
• Neck pain	• Cold hands and feet
	• Restlessness

Psychological Symptoms

• Crying spells	• Feeling trapped
• Decreased interest in sex	• Impatience or easily angered
• Apathy	• Feelings of impending doom or danger
• Thoughts of death or suicide	• Confusion
• Lack of pleasure in things you usually find enjoyable	• Memory blanks
• Feeling lonely and isolated	• Persistent worrying
• Poor concentration, including daydreaming	• Feeling depressed
• Nightmares	• Binge eating or binge drinking
• Inappropriate feelings, including guilt, shame, embarrassment, hopelessness	• Overuse of alcohol, drugs, or medication

Talk, Talk, Talk!

When reading the literature and research on police stress, what stood out for these authors was the reluctance that the majority of officers have to talk about the traumatic and stressful event they have had to face. Some officers felt that talking about it would make them appear weak. Others thought that talking about it would make it too real for them to handle. However, keeping feelings bottled up inside for years takes its toll. Officers need to work through the incident, understand their feelings, and bring closure to the experience. In one case, the officer witnessed the death of a friend in a car accident. The drunk driver who caused the accident was not prosecuted. Only years later did he talk with a peer counsellor and get the sense of completion that he so badly needed (Anderson et al., 1995, 91–94).

While many police officers recognize the value of talking things out, the problem is who to talk to? While talking to fellow officers may be a good idea, some are afraid that they may look "sissy" or ineffectual or not tough enough to do the job. However, many officers find it easy and rewarding to talk to peers about their stress. Fellow officers often understand what the person is going through because they have already "been there" and understand the stresses of police work. Younger officers may benefit from the counsel of older officers or other mentors. In line with this idea, many services offer free peer coun-selling: trained police officers with skills in therapy, stress management, and psychology.

It is important to develop a network of support and include in this network people who are not in law enforcement or a related profession. Sometimes, a good friend, a golf game, and talking about sports is the best medicine!

Prepare for Court Appearances

To reduce the stress of court appearances, prepare for them. Here are a few suggestions to help you reduce the stress of testifying in court:

- **Have your reports/memo book in order.** Write your notes as soon as possible after an incident. Develop your own personal style of organization and make sure that all notes are complete. Then if you do have to testify, you will be reassured that all your files, memo book, and any notes are neat, organized, and complete.

- **Draw pictures or other visuals.** Over time, memories can become blurry. Draw pictures of the scene, label items, use arrows to show movement, and number the sequence of events. Properly title and date the drawing to supplement your report.

- **Use memory devices and techniques to aid recall.** Under intense examination when you are nervous, using memory techniques can aid recall. When we are nervous, we can forget things, and you do not want to appear forgetful or unsure of your facts in court. For example, use the first letter of each word for the reasons you stopped a driver: *A.* appeared drunk, *S.* Swerving, and *S.* Speeding.

- **Know the "players."** Find out information about the lawyers, judge, and others involved in the case.

- **Meet with the Crown attorney.** Find out the questions you will be asked and get an opinion about possible questions from the defence attorney.

- **Mentally rehearse the court appearance with positive outcomes.** Often we focus on what could go wrong. By rehearsing the situation positively, you will increase your confidence. As part of the rehearsal, carefully review the case and your answers to possible questions.

- **Relax while waiting to testify.** It may be very difficult to relax, but try deep-breathing or use mental imagery. One police officer stated that he visualizes the defence attorney or judge as being naked and this helps him relax.

- **Stick to what you know.** The defence may try to get you to offer opinions or to be more accurate, by asking such questions as "So exactly how far away were you from…?" Since you did not bring a ruler, if you state an exact number of metres, you open yourself to questions about accuracy. It is best to stick with what you know and give a range, such as between 10 and 12 metres, which is what you know and is in your report (Anderson et al., 1995).

- **Remain objective.** A police officer's job in court is to present the gathered evidence, not to convict people. An officer who appears to be objective (not out to persecute the accused) is a much more credible witness. Further, this type of attitude takes away some of the personal stakes in the outcome, and reduces stress.

Keep Your Body in Shape

Diet, exercise, and proper rest are three strategic areas of management that will help both the body and mind continue to battle the stress of police work. Diet is important because nutrients, including vitamins and minerals, help the body fight infection, boost the immune system, and help maintain muscle fitness. Proper diet also improves several brain functions, including such important skills as reaction time, coordination, eyesight, and problem solving and decision making.

Exercise is also important. Regular exercise lowers blood pressure, releases hormones that make you feel good, boosts the immune system, and gives you the strength and endurance required for some aspects of the job.

While rest includes sleep, it also includes time for relaxation. One skill—napping—is beneficial for managing stress as well as the rigors of shift work. Some people become very good at napping, taking 15- to 20-minute naps a couple of times per day. For many officers, the profession becomes all they can think about. Spending time with family and friends can be a good way to unwind. It may also be important to let people know that when you are unwinding, you do not want to answer questions about your job, such as "Have you ever shot anyone?"

Use Alcohol and Medications Moderately

While it may be tempting to wash stress away with a few drinks or other medications, overuse or abuse can create additional stress. Recent statistics indicate that alcohol abuse by police officers is nearly double that of the general population (Violanti, 1999). In an article from *Maclean's*, a 1989 report from the Clarke Institute concluded that more than one-third of the RCMP's regular and civilian employees drank over the level recognized by the World Health Organization as damaging to health: more than three drinks per day (Corelli and MacAndrew, 1994). This paper also reported that over 600 members were experiencing distressing side effects relating to prescription and over-the-counter drug use.

Alcohol and drug abuse are real problems facing police services today. If this is true, then it is up to the individual to monitor alcohol and drug use. Some suggestions for limiting alcohol abuse are to drink no more than three drinks per day, never drink on the job, and cease drinking alcohol completely at least 12 hours before the next shift. Spending social time with people who do not drink reduces the opportunity for drinking. On days off, to think of drinking before 6:00 p.m. as a personal taboo is also an effective strategy (Dubrin and Geerinck, 2001).

Use Relaxation Techniques

Since not all stress can be directly confronted and can build over time, finding ways to relax are crucial for stress reduction. Here are a couple of strategies that people find useful.

Deep breathing The major benefit of deep breathing is that it can be practised anywhere and anytime. Waiting for your turn in court, driving to a gruesome murder scene or on the way to deliver bad news to a family are all good opportunities to practise this simple strategy. For those who are interested, the technique is presented in the Skills Practice box below.

Skills Practice: Deep Breathing

Inhaling and exhaling slowly and deeply is a powerful stress reducer for many people. Deep breathing has immediate and long-term benefits such as lowering the heart rate, lowering blood pressure, and increasing skin temperature. It may also help you to relax emotionally so that you can think more clearly and gain perspective (Dubrin and Geerinck, 2001). Before using it on the job, learn how to do it so that you can use it whenever and wherever you need it. Here are the basic steps to learn this technique:

1. Sit or lie down in a quiet spot. We recommend sitting, because this may be the position you use on the job.

2. Place one hand on your belly, the other in the centre of your chest. Breathe several times. The hand on your belly should move more because it indicates you are breathing from your diaphragm (breathing deeply).

3. Now inhale slowly, filling your lungs. As you exhale slowly, push air out from the bottom of your lungs.

4. Take long, slow breaths. If you get dizzy or light-headed, you are breathing too quickly.

5. As you inhale, elevate your shoulders and collarbone slightly to fill the lungs with air (sit up straight).

6. Once you have mastered the breathing, you can add some visualization or thoughts such as breathing in calmness and exhaling worry (McDonald, 1995).

Once you have mastered this technique, you can use it anywhere and at any time. One student reported that he used this strategy while waiting for an interview with a police service. It must have worked—he got the job!

Achieve the relaxation response through informal meditation The **relaxation response** is a bodily reaction that you experience when completely relaxed; respiration and blood pressure is lower, heartbeat is slower, and muscles are relaxed.

One way to achieve this response is to use informal meditation. We use the term *informal meditation* because there are other meditation techniques such as transcendental meditation that may require some formalized training. The informal method here should be practised twice daily for periods of 10 to 20 minutes. Four things are required to practise the relaxation response: a quiet place, an object to focus on, a passive attitude, and a comfortable position. Then close your eyes, relax, and concentrate on something such as a word, phrase, or prayer. Do not let other thoughts intrude for the time period (Benson, 1995). Ten to twenty minutes per day is all it takes to learn and use this strategy.

Develop hobbies and interests outside of policing

Developing a variety of hobbies and interests lets you unwind and put the stresses of police work aside for awhile. Hobbies can include anything that you enjoy doing including sports, crafts, and artistic pursuits.

ADMINISTRATIVE STRATEGIES

While this is not a text about police administration, it is useful to quickly and informally examine how police administration can assist officers with stress management. One of the stressors listed for police officers is lack of support by managers. One strategy points out the need for training police managers in techniques such as conflict resolution, communication skills, recognizing symptoms of drug or alcohol abuse, and stress management. Managers need to be able to recognize officers who are under stress, then provide support for them.

Second, police services require good counselling personnel to assist officers with a variety of problems. Counselling areas should include assistance and training for stress reduction, critical incident counselling, and help for officers who have post-traumatic stress disorder. Again, management plays a large role by dispelling any myths that an officer requiring help is somehow undependable or weak. Only if a service demonstrates that counselling is effective will officers seek the necessary support in their employee assistance plans. One strategy, using peers as counsellors, may be effective, because the counsellors are trained police officers who "have been there" (McKenna, 1998). Also, support must be immediate in such events as suicide by cop or other critical incidents.

Third, services must provide programs to help police officers manage critical-incident stress. Peer support programs have been very effective, especially when peer supporters are the ones who recommend professional intervention. Many officers are more likely to take advantage of professional counselling services if the referral comes from a fellow officer. Peer supporters can act as bridges to professionals (Finn and Tomz, 1998). By being offered empathy and credibility, traumatized officers receive immediate support and validation for their problems. Many services match the peer supporter with the officer who has experienced a similar event. Peer supporters can also be used for other types of stressors including financial or marital problems. Note that peer supporters require training, and care should be given to their recruitment and selection (Finn and Tomz, 1998).

POST-TRAUMATIC STRESS DISORDER

A special kind of stress seldom covered in textbooks is post-traumatic stress disorder (PTSD). When first writing this chapter, there was no initial plan to include a section on this disorder. But as research continued, one thing became very clear: many officers have lived and are living through this disorder. Some who have experienced it have killed themselves. This book would not be complete if we did not discuss the severe inner conflict and turmoil created by PTSD.

Many critical incidents that happen to police officers cause extreme stress and may be more difficult to cope with than the more normal stressors of police work. For example, such events as shooting a person, watching a partner get shot and killed, having a hostage situation end with the death of the hostage are extreme circumstances that even the most seasoned officer can have difficulty coping with. **Post-traumatic stress disorder** is the development of characteristic symptoms after exposure to extreme traumatic stress that involves direct personal experience of death or serious injury; threat to one's physical integrity; or witnessing an event that involves death, injury, or a threat to the physical integrity of another person (APA, 1994). This disorder is emotional, psychological, and physical. Often because people feel that death and destruction is part of law enforcement work, police officers feel that they should not or would not be affected by such events. However, no one is immune to the effects of these traumatic events.

Post-traumatic stress disorder (PTSD) may develop suddenly, or it may develop over time, with symptoms gradually worsening. A person with PTSD often does not recognize that he or she is experiencing PTSD, and it can be difficult to diagnose, because many try to hide the symptoms from friends, family, and co-workers. Note that post-traumatic stress disorder is different from post-traumatic stress. According to one researcher (in Mock, 2001), 20 to 30 per cent of police officers working in urban areas will develop a reaction to post-trauma stress during their lifetimes. Most officers can deal with post-trauma stress caused by a critical incident, but some will be unable to cope and will develop post-traumatic stress disorder. PTSD is much more devastating, is long-term, and can be extremely debilitating. Many police officers retire or end their careers in policing as a result of this disorder.

The symptoms of PTSD are similar to those of stress. The difference is that the symptoms are more severe, pervasive, unusual for the person, and continue to get worse over time. For example, bowel problems (a normal stress reaction) escalate in PTSD and may include blood in the stool and irritable bowel syndrome (IBS). Also, the symptoms must be unusual for the person. For example, many people have bowel problems due to IBS. This does not mean they have post-traumatic stress disorder. Below is a list of some of the possible symptoms of PTSD (Mock, 2001). For the complete list of symptoms, visit the Web site of Jim Mock, which can be found at the end of the chart.

Often the person will try to hide these symptoms in an effort to maintain normalcy and maintain the impression that everything is fine. PTSD does not go away; things will get worse, and the person does need help.

Many police services recognize that officers need critical-incident debriefing as soon as possible after the event. The often lengthy time between the event and debriefing often leads to the early onset of symptoms, including perhaps the false belief that everything is all right. The officer needs to talk about the experience in an environment of support, without defending actions or becoming defensive. The issue at this point is not the right or wrong but the emotional trauma of the event.

TABLE 10-2	Symptoms of PTSD

Intrusion

Extreme nightmares

Extreme paranoia

Sense of shortened future, impending doom

Avoidance

Depression

Isolation, especially from loved ones

Absenteeism from work

Addictions

Poor hygiene

Memory loss or poor recall

Arousal

Worse than usual problems with police management and/or the public

Increasingly cynical

Exaggerated startle response

Sudden outbursts of anger or rage, especially over-reaction to the situation at hand

Hyper-vigilance

Work becomes a crusade

Extreme hyperactivity

Somatic Problems

Problems urinating

Intestinal pain

(see other physical symptoms in earlier chart)

Source: Jim Mock (2001) Web site: home.socal.rr.com/jpmock/ptsd/recog.htm

Consider This...

One officer states, "Afterward, I just felt numb. When I came back to the station to meet with the counsellor, she just let me sit there, numb. But I knew she was there, and when I started to talk, she let me talk and talk without interruption. She knew I would have done anything else if I could have and it was the right thing."

This officer shot and killed a 14-year-old youth after the boy had shot and fatally wounded a shopkeeper in a botched robbery attempt.

You may ask, "Why do I need to know about PTSD when I am not even a police officer yet?" When talking to officers who have experienced and continue to experience this disorder, the answer is simple. Forewarning is foreknowledge. In other words, if you learn now that critical incidents will have a profound effect on you that may last for a time, you will be more ready to deal with them. You will be more alert to the pervasive effects of stress and seek help earlier and perhaps prevent an early end to an interesting and rewarding career.

SUMMARY

As the last chapter in this text, stress is explored from both a psychological and physiological viewpoint. Dealing with the conflicts, hassles, and routines of police work can all lead to stress. A solid knowledge of stress will help you to become and stay an effective officer.

Stress and stressors were defined, and the reactions to stress were discussed. Stressors or stressful events have four characteristics: they are unpleasant, unpredictable, and ambiguous, and they appear to be irresolvable. When responding to stressful events, the body reacts physiologically in three stages according to the general adaptation syndrome consisting of alarm, resistance, and exhaustion, if the stressor continues for a protracted length of time. While stress is often perceived of as negative, positive stressor eustress can occur, which also taxes the body's ability to cope.

There are many sources of stress. The common ones include life events, everyday hassles, social and family problems, physical and mental health problems, financial problems, and personality factors (including Type A behaviour, belief in an external locus of control, negative affect, and stress sensitivity). Several stressors of police work include the life stress events characteristic of law enforcement, shift work, problems with police supervision, dealing with death and severe injuries, testifying in court, dealing with members of the public, suicide by cop, and critical incident stress.

With so many potential sources of stress, prevention and management of stress becomes very important for police officers. First, recognize your personal symptoms of stress, because such symptoms vary from person to person. Once you recognize your symptoms, it is important to manage them and prevent them from worsening or becoming debilitating. Several strategies were presented to choose from and included developing a support network (talk, talk, talk), preparing for court appearances, keeping your body in shape, using alcohol and medications moderately, using relaxation techniques, developing hobbies and interests outside of police work, and using support from administration (if it exists).

The last section of this chapter ended with an examination of post-traumatic stress disorder, an often debilitating reaction to critical incident stress. Knowledge of this condition, including the causes and symptoms, may help you to avoid and manage this type of reaction to traumatic events that may occur in your policing career.

CASE STUDY

Post-traumatic Stress Disorder and Gene's Story

This case is a true case of a police officer. He has given us permission to tell it in order to help new officers understand post-traumatic stress disorder and its long-term effects on a very competent and able officer. At the time, Gene was a field training officer with a new partner of two months.

"I was on call in a city park where a lot of youth hung out. A drug exchange was supposed to go down there. I pulled in with my marked squad car with my partner. I saw a person who I knew had his driver's licence revoked. I held my hand out the window to stop him, because we were driving in the opposite direction. He stopped, got out, walked up to my window, and from behind his leg he pulled out a gun and pointed it between my eyes. There was some conversation. He told my partner not to move or he'd kill me. After a short period of time, he tried to pull the trigger. At this point, I lose memory.

"My next memory is of the suspect standing in front of my squad car, still pointing the gun through the windshield. My partner was gone. I got out and called for help and took a position behind his car. I ordered him to lay down his gun or I'd shoot. He said, 'Shoot me.' He continued to ask me to shoot him. I was waiting for legal qualification to justify the shoot. He kept his gun pointed at the ground. I manoeuvred around the cars in the parking lot, waiting for legal justification. Other squads then arrived. There was a standoff for five minutes. He then raised his gun, fired a shot into the ground, and another officer killed him with a shotgun.

"I later learned that during my memory loss, my partner tried to shoot the suspect, but the suspect made him lay down his gun, saying he'd shoot me if he didn't."

Gene found out later that his partner jumped out of the car. He tried to draw on the suspect over the top of the squad car. The suspect told him to drop his gun or he would kill Gene. His partner ran from the squad car and took a position somewhere else. The suspect ordered him several times to drop his gun or he would kill Gene. The partner finally dropped his gun and took cover away from the site until it was over.

"Three months later, my doctor prescribed Valium because I said I was finding the work stressful. At the time I did not relate the stress to the incident. The zeal and dedication I had for the job began to drop off over the next two years although I stuck it out for another nine years. Anger began to build toward my supervisors, with the anger sometimes becoming very intense. Gun calls were particularly difficult, with heightened fear. It was as if I knew all too well the possible consequences of high-risk calls and feared them considerably. But in order to fulfill the obligations of the job, I had to deny or set aside the emotions in order to perform well. I became very good at denying emotion, which I later learned is called detachment. One year after the incident, I began to use the bathroom 5 times per day. After two years, it was 15 times per day. I had constant pain in the left side of my colon, and found out this condition is called hyper motility of the colon. I asked for and got inside station duty. Anger situations easily pushed my blood pressure up to 150 over 120 (anything over 140 over 90 is considered high). Fear situations such as going to the dentist pushed it so high that the dentist would not work on my teeth. My lieutenant and captain sent me to a psychologist, saying I had PTSD. Eight years after the incident, I was running to the bathroom 10 to 15 times per day, and my blood pressure would spike regularly. When I left work for two weeks, all the symptoms subsided. Then I began to have severe pain in the colon during the middle of the night. The pain was so intense it doubled me over and gave me cold sweats. About 20 minutes after the pain, I would have diarrhea. This happened nightly before my retirement.

"I finally ended up in the chief's office crying. I didn't know what was wrong, but I was very sick. I found out it was depression and anxiety. The chief said I should find a lawyer and retire; the traumatic incident had done its damage. I got a lawyer, as he said. The medical reports went in. I could no longer return to work. On the other hand, the city said that while I could not return to work, they didn't know if they could agree to retirement. With that leverage, they had me sign papers relieving them of all medical and financial responsibility and forced me to waive all my rights under the employee contract.

"This once again placed me in a situation of complete helplessness. I got really sick now and ended up in a psychiatric ward in a catatonic state. When I was discharged, I signed their papers as a way to get out from pain of the stress. I was then placed on, not a city retirement, but a state retirement. That way the city paid nothing! At first, United Way contributions paid for half of my medical care. Later, I turned the bills over to the insurance company, claiming depression. This made it look unrelated to the job, so that the insurance company would pay.

"Almost immediately after leaving the job, the colon problems ended. It took several years before I stopped having daily panic attacks brought on by the bureaucratic retirement process. During the six months after signing for retirement, I had panic attacks and suspicious thinking that the state or the city would simply drop me from retirement. I continue to have an exaggerated fear response but not nearly as much as when I was working. If the insurance company doesn't pay a bill that they should have, I have an exaggerated anger response."

Questions

1. Identify Gene's symptoms of PTSD.
2. Why do you think the symptoms became worse over time?
3. How did Gene's department let him down?
4. According to the information in this chapter, how should his case have been handled?
5. If handled properly, where might Gene be today? How would his life be different?

KEY TERMS

Circadian rhythm: The human 24-hour cycle of activity, ranging from sleep to activity.

Critical incident stress: Stress resulting from a traumatic event or a series of traumatic events.

Distress: The term coined by Hans Selye to describe negative stress.

Everyday hassles: Minor annoyances that can create stress.

External locus of control: Belief in external locus of control is the conviction that events are beyond personal control, so things that happen are a matter of fate.

Eustress: A term coined by Hans Selye to define positive stress.

General adaptation syndrome: Three stages of the body's reaction to stress: alarm, resistance, and exhaustion.

Homeostasis: The balanced or steady state an organism tries to achieve for survival. When the body is not in homeostasis, the organism is motivated to make adjustments to achieve it once again.

Internal locus of control: Belief in internal locus of control is the conviction that events are within personal control, and outcomes can thus be changed.

Negative affectivity: A personality tendency to experience aversive emotional states including feelings of nervousness, tension, and worry, and a predisposition to experience emotional stress.

Post-traumatic stress disorder: A *DSM-IV* disorder that usually results from extreme and traumatic stress or critical incident(s), which may develop rapidly or over a period of time.

Relaxation response: The body's reaction to complete relaxation, including lowered blood pressure, respiration, and heart rate, and relaxation of muscles.

Stress: A reaction to an event that requires an organism to adjust in some way.

Stressor: An event or situation that leads to stress.

Type A behaviour: A personality syndrome characterized by time urgency, free-floating hostility, impatience, and aggression.

 # WEB LINKS

http://depression.mentalhelp.net
A site devoted to depression and includes information on how to get help for depression.

www.ptsdpolice.com
A site devoted to post-traumatic stress disorder for police officers and their friends and family.

www.heavybadge.com/efstress.htm
An article by Police Officer Dan Goldfarb on the effects of stress on police officers.

REFERENCES

American Psychiatric Association (1994). *Diagnostic and statistical manual of mental disorders* (4th ed.). Washington, DC: Author.

Wayne Anderson, David Swenson, and Daniel Clay (1995). *Stress management for law enforcement officers.* Upper Saddle River, NJ: Prentice Hall.

Herbert Benson (with William Proctor) (1995). *Beyond the relaxation response.* New York: Berkley Books.

A. Bandura, D. Cioffi, C. B. Taylor, et al. (1988). Perceived self-efficacy in coping with cognitive stressors and opioid activation. *Journal of Personality and Social Psychology, 55,* 470–88.

Robert A. Baron, Don Byrne, and Gillian Watson (2001). *Exploring social psychology.* Toronto: Allyn and Bacon.

D. Baxter (1978). Coping with police stress. *Trooper, 3*(4), 68–73.

A. C. Billings & R. H. Moos (1984). Coping, stress, and social resources among adults with unipolar depression. *Journal of Personality and Social Psychology, 32,* 114–29.

John Carpi (1996). ... Stress... *Psychology Today, 29*(1), 34–44.

Peter Y. Chen & Paul E. Spector (1991, June). Negative affectivity as the underlying cause of correlations between stressors and strains. *Journal of Applied Psychology,* 398.

Rae Corelli & Barbara MacAndrew (1994). Booze and the badge. *Maclean's, 107*(13), 52–57.

Richard J. De Paris (1998, December). Organizational leadership and change management: Removing systems to community-oriented policing and problem solving. *The Police Chief,* 68–76.

T. M. Dembrowski & P. T. Costa, Jr. (1987). Coronary-prone behavior: Components of the Type A pattern and hostility. *Journal of Personality, 55,* 211–35.

Andrew J. Dubrin & Terri Geerinck (2001). *Personal relations for career and personal success.* Toronto: Prentice Hall.

Peter Finn & Julie Esselman Tomz (1998). Using peer supporters to help address law enforcement stress. *FBI Law Enforcement Bulletin, 67*(5), 10–19.

E. A. Holman & R. C. Silver (1998). Getting "stuck" in the past: Temporal orientation and coping with trauma. *Journal of Personality and Social Psychology, 74,* 1146–63.

T. H. Holmes and M. Masuda (1974). Life change and illness susceptibility. In B. S. Dohrenwend and B. P. Dohrenwend (Eds.), *Stressful life events: Their nature and effects.* New York: Wiley.

T. H. Holmes and R. H. Rahe (1967). The social readjustment rating scale. *Journal of Psychosomatic Research, 11,* 213–18.

Arthur W. Kureczka (1996). Critical incident stress in law enforcement. *FBI Law Enforcement Bulletin, 65*(2/3), 10–17.

Walter Lippert & Eugene R. Ferrara (1981, December). The cost of coming out on top: Emotional responses to surviving the deadly battle. *FBI Law Enforcement Bulletin,* 6–10.

Sue McDonald (1995, October 24). Take a deep breath. *Cincinnati Enquirer,* p. D3.

Paul F. McKenna (1998). *Foundations of policing in Canada.* Scarborough, ON: Prentice Hall.

Jim P. Mock (2001). Recognizing police officers with posttraumatic stress disorder. *Road runner.* http://home.socal.rr.com/jpmock/recog.htm

——— (2001). Stress. *Road Runner.* http://home.socal.rr.com/jpmock/ptsd/ptsd.htm

Ray H. Rosenman (1975). *Type A behavior and your heart.* New York: Fawcett.

I. G. Sarason, J. H. Johnson, and J. M. Siegel (1978). Assessing the impact of life changes: Development of the Life Experience Survey. *Journal of Consulting and Clinical Psychology, 46,* 932–46.

Hans Selye (1974). *Stress without distress.* Philadelphia: J. B. Lippincott Company.

James D. Sewell (1981, April). Police stress. *FBI Law Enforcement Bulletin,* 9.

Mike Simpson & Suzanne Richbell (2000). British policing and the Ottawa shift system. *FBI Law Enforcement Bulletin, 69*(1), 19–27.

Shelley E. Taylor, Letitia Anne Peplau, and David O. Sears (2000). *Social Psychology.* Upper Saddle River, NJ: Prentice Hall.

L. Territo & H. J. Vetter (1981). Stress and police personnel. *Journal of Police Science and Administration, 9*(2), 195–208.

Clinton R. Vanzandt (1993, July). Suicide by cop. *The Police Chief,* 29–30.

John M. Violanti (1999). Alcohol abuse in policing. *FBI Law Enforcement Bulletin, 16*(1), 16–19.

J. M. Violanti and D. Paton (1999). *Police trauma: Psychological aftermath of civilian combat.* Springfield, IL: Charles C. Thomas.

J. W. White, P. S. Lawrence, C. Biggerstaff, et al. (1985). Factors of stress among police officers. *Criminal Justice and Behavior, 12*(1), 111–28.

Index